How to Raise and Invest Venture Capital

How to Raise and Invest Venture Capital

Edited by

Stanley M. Rubel

Edward G. Novotny

Presidents Publishing House, Inc.

New York, New York • 1971

Printed in the United States of America by
The Book Press

Library of Congress Catalog No. 77-163646

ISBN 0-87856-006-8

Designed by Elliot Epstein
Manufactured in the United States of America

FIRST PRINTING

. . . to the entrepreneurs, toiling from dawn to dusk, pursuing their dreams against the fates . . .

. . . to the venture capitalists who help make these dreams reality . . .

. . . and to Suzanne and Sandra.

CONTENTS

PREFACE

A reporter for a wire service admitted to me recently that he had not sent out a story on a local convention of venture capitalists because he did not know what they were. It sounded simple, he said, so simple that the name was confusing. Besides, he pointed out that he never met anyone who admitted that they "venture capitaled" for a living.

He was right. Very few people are familiar with the venture capital industry because, until recently, this unique area of finance was practiced by a handful of publicity-shy investor groups and managers of upper-class fortunes.

We tend to forget, for instance, that America was practically founded as a venture capital deal. The early American colonies were capital investments backed by foreign "adventurers." Even then, there was nothing new about a group of businessmen pooling their money in a high-risk venture to reap high returns on their investments.

History is practically an audit of venture capital investments. When men climbed aboard ships to sail the seas or trekked to the East in caravans, it was not curiosity but profit that motivated their efforts. One wit has noted that Adam was probably in the midst of measuring the apple market potential when he and his companion were driven to less comfortable environments.

And little has changed since.

The vessels now search among the stars and in the dark of the seas. Man's potential for profit is limited only by the depth of his imagination, his ingenuity to convert a dream into reality. The glamor stocks of tomorrow are now only vague scratch-pad jottings of young men who are just finishing school. The great stories are yet to come, and when they do, you will probably find a venture capitalist on the ground floor.

Today's tight money market policies and the increasing capital demands of new business have turned the nation's business spotlight on the venture capital industry. More newspapers and magazines today are writing about the activities and the dramatic successes of venture capitalists. Venture capital operations are being formed as subsidiaries of corporations, banks, insurance companies and mutual funds, and an increasing number of enterprising individuals and new investor groups are emerging on the scene.

The view here of this unique investment industry will be from the pilot's seat, through the eyes of the leading men in the field. Their insight into venture capital operations has been developed through daily trials and tribulations, working with an endless variety of venture capital situations.

These venture capitalists first expressed their views in a series of unique panels and discussions on "How To Raise Venture Capital." The sessions, held during 1970 in New York and Los Angeles, were sponsored by Corporate Seminars, Inc., a New York-based management education organization that has served the community since 1966 by offering in-depth analyses of problem areas of vital interest to corporate policy-makers.

Subsequently (for the purposes of updating the material for this book), the authors have revised their comments to reflect interim changes in the country's economy, and the effect of such changes on the venture capital industry. The reader will note many differing viewpoints among the authors here. Perhaps the one most consistent thread that runs through the venture capital industry is that virtually every practitioner has his own ideas, concepts and practices which, in most cases, he feels are superior to those of others in the field.

We have attempted to cover the industry from both sides of

the investment situation, eliminating excess verbiage and duplication of material wherever possible. The result, we feel, is the best of material presented in a readable and interesting format.

Primarily, this book is designed to provide information to three major groups concerned with venture capital:

. . . individuals or organizations with capital to invest,

. . . individuals or firms acting as consultants in seeking capital,

. . . businessmen looking for capital to finance a new or emerging enterprise.

We do not profess to cover every detail of this complex business, but we feel the reader will have been given a much clearer idea of the nature of the venture capital industry.

The results of this effort would not have been possible without the help of many people across the country who contributed their knowledge and editorial expertise to this work. My co-editor, Mr. Stanley M. Rubel, and I thank the authors of the chapters that follow, and we are grateful to the many venture capitalists and associates who took valuable time to review the material. We also gratefully acknowledge the efforts of the corps of assistants and secretaries who toiled over the manuscript for so many weeks.

We are particularly indebted to Robert Jones, executive editor of Presidents Publishing House, and Mr. William Colvin, president of Corporate Seminars, Inc., who made this book possible.

EDWARD G. NOVOTNY

INTRODUCTION

The success of American business can be attributed to ambitious men who were willing to gamble their time and fortunes to create major companies. Many of these men initiated their operations out of garages, borrowed capital from everyone they knew, worked around the clock and never took "it can't be done" as a final answer. Major enterprises that are now household words and highly-respected big board companies were started on a shoestring, most of them experiencing a period of crisis in their corporate history.

The idea of venture capital is to duplicate this process—to back new and early-stage companies that appear to have growth prospects for achieving major status over a period of time. From the entrepreneur's point of view, launching a new venture is becoming both easier—and, in some ways more difficult.

At this time in the business history of our country, there are probably more opportunities for small businesses than ever before. The level of corporate activity is incredibly high, even during recessions. The constantly-changing needs of people as well as companies give rise to an endless string of opportunities.

The entrepreneur, however, finds it increasingly difficult to obtain sufficient funds from sources such as relatives, friends, and suppliers in order to successfully finance a new venture, or one that is at an early stage of growth. Usually, it takes more equipment, inventory, development cost and marketing expense to launch a venture than was the case a decade ago. The mere fact that the dollar has eroded about 35 percent in value over the past ten years is a factor in this escalation.

Furthermore, it now takes greater business skills to launch and run a new business successfully. But the rewards for the successful entrepreneur and his backers are probably greater now—and for the coming decade—than ever before.

The stock market seems to have become far more receptive to small company securities, a trend which shows signs of continuing. In the period of 1968 and 1969, over $2.2 billion of stocks in small and early-stage companies were sold to the public. Although many of these securities declined precipitously during the down markets of the mid 1970's, they recovered more quickly in early 1971 than in any previously comparable period.

More and more, corporate executives and younger businessmen tend to react against the structured life in a large corporation. Although the large corporations continue to command an increasing percentage of the assets of the country, talented executives in all walks of corporate life are evidencing signs that they would like to find some way to start their own companies or become associated with a small growth-type business.

Although venture capital investing is an old business, an interesting trend has been developing in the past decade. More venturing is being done by organized firms, whose sole function is to make high-risk investments in early-stage companies. As in the operation of a small business, venture capital investing is also becoming more difficult, requiring a more professional or disciplined approach to achieve satisfactory results. Starting with the organization of the SBIC industry in 1958-1960, and continuing with the formation of large venture capital corporations and partnerships in the 1968-1970 period, venture capital is becoming more institutionalized and the people operating in the field more visible and understandable. There are now 450 such firms in the country, and the number appears to be growing.

This book represents a compilation of the views and experiences, operating techniques and practices, and evidence of financial rewards and failures of various industry leaders who are associated in various ways with the venturing field. These people are partners or officers of venture capital partnerships or corporations, SBIC's, investment bank firms, private placement consultants, and many others who are involved in the venture capital process.

The doctrine of quality management in a new venture emerges as a prime requisite for most of the people in the venture capital industry. There is almost a unanimous feeling that it takes a superlative manager-entrepreneur to move a small company into the big leagues. Not so clear is the fact that no two venture capitalists will agree on a man's potential as a super-manager after an interview or a series of meetings with him. There is a great deal of latitude in interpretation between different venturers.

A prime requisite for the entrepreneur in order to launch a venture successfully is that he have unbounded energy, optimism and the willingness to keep plugging away at the financing needs of the business until they are properly fulfilled. Sometimes he will get lucky and find financial support from one of the first venture capital firms or SBIC's he approaches. More likely, though, he will require many months of painstaking exploration in the money markets to find someone interested in his company or project.

It is an oft-repeated maxim that there is sufficient capital in this country for the right venture capital opportunity. This is true but meaningless for the small business executive or entrepreneur who must invest months of his time to find "that interested source"—and then negotiate equitable terms for the investment.

This book has been compiled to aid such businessmen who are seeking funds for their company or special project toward a better understanding of how venture capital operates, what the companies in the business are seeking and what they will require from the companies they choose to back. It also touches on many skills and experiences venture capitalists can bring to a smaller-sized company that does not ordinarily obtain funds in this manner.

The book also discusses these matters from the standpoint of the venture capitalist who often does not know how his counterpart in another part of the country, or even in the same city, might be operating.

From any point of view, the venture capital industry is one of the most interesting and exciting areas of the financial community. In many respects, the industry is still in its infancy and likely to grow to even greater proportions in the coming years. It is from this area that the next Xerox or Polaroid or Digital Equipment Company will emerge for those venturers and entrepreneurs who are prepared to work together to achieve the American dream.

STANLEY M. RUBEL

How to Raise and Invest Venture Capital

1
THE VENTURE CAPITAL INDUSTRY

Stanley M. Rubel

The venture capital business has been surrounded by a great deal of mystery over the years. The mystique seems to stir men's minds and imaginations. Perhaps it is that venture capital is a little like sex—the only way you can really learn about it is from practical experience.

VENTURE CAPITALIST/ASTRONAUT: THE CHALLENGE OF THE 70's

A few months ago, at our request, a leading psychologist, Dr. David Campbell at the University of Minnesota, sent a questionnaire to venture capitalists throughout the country.

On the basis of responses from a majority of these people, Dr. Campbell concluded that venture capitalists have about the same degree of "adventuresomeness" as the nation's astronauts. Today's venture capitalists possess the leadership characteristics needed to solve the challenge of the 70's: they are at home in the world of ideas, oriented to knowledge and power, flexible, open-minded and oriented to innovation.

Mr. Rubel is president of Capital Publishing Corporation in Chicago, Ill., publisher of SBIC/VENTURE CAPITAL, and senior associate of S. M. Rubel and Associates, and Vencap Fund, Ltd.

During the next ten years, this country will be called upon to solve the problems of pollution, poverty, over-population; and we will be constantly pressed to turn our technological advances in space and electronics to consumer markets in an effort to improve the lot of our fellow men. Many of these problems will be solved by smaller-sized companies that have received key financing and guidance from venture capitalists because their primary goal is to seek such situations.

As major industries become more dominated by the large corporation (a present-day trend which will continue), increasing opportunities will spring up for the service business or specialized manufacturer, the distributor or retailer who can innovate, change, move quickly and take advantage of new opportunities.

These are the kinds of companies in which venture capitalists are interested, and the industry has not done a bad job with them. For the past three years, for example, SBIC (Small Business Investment Company) and venture capital companies have far outperformed the go-go type mutual funds, and many of the companies they have assisted have now become major corporations in this country. However, far from being self-satisfied, these firms are seeking new investment opportunities, and many of them feel that the 70's will truly be "the golden age" of venture capital.

THE VANTAGE POINT OF VENTURE CAPITAL

Before delving further into the mysteries of the venture capital business, more should be known about the vantage point from which we in the business view our industry, where our knowledge comes from, and how we can make claim to knowing something about this business.

Our firm has a unique vantage point: SBIC/VENTURE CAPI-

TAL is the only monthly journal that analyzes and reports on the venture capital business. One of our aims is to provide detailed studies of companies in the industry—what they are doing and why. We also provide a variety of other kinds of news information about the venture capital and SBIC industries. Our *Guide To Venture Capital Sources* is the only comprehensive directory of over 450 venture capital firms in the country. The National Venture Capital Foundation, conceived some years ago, dedicates itself to improving communication with the general business community regarding venture capital and SBIC investing. Vencap Fund is a private venture capital partnership.

In the decade which we have devoted to these endeavors, we have been able to gain much insight into what the business is all about, and to develop personal relationships with people in the business to find out how they really operate.

Despite our years of specialized experience, it would be presumptuous to say that we thoroughly understand the venture capital business. It is constantly changing. What is true today may not be true tomorrow; much of what was applicable three months ago does not apply now. In this dynamic business, where the rules of the game change continually, one never stops learning.

SOME WORKING DEFINITIONS

In trying to understand this business, some working definitions are helpful. In one typical definition, venture capital is related to financing startup-type businesses—companies that either are in the embryonic stage or not yet in operation. This is certainly a part of the venture capital world and probably the one that is most generally accepted.

However, there are many people in the venture capital business who do not finance startup-type ventures at all; or if they do, the occasion is rare. These people will finance a business that has been operating for a year or two, perhaps as long as five or ten years. The business may be expanding, or may need additional capital for operations. The degree of risk in the situation places it in the venture capital area, rather than on the bank or insurance company loan level.

Venture capital is also used to influence management changes, new ownership, and a wide range of other financial situations. It is important to keep in mind the fact that venture capital financing can occur in two, three, or even four stages.

The first stage is the startup, when capital is needed to put a new company into business.

In most cases, the second stage of financing will occur after the company has been operating for a year and has developed a prototype or perhaps limited production; now it needs capital in order to begin manufacturing operations.

A subsequent stage occurs when the company develops a proven demand in the market through substantial orders for its product. In order to meet delivery schedules, it now needs financing to expand the business.

The progression of financing stages goes on to the point when the company eventually sells its stock to the public.

Any of these various stages of financing could be considered a venture capital investment, and there are venture capital firms or people who are interested in one or all of the stages of a company's growth before it becomes a publicly-held company.

Primarily, venture capitalists finance private companies; sometimes, however, they will invest in a publicly-held company for which it is not practical to solicit additional public financing.

Trying to define venture capital may be somewhat confusing, and the same difficulty is encountered in trying to define the various methods of operation in the venture capital business.

There are varying degrees of interest and participation in the business—from being an active partner in the firm to being a totally passive investor—with all the gradations in-between. Many people operate successfully as passive venture capital investors by taking small portions of deals from others.

TO DEAL OR NOT TO DEAL: LEARNING FROM THE VICTIMS

Perhaps the most significant information about this business may be gleaned from specific situations . . . how they were evaluated and handled.

Understandably, venture capitalists prefer to point out the deals that have been successful—where the combination of skills resulted in substantial profits or in working out overwhelming problems. But the venture capitalist is, after all, human; and 'to err is human." Consider a few cases in point . . .

The Portable "Guided Tour" No One Took . . .

Several years ago, some people invested $250 thousand in a company that was developing what appeared to be an exciting new concept in the use of tape recorders. Small and lightweight tape recorders had made their recent appearance on the scene, and these people had developed a portable "guided tour" designed for museums, art galleries, zoos and other public-attracting places. The idea was based on the belief that visitors at zoos or museums rarely understand the significance of the exhibits, and that utilizing the portable guided tour would enable them to get much more out of their visits.

It seemed a great idea. It had been tested and appeared to be successful in one or two pilot projects. The business seemed to have major potential in view of the significant number of such public and private institutions throughout the country.

But some two years—and an additional $150 thousand—later, the company was obliged to shut its doors. Not only had two competitors unexpectedly emerged, but also fewer museum visitors were inclined to use the equipment than had been earlier assumed. Apparently, people simply wanted to look and enjoy themselves without any educational concern. Furthermore, the vandalism and maintenance costs were much higher than had been expected. Too many museums finally concluded that the entire program was more trouble than it was worth.

The venture capital company which had invested in this new concept got zero dollars return on its $400 thousand investment. It was, incidentally, one of the most successful venture capital firms in the country.

Putting it on Tape, Classically . . .

In a somewhat different vein, another classic example occurred in the early 1950s when one of the biggest current venture capitalist concerns came to the conclusion that the magnetic tape recorder business was going to emerge as a major industry. After studying the field carefully, they concluded that there were two companies in the country, both in embryonic stages, both with great potential for becoming leaders in the industry.

Both companies were open to major investments. One, however, provided an opportunity for negotiating much better terms, a greater piece of the action for a given amount of money. After some agonizing reappraisals, the venture capital firm decided to go with the manufacturer that offered the bigger share of the cake.

Although both companies got off to a rapid start, the competitor was able to do an exceptional job of designing new products as well as developing strong, direct channels of distribution. The company which had been backed by the venture capital firm ended up distributing through a larger manufacturing firm in their industry.

Although the volume of the venture capitalist company grew significantly, they had devoted substantial amounts of research and development money to products which could not be developed successfully.

On the other hand, the products of the competitor became recognized as the standard for the industry and the company won the top spot as the industry leader. At last count, this company's shares are traded on the New York Stock Exchange, with a volume of over a hundred million dollars. A dollar invested at the outset has multiplied several hundred times since. Meanwhile, the venture capital firm's company drifted sideways and eventually sold out to another concern of rather mediocre quality; and it, in turn, finally sold out to a third company. The venture capitalist, after investing for over ten years, eventually got its money back; but it never made a penny on the investment.

Pulling out of a 60-Second Picture . . .

A third case in point illustrates what can happen in the venture capital business from another point of view. Back in the late 40's, one of the more astute venture capital groups was among the group of investors who backed the original Polaroid Corporation. In Polaroid's earlier years, the company went through various false starts and a variety of research and development projects before finally breaking through with its self-developing film.

At one point, the venture capital company had about $600 thousand to $700 thousand invested in Polaroid, and it became very apprehensive when the company was showing substantial losses during the early years. Many of the projects that showed original promise failed to have the type of growth or profit margins that were anticipated. At one point, in fact, the investment was considerably under water.

Polaroid finally reached the stage of becoming publicly-held and its shares climbed back to the original purchase price of the investment group. After investing in the company for about five years, the venture capital group sold its shares in the over-the-counter market and heaved a great sigh of relief at being rid of what they considered to be a very troublesome investment. It is staggering to guess what one of those dollars invested then would be worth now—five hundred dollars, a thousand dollars?

The subsequent growth of Polaroid proved to be such a shock, actually, that the venture capital company went out of business for many years.

"Cases in point" such as these are cited here merely to illustrate the risk factor that is inherently a part of the venture capital business. The financial rewards and satisfactions that can be had, however, are immeasurable. To quote Charles Lea, who operates a venture capital division of New Court Securities, "The venture capital business consists of six years of blood, sweat and tears, followed by six months of glorious pleasure." This industry abounds with success stories . . .

TAKING A LOOK AT A LEADER IN THE INDUSTRY

American Research and Development is often cited as the nation's most successful venture capital company—and indeed it is. Starting after 1946 with a few million dollars, and following with two or three public offerings that raised capital to about $15 million to $20 million, the company now has total assets which would be worth a little over a half-billion dollars, including assets that have been spun off over the years.

A good deal of that gain results from present holdings in Digital Equipment, a company that American Research helped get started in the late 1950's. George Doriot, president and founder of American Research, was an eminent professor at Harvard University, and he has been an exceedingly patient man with his investments. He is often accused of staying too long with companies he invested in, bending over backwards to continue to support companies long after their potential has faded. He is slow to get into new investments—and even slower to get out of them.

General Doriot's philosophy points out one of the major differences between the venture capital business and currently popular methods of running a portfolio of securities.

The securities portfolio manager is almost afraid of becoming too familiar with the company in which he has invested. He is overly concerned about close personal relationships with the people who run these companies. He knows he will have to liquidate his position, often on very short notice if he expects or anticipates that market conditions will deteriorate.

The venture capitalist's point of view, however, is just the opposite. It is essential to him that he establish the right kind of personal relationship with the company in which he has invested. Often, the guidance and assistance that he provides to the companies have a significant bearing on the ultimate success of the struggling business and his investment.

He certainly cannot afford to develop a reputation for letting a company down, or risk other negative implications that in-and-out type trading could create. He may be forced to remain in an investment long after a cold, impartial investment decision might dictate his selling out of his position.

In addition, he is subject to the multitude of restrictions of the

Securities and Exchange Commission, which also prevent him from selling when he would like to move.

CREATING A SUCCESSFUL VENTURE CAPITALIST: SOME INGREDIENTS

One of the major difficulties for the venture capitalist is that when he makes an investment, he is forced to look down the road five or maybe ten years ahead. He must make a judgment about a man, or a group of men, without really knowing them in depth or having enough background in psychology to be able to make that kind of judgment in the first place. He makes the most difficult decisions in the financial community, but never has enough information about the decision, although he may have exhaustively researched many areas. There are always a multitude of unknowns that are totally unpredictable. After he has made the investment, he will then be stuck with it for five to ten years—unless he is lucky enough to fall into the kind of market that existed in 1968 and 1969.

Most of the people in the venture capital business have been trained primarily, of course, in the financial and business community; an even better training, however, might very well lie in the field of philosophy or psychology or sociology—or any other field that could offer better insight into the areas that cannot be measured in dollars and cents.

In the long run, the two personal qualities needed for the venture capital business are a strong measure of guts and a large measure of luck.

It is difficult to be specific about just who is in the venture capital business, how much money they represent, how much money they have made on their investments—and many other specifics that would be helpful in trying to figure out what the industry is all about. We have organized some of this information, though, in our *Guide To Venture Capital Sources*, a comprehensive directory of over 450 venturing firms in the country, which includes about 100 SBIC's.

SBIC's: ORGANIZED VENTURE CAPITAL

The oldest organized form of the venture capital business is the SBIC industry—the 325 Small Business Investment Companies licensed and regulated by the government's Small Business Administration. Because they must report to the government, it is possible to acquire specific information about what they are doing and what effect they have had on companies they have financed.

It is fair to assume that the SBIC industry's activities are somewhat representative of the activities of the entire venture capital industry.

Currently, the SBIC industry has assets of about $600 million to $700 million, and has provided a total of $1½ billion in financing to small businesses throughout the country.

Statistics also reveal that every dollar of investment by SBIC's has helped their small business customers borrow an additional $1.36 from banks and insurance companies. All told, the SBIC industry has resulted in a cash flow to small businesses of approximately $3½ billion over the past decade.

The government has invested about $250 million in the SBIC program. In terms of leverage, this means that the government has had a successful program. Based on our estimates, the government has indeed actually made a profit on the SBIC industry. In 1969, we calculated that the government netted approximately

$13 million, after paying expenses related to the program. For the preceding year, the profits were about $6 million or $7 million.

SBIC Investment Returns: Outperforming the Go-Go's

SBIC's investment returns have been quite impressive in recent years, particularly over the last six or seven years. During that period, the top ten or fifteen publicly-held SBIC's and venture capital companies outperformed the leading growth funds, as well as a variety of other indexes. Many of the leading companies have been able to show an annual return on capital of 20 to 70 percent, not compounded.

Because of the difficulty of getting started in this business, the average return over the history of the entire industry has been about 5 to 10 percent per year for the combined SBIC industry. Some of the leading companies have shown between 50 and 75 percent annual growth and a few have shown over 100 percent. In 1969, for example, the Dow-Jones Industrials dipped some 15 to 18 percent while growth funds and others dropped to 20 to 30 percent; but the SBIC and publicly-held venture capital companies slightly declined in asset value by only 3 to 4 percent.

This was also the third straight year in which these companies vastly outperformed the kinds of investment companies that have attracted a great deal of publicity.

What effect have SBIC and venture capital activities had on small businesses? Based on data also accumulated by the government, companies that are in the portfolios of SBIC's have shown, over the last three years, an average growth in sales, profit and employment of 20 to 25 percent per year—far above the national average of 3 to 7 percent for those same years.

We estimate that the SBIC industry has created about three hundred thousand new jobs and has given birth to a great many new companies that otherwise could not have been formed, many of which have grown into giants in their fields.

CLASSIFYING THE INDUSTRY

Our classification of the organized venture capital industry would show a variety of different components.

First, the organized industry consists of companies that are steady, and not fly-by-night operations. Brokerage firms who have customers' accounts, who can go into venture deals today and, if the market turns, will have no interest in venturing, are not considered venture capital firms.

Venture capital companies, for our purposes, are those who either have a specific capital structure or allocate capital to these ends, and whose only purpose for being in business is to make venture capital investments, regardless of the type or area in which they invest.

The industry can be broken down into the following components:

There are the SBIC's, of which there are approximately 325; 25 are publicly-held, 75 are owned by commercial banks, and the rest of them are independently-owned. About 125 are clearly devoted to venture capital.

There are five publicly-held venture capital companies, including American Research, Greater Washington, Capital Southwest, and others. We estimate that there are some 150 to 200 private venture capital partnerships and family investment firms that are primarily interested in venture capital investing.

In the last few years, there has been a new development: a number of major corporations have set up subsidiaries to operate in the field of venture capital investing. We estimate that there are some twenty-five to thirty-five such firms. Also, in recent years, we have seen a number of investment bankers form venture capital firms in which they took a leading role or, in some cases, the entire action. We estimate that there are some twenty to thirty brokerage firms of this type who have organized specific venture capital operations.

In the last couple of years a new type of firm has been organized—the "letter stock" or "combination fund." These are firms that buy letter stock deals, make venture capital investments and also buy publicly-held companies. They change the percentage of participation in these fields according to the demands of each situation.

Besides these specific forms of organized venture capital, there is a wide range of individuals who make venture capital deals on their own, as clients of a brokerage firm, or as clients of a law or accounting firm. With a few exceptions, there is no way of knowing who those people are, how much they invest, when they invest or how they operate. Strangely enough, it may well be that this is the largest single segment of the entire venture capital industry.

There are also many differences in the ways these various types of funds operate.

SBIC's

SBIC's are located throughout the country. In the main, they tend to invest in nontechnical-type businesses, although there are quite a few SBIC's in various parts of the country that are heavily engaged in technological companies.

SBIC's cannot take control positions; this is one of the regulations of the Small Business Administration under which they operate. Many of them structure investments with debt and notes, along with options, convertible features, or a smaller portion of their investment in stock. The reason they do this is that the

SBIC's borrow from the government and pay interest rates. They then offset that interest expense with the interest income.

As noted earlier, the SBIC's are the only venture capital businesses that can be specifically measured in terms of their activities. They have a trade association and are organized and identifiable.

Venture Capital Companies and Partnerships

Another major area of this industry is private venture capital partnerships and venturing firms. Such firms would include Gardner and Preston Moss, and Graylock Management Corporation in Boston, Data Science Ventures in Princeton, Heizer Corporation in Chicago, New Business Resources in Dallas, Hale Brothers, Mayfield Fund and Arthur Rock in San Francisco, Goodman and Mautner and Hohenberg Associates in Los Angeles, and Gunwyn Ventures, the Island Company, New Court Securities, Bessamer Securities, and Venrock Associates in New York. Most such firms are located in New York, Boston, Los Angeles or San Francisco; and most of them tend to specialize in technology-type businesses. Some of them finance the startup-type situation. Frequently, venture capitalists who finance startups will take more than 50 percent control of the company and offer management incentives to buy back some of their stock after a certain performance level has been reached.

Although, within the last few years, these groups have tended to prefer startup and early-stage financings, it is not at all certain that they will continue to do so. In 1968 and 1969, the pressures of the new issue market considerably raised the equity price of second- and third-stage financing deals which have been sold to the public generally, thus forcing the venture capital partnerships into early-stage financings. With the new issue market seriously hampered, it is quite conceivable that the venture capital partnerships will move more heavily into second- and third-stage financings, inasmuch as the terms of the financings can be arranged on more sensible bases.

Private venture capital groups are also staffed with professional people, as are SBIC's. They tend to be active in the business of their portfolio companies, taking a constructive attitude toward the company as the long-range investors.

Venture Capital Divisions of Major Corporations

With a few exceptions, venture capital divisions of major companies—such as Monsanto, Singer, General Mills, S & H, Standard Oil of New Jersey, General Electric and other similar operations—are just getting into the venture capital business. It is not yet clear what specific investment policies these new divisions will maintain. In the past, some of these divisions have been established to serve as a training ground for new personnel for the parent company, or as an eye and ear for new technological developments that could become future divisions of the parent company. In most cases, the subsidiaries have been set up because they appear to be attractive profit centers.

Affiliates of Investment Banking Firms

Many investment banking firms have set up subsidiaries or related firms to do venture capital investing. These include Advent Companies (Tucker Anthony & R. L. Day) in Boston, Becker Technological (A. G. Becker & Company), New York, Ungersmith Securities (F. S. Smithers, Inc.), New York, and several others in New York. These people are active venture capitalists. They operate in much the same way as do private venture capital partnerships.

New Public Investment Companies

The letter stock and combination funds are the newest addition to the venture capital scene. The funds include, among others, the Inventure Capital Corp., SMC Investment Co., Diebold Venture Capital Corp., and Value Line Development Capital Corp. These people lean toward passive investing, although some of them have active venture capital divisions. They tend to buy deals and placements from the brokerage community. Each individual manager controls substantially more money than do most venture capital partnerships.

Insurance Companies, Pension Funds, Etc.

In recent years, many insurance companies, pension funds, bank trust departments and others have established venture capital divisions. These groups tend to be passive-type investors and generally participate in third-stage or fourth-stage financings. Some six or more have venture capital activities that operate similar to private venture partnerships.

Investment Banking Firms

The investment bankers have been probably the most active of any group in the venture capital field during the past three years (until early 1970). Certain firms—such as Lehman Brothers, Inc., White Weld & Co., F. S. Smithers, Inc., Burnham & Co.—have maintained active venture capital operations for many years. In recent years, small firms have been established to engage in venture investing and corporate finance—firms such as Weis, Peck & Greer, New York, and Hambrecht & Quist and Robertson, Coleman & Siebel on the West Coast.

However, most regional and national investment banking firms run hot-and-cold with the venture capital business. When times are good, they package and sell venture investments at a brisk rate. But in the types of markets that developed after May, 1970, most of these people have closed their venture shop to await a brighter day.

Individual Investors, Relatives, Friends, Clients, Etc.

This group, which cannot be measured, probably represents the largest single source of venture capital. Although there are certain individuals who have developed excellent reputations as venture capitalists, most of the capital remains hidden from view and tends to be best identified by investment bankers and specialized "deal" men who help package ventures for a fee.

Furthermore, as many businessmen discovered in April and May of 1970, the new issue market is very fickle. While it may offer some advantages during its strong and active period, when the market sours, the businessmen whose timing was not perfect find themselves with major expenses for SEC registrations and professional expenses—and no money to show for their time and trouble. The venture capitalist is a far more predictable source of financing.

In terms of the types of deals made, there is practically no way to be specific. The only possible way to make any kind of judgment is to seek out the facts about specific investments made by the venture capital people.

In recent years, alternative sources of funds have been available to small businesses. Companies could go directly to the public with a stock offering in order to raise needed capital. There are specific advantages in dealing with venture capitalists, regardless of whether the company can or cannot go public. These include management counsel, financial advice, contacts at all levels and the availability of follow-up financing if needed. These advantages should be considered by companies who are interested in obtaining growth capital. Aside from the money aspects of the business, there are many other advantages in dealing with venture capital companies.

THE DYNAMICS OF THE VENTURE CAPITAL INDUSTRY

Venture capital is an exciting business. It can be highly rewarding, not only in terms of money, but from the standpoint of personal challenge, as well as the unique personal relationships that can develop. The venture capitalist primarily deals with dynamic, young, aggressive businessmen. One of the reasons many venture capitalists are in the business must be that there is no way they can possibly go stale if they are successful. They must stay on their toes, be alert, learn constantly. Compared to practically any other area of the financial community, venture capital is undoubtedly the most exciting profession for the adventuresome (but patient) individual, and the most rewarding for the well-managed and aggressive young company.

2

THE ART OF VENTURE CAPITAL INVESTING

Don A. Christensen

After learning the problems of operating a publicly-owned SBIC (Small Business Investment Company), many people wonder how such organizations can make money. Be assured, it is a profitable activity.

We will recount here some of one firm's experiences over the last ten years of investing in high-technology ventures. For perspective, some background on Greater Washington Investors—and how we came to enter this business—is in order.

OUR BEGINNINGS

Greater Washington was organized in 1959 by a group of businessmen in the Washington area to provide a source of capital for technical companies operating in the District of Columbia.

Washington, D.C., has the highest per capita number of technical people of any major city in the United States. It has constant

Mr. Christensen is President of Greater Washington Investors, Inc., in Washington, D.C., one of the two venture capital firms listed on the New York Stock Exchange, and the only one listed with an SBIC subsidiary.

spin-offs from the various government agencies. There are also small technological companies in this city that have built up and have their own spin-offs. All this creates a demand for venture capital.

In Washington particularly, we did not have local sources of capital for technological companies. Existing local financial institutions were largely retail-oriented and real estate-oriented; they were not industrially-oriented.

At the time Greater Washington was formed, there were relatively few national venture capital activities. There were a few partnerships—the Whitneys, the Rockefellers—but they seemed unapproachable. One small over-the-counter company called American Research and Development had $15 million in assets, but the firm was not well-known. ARD now has over $600 million in assets.

In forming Greater Washington, it was not our intention to become an SBIC. We planned to operate, like American Research and Development, as a publicly-owned venture capital company. However, we recognized that the federal government through its SBIC program was trying to accomplish on a national basis what we were attempting to do locally: to provide sources of long-term debt and equity financing for smaller businesses.

There was a great deal of publicity surrounding the SBIC program in 1958-59. One SBIC, Electronics Capital, had gone public. It became clear that our objectives of forming a publicly-owned venture capital company would be best achieved through a similar route, so we elected to become an SBIC. In April of 1960, when we became the second SBIC to go public, we raised $4½ million through a public offering. By May of that year, we had high hopes and $4.8 million in the bank—but very little experience in conducting venture capital activities.

THE VENTURE CAPITAL ROLLER-COASTER

By the end of our first month, we had made a major investment. We invested $900 thousand in a company called CEIR, a local company which in time gave us the most outstanding roller-coaster ride in our history.

CEIR was formed to take over a government contract for computer services. Originally a not-for-profit company, it was soon converted to a profit setup. At the time of our investment, the firm had a profitable service bureau operation in Arlington, Virginia, with great hopes and plans to expand internationally, even though it had a small market for its shares. Our $900 thousand was invested in debentures, convertible at a price of eight dollars per CEIR share.

We were excited about this venture. It was a big one for us, representing 19 percent of our capital. We knew that whatever good happened for CEIR would be good for us, so we were very pleased some months later, when the astute New York investment banking firm, Lehman Brothers, bought $1.8 million of CEIR common stock at $28 a share—three-and-a-half times what we had paid a few months earlier. As so often happens, the public market responded enthusiastically to this show of support and CEIR stock soon reached a $90 high. Thus, within less than a year, we saw our $900 thousand investment climb to approximately $10 million in market value—more than twice what we had raised in our own public offering. Apparently, venture capital was a quick way of making big money.

The investing public occasionally gets carried away by their enthusiasm, so it was not surprising that CEIR stock came down in price a little. When it dropped to the $40's or $50's, we were reassured in our commitment by the fact that another major investment banking group, a mutual fund group, Investors Diversified Services of Minneapolis, bought $1 million worth of stock in the mid-$40's and lent the company $2 million in debentures, convertible at $55 per share escalating with time.

Soon there was a little more deterioration in the price, but IDS was undaunted and dollar-averaged with another $1 million stock when CEIR stock prices fell to the mid-$20's. Finally, when the price sank to $3⅛, we could find no more investment bankers willing to put in money, so we sold the company's equipment to Booth Leasing and leased it back. Fortunately, the capital provided by this move enabled the company to turn around.

Here is an example of an investment that roller-coastered within less than two years: the value went from what we had paid to ten times that amount, and then down to about one-thirtieth the amount.

Greater Washington needs little sympathy in that we did not fare too poorly at the end. When we realized what was occurring, we distributed about $1 million in holdings to our shareholders. They were free to do with it as they pleased. Ultimately, we sold the balance of our holdings so that our final return on the investment was about 140 percent.

Because the stakes are high in this business, it is critical for the venture capital firm to make the most of each and every lesson, win or lose. From the CEIR case, we learned a fundamental truth about investigating prospects: good management is essential, but it is also vital to identify where the real strengths lie within a management group. We were not aware of the fact that one of the founders who died at about the time we made our investment had contributed great strength and financial responsibility to the company.

Not so incidentally, the company had another kind of problem —believing its own publicity. Reading about one's own success in the newspaper, even when the copy is self-generated, is likely to result in a glorified impression of oneself. Also, being out there in front with everyone else following reinforces the impression that one is on the right track.

In light of the CEIR experience, we also developed a policy of disposition by cashing in investments. As distinguished from some venture capital operations, we tend to hedge our bets by cashing in as the company matures. After holding an investment for about five years, we begin to liquidate it from our portfolio and to realize the capital gain, so that in ten or fifteen years it will probably be totally eliminated. The actual decision to sell relates to possible alternative uses of funds. At certain times, there are so many possible investment opportunities that we can see great areas in which to put our funds to work. At other times, what we are really saying is, "If we cash this in, it is going into Treasury bills or commercial paper." At that point, the inclination is to not cash stock in as rapidly.

Our fundamental objective is to realize 25 percent compounded growth rate on our assets. This is not a very great goal. We would like to be able to do better. In studying our portfolio, we determine: is this meeting our basic investment objective, or should we take that money out of the mature company and put it back into small ones.

Getting One up on the Government—the Hard Way

One of CEIR's major mistakes was to order two huge computers. When IBM came out with what was known as the "stretch computer," a unit alleged to be the biggest and best of all time, the federal government ordered one. CEIR went one better—they ordered two! They were not even around to receive the computers. We had to bargain our way out of that contract for several hundred thousand dollars in penalties.

Other CEIR problems came with expansion. Expansion is the name of the venture capital game. It is easy to expand but much more difficult to contract. CEIR expanded and, as an example, we ended up with leases on beautiful pieces of property all over the United States. We could neither use them nor dispose of them. We had, for example, one hundred thousand feet of land on Wilshire Boulevard in Los Angeles. Although it was fine property, there happened to be millions of feet of unused property on Wilshire Boulevard at the same time.

The key factor here is management. Too often, the feeling is that if a corporation lacks adequate management at the start, it can be brought in later. The CEIR Board of Directors agreed with this principle. They hired one of New York's most prestigious management consulting firms to come in and straighten out the problem. After about $300 thousand in management consulting fees, the company wound up with new operating management which the consulting group had recruited, and a whole set of new procedures on the way a business should be run. Two years later, the new management was gone and the procedures were in disuse. It simply is not that easy to bring new management into a situation.

The most unnerving fact about the CEIR story is that we had a tremendous technical opportunity. In 1960, the service bureau and computer industry was on the verge of major expansion. We invested in it; but the fact that we did not bet on the right horse is, in a sense, beside the point. It was not the fault of the industry or the company's business potential; it was management weakness that scratched us from the race. Money is put on people just as much as on technology.

Greater Washington's major problems with CEIR occurred in 1962. A number of other problems also developed in our portfolio and in almost all SBIC portfolios at that time. Losses come quickly in the venture capital industry; gains take a lot longer.

GROWING UP WISER—AND STRONGER

In 1962, we faced up to our losses and set up a reserve fund. We ultimately took about $1½ million in losses. This was actually less than the average for all SBIC investments made during that period of time, which ran in excess of 20 percent. From 1962 to 1970, our losses were only $13,200, but undoubtedly there are more coming. Since 1962, we also built a balanced portfolio, and we have gathered a very strong venture team, going to a two-tiered management setup in mid-1968.

Our current staff at Greater Washington reflects quite a variety of backgrounds and abilities. There is a vice-president with degrees in economics and law; he has been very effective in helping portfolio companies through much of the legal maze that slows up small companies. Another colleague has a doctorate in physical chemistry from the University of Paris. A man who runs our Houston office has an electrical engineering degree. One of our younger men has a law degree and practiced for several years at the SEC. He is useful in terms of our own regulatory situation, as well as helping our portfolio firms. Expansion plans will require that a junior man come aboard soon.

One deterrent to attracting and holding a good staff for a publicly-owned venture capital firm lies in the difficulty of providing incentives. We cannot personally invest in our own portfolio companies. We cannot have profit-sharing other than profits which would qualify under Internal Revenue—limited to 15 percent of salaries. As things now stand, good incentives do not exist for the American Research and Developments, the Greater Washingtons and other publicly-owned venture capital companies.

We fought this problem for many years. There are potential solutions, but they are still in the distant future. What we do offer that enables us to attract new men and to keep them for five to ten years is possibly the best post-graduate course available in entrepreneurship. Whether or not we will be able to keep them for a longer period of time is hard to say. We know that key men have left American Research to go into venturing partnerships. Things might be different if we were able to get participation in profits without limitations for our key personnel.

In 1968, we moved to a wholly-owned subsidiary SBIC activity, leaving the parent company with a new name—Greater Washington Investors—as a venture capital investment company. In February 1969 we had a rights offering to raise additional capital. This enabled us to be listed on the New York Stock Exchange. In 1970 our total assets were approximately \$25 million, net equity slightly in excess of \$20 million, and a portfolio of forty-five companies which cost us approximately \$12½ million and have a present value of about \$22 million—all this, after realizing some \$5½ million in capital gains over the last five-and-one-half years.

VENTURE CAPITAL: A WORKING DEFINITION

We see venture capital as the merging of men and an idea with tangible resources to create something of value. It is a combination of a variety of factors, with unique contributions made by each element of the formula. The practice of venture capital is to bring these elements together to achieve the values; and it requires a number of special qualities, such as faith and optimism —faith in men, in technical innovation and in the American free enterprise system.

Venture capital is a young man's business. The bright, young fellow brings his idea into the office and describes how he is going to set the world on fire. The scene is not a new one . . . his unrealistic attitude, like that of all his predecessors, can be discouraging. It is important to keep young in outlook, of course, but faith and optimism must be tempered by realism. Imperfections must be recognized—in men, in ideas, in our very way of life.

Not all men can operate in a changing environment or an evolving situation with the same effectiveness as they can when conditions are static. A group of men who have been very effective as staff members in a corporation may not possess the overall skills for successfully managing a new venture. Similarly, a man who has been able to form a company may not be the leader who is able to carry it through when organizational rather than entrepreneurial skills are required.

Timing is exceedingly important. An idea that is perfect for today may not have been a viable enterprise last year, and may not be one a year hence. We keep in touch with a number of ventures in which we have not yet invested. It is anticipated that one day they will reach a point when it will be appropriate for us to invest. We believe these companies understand that in this way they can leave a little less time for securing capital because they have greater assurance of being able to work something out with us.

The time it takes to complete a venture investment between first contact and the final dollars varies from ten days (in one instance at our firm) to perhaps ten years. It depends on how complicated a situation is, how much analysis is involved, the kind of people with whom we are working. Anyone who is seeking venture capital should allow an absolute minimum of three months, and would be much better off allowing six to nine months, with the earlier months devoted to educating the venture capitalist. The most difficult part for the venture capitalist is putting the first dollar into a situation; he does not know that much about the deal. He really becomes educated after that first dollar, and then it is much easier to do his job.

Finally, the venture capitalist has to be realistic about the free enterprise system. In venture capital, one bets on the underdogs. The companies that we back are competing against major corporations with greater resources in dollars and manpower. It takes a great deal of luck as well as hard work to make it under those circumstances. Besides his faith, optimism and realism, the venture capitalist has to be equipped with iron guts. He must possess the ability to stand up to the inevitable problems that develop.

A small company is not unlike a small child. He is sent off to school in the morning perfectly happy. He comes home with the sniffles. By the time he is put to bed, he has a temperature of 105 degrees and the parents are up all night worrying. The next morning he awakens in perfect health again. It has not been an excruciating experience for the child, but it was for the parents . . . and the parents in our case are the venture capitalists.

It should be pointed out that venture capital investment does not mean operating the business. The venturer is a minority investor standing on the front line with his money at risk, but without control over the situation. It is a viable industry, but a difficult one. Many of those who have left the industry have done so because they could not stand the heat. They faced up to the losses and decided that this was too hard a way to make a living. Another reason that many of them have moved on to operating companies can be readily understood by explaining our stock-pricing policies.

In early 1970, Greater Washington had a net asset value of $18 a share. Our market price was $12½. We are selling at about two-thirds of our underlying asset value. When Growth Capital (an SBIC which became publicly-held at about the same time as Greater Washington) switched from being an investment company to becoming an operating company, their stock roughly tripled in price. An operating company, then is measured in terms of an earnings formula, rather than net assets.

Now that we have some idea about what the venture capitalist is like, let us caricature him this way: he has two large feet, one firmly planted on the ground, the other taking a giant step forward; a skinny body due to working so hard; a cast-iron section somewhere in the middle; a very long neck with his head up in the clouds; and radar antennae so that he can see reality.

This is our venture capitalist, complete with all the basic elements for success in his business.

PRACTICING THE BLACK ART

The practitioner of this black art of venture capital spends a great deal of time in airplanes and rental cars . . . and very little time at home with his family watching television.

General Doriot, president of American Research and Development, to whom we all look as the revered leader of the public venture capital activity, said this about the field:

> "It is almost impossible to give a fair idea of the problem of launching new companies to anyone who has had no contact with it. The stories of success are well-ignored, and, of course, memory is short. It has been said of venture capital that if you get your money back you are successful. If success is obtained beyond that, you should be modestly satisfied.
>
> "The story of progress, be it in a laboratory, or industry, or commerce, is made up of failures and successes. One must learn from the failures, accept them with courage, and take success wherever it comes with modesty.
>
> "Today, venture capital seems very fashionable. Let us make an effort to understand it so that we do not spoil it, wreck it or come to the false conclusion that we should ignore it and start looking for other forms of financial excitement.

> "The words "newness" and "innovative" have become very popular, very acceptable, very tempting. Newness is supposed to solve all our problems, whatever they may be. There is nothing wrong with that as long as it is understood that in themselves they have very little meaning unless proper selection is made, and useful, constructive light is imparted to the idea. One builds soundly and fairly quickly because new ideas have very short lives.
>
> "A new idea in itself may be worth very little unless it can be the beginning of a family or succession of useful, related ideas."

With all the enthusiasm that exists for venture capital today, we should take his words to heart.

In the case of Greater Washington, what do we look for in high technology investments? The standard answer is—people; but it is not really as simple as that.

The venture capitalist's vision must be tempered by realism on the question of technological opportunity. We invest in technology because we see an opportunity for a small company to be formed, to grow rapidly and to generate capital gains for us and for management. We must take care to remember, however, that rapid change is always accompanied by great uncertainty and great risk.

SIMMERING THE MANAGEMENT STEW

Harper Woodward, another renowned venture capitalist, in a speech at Penn State University more than fifteen years ago, spoke of the ingredients that the Rockefeller family looks for in their venture investments. He spoke of a "management stew." Our recipe is somewhat different, but borrowing his concept or menu, here is a list of the ingredients we look for in this stew.

Ingredient No. 1: Technical Excellence

At the top of the list is technical excellence—in a promising field. There are several important aspects to these few words. Excellence is difficult to judge, especially when considering an economic environment. A man may have great technical excellence as an academician, but he may be unable to hold his own in the world of free enterprise. The technology must have practical application. This man has to make trade-offs—recognize the necessities of trading off costs and time with what he hopes to achieve technically. This requires the adoption of expedient alternatives which often are against the wishes of technically-oriented people.

Then Add a Pinch of . . . a Promising Field

Second—the matter of a promising field. There is no general agreement on the definition of this phrase. We in the industry tend to become enchanted by different technologies, when we should be objective and ask: is there an opportunity for a small company in this particular field?

Not all exciting technological fields are suitable for a small company. The choice has to be one whose financial requirements are on a level with the company's available resources. It must also be one for which the market is not so attractive that major companies are coming in after the kill. We often prefer to find and develop a smaller market—for example, a rapidly expanding $10 million to $20 million market that may be unnoticed at the moment, rather than the $100 million market in which the payoff is sufficiently large to attract the bigger companies.

Timing, too, is exceedingly important in sizing up a potential market. In space technology, the critical threshold in space flight is referred to as "the window." There is a window for technological ventures. If we are too early, we find ourselves pioneering and pouring dollars into an effort to create a market which does not exist. If we are too late, we find ourselves up against entrenched competition and are at an immediate disadvantage.

Mix In Carefully . . . Business and Financial Management

The third ingredient of our stew is business and financial management . . . easy to take for granted when it is there, but one of the most delicate ingredients to stir in without curdling.

There is great reluctance among technical entrepreneurs to accept a financial person into their family as an equal. We sometimes refer to this as "the Ph.D. Syndrome." The technical people whom we back have so much intelligence and self-confidence, they think they can do everything single-handedly. One of our major sales activities is to get them to recognize that they need a team and help other than their own skills.

Our experience has shown that when we have been successful in venturing, our team has always included a strong financial man. Two of our investments, Conductron Corporation and Data Products, are good examples. In both cases, a strong, capable, technically-oriented president had a management-, financially-oriented individual who carried considerable weight in the organization as the right-hand man. This is an important combination.

We did an interesting startup venture in Phoenix in 1969. Two bright young engineers came to us with an idea to form a company to manufacture a special disk file, a mass-memory unit to be used with computers. We examined it, and the project made good sense in terms of the market, the technology involved and the young men's abilities. One of the partners was clearly a leader and had good marketing sense. The other was very strong technically. The group lacked, however, someone with real business experience.

We told them we were interested in their project, but would be unwilling to invest in it unless they added the necessary third ingredient; and we were not going to find the man for them. That was their responsibility.

They perservered, and went to various banks among their contacts in Phoenix, and came up with a good man who was made a member of the team of equal status with the first two. Considerable credit goes to him for getting the company launched in a very effective way. Incidentally, that man has since moved on to perform a similar role in another startup venture in which we participated.

One important word of caution at this point: the venturer should be wary of the source of ideas. If, for instance, there is the possibility that the group seeking backing may have taken some trade secrets or proprietary products from their previous employers, we would demand that the new venture's management group sit down with us and their previous management, and discuss just what they are going to do to see how their former management feels about it.

In the Phoenix case just mentioned, for example, we made certain that the engineers and their counsel discussed the plan and, if possible, put in writing a tacit agreement with their previous employer that there were no objections if they went into this business.

This is a tough area in which to take risks because if the previous "owner" of the proprietary information is a large company with blood in its eye, right or wrong, it can put the new organization out of business before the matter has been finally litigated. This does not make a sound venture.

Thicken With . . . Maturity and Judgement

Fourth: maturity and judgement are also needed. A look at the successes of the young companies that have been venturers reveals that the management groups are not old folks, but they have maturity. They are able to grow with the organization, to delegate as the situation gets bigger, to become a smaller fish in a bigger pond.

In this regard, we always look carefully at the experience of previous investors with people in whom we are interested, because it is in the management-investor relationship that maturity can be observed.

Add Spice . . . With a Leader

The fifth ingredient—at least one executive. He may be a technical man or a financial man, but he must be someone who understands the role of an executive.

We make sure that he is personally committed, and in measuring the commitment of a founder, we like to see lush green dollars. The arrangement is healthier if the management of a portfolio company contributes some of their savings, some of their hard-earned dollars to it, too. In the case of the Phoenix company, the management group purchased 40 percent of the equity for $80 thousand. We and an associate (another venture capitalist) purchased 60 percent of the equity for $120 thousand.

We each paid the same price, but they sweetened theirs by committing themselves, and we sweetened ours by lending the company in excess of a half-million dollars, which was what the financial plan required.

. . . And Some Incentives

The sixth ingredient is management incentives. We contribute what we can in the way of help by putting up the money, but we are betting on the management team, and they must have incentives. These should match the venture capitalist's objective. We are involved in trying to obtain a capital gain and the incentives for management should also be oriented toward capital gains. We do not use limitations on salaries or expense accounts, mainly because they are unnecessary if we are backing the right sort of team; and they are unbelievably difficult to police under any circumstances.

We prefer to see a management team that is capital gains-oriented—one that recognizes that if they do not take the extra dollar in salary they can then bring it down to net, and the fifty cents after taxes that results can be capitalized at thirty-times-earnings; it now becomes fifteen dollars instead of one dollar.

We have tried a number of incentive approaches. In some cases, we used variable ratios of our conversion or our percentage ownership, depending on how successful the company is in meeting its objectives. If management does what they say they are going to do, they should end up with more than they would if they do not meet those objectives.

We have also used approaches in which a major option—as much as a third of the company—was given to the management group at a price significantly above the investor's price. With this plan, once we have made a stated return, the management group would then be able to make an additional return beyond that.

And a Drop of Confidence and Optimism

Among the other ingredients in our stew are confidence and optimism—not blind optimism, but a belief that is based on knowledge of the industry and knowledge of the technology involved. We do not succeed unless we believe we are going to succeed. The problems along the road for a young entrepreneur are so great that he must have a high level of confidence.

And a Drop of Honesty and Integrity

The last ingredients are implicit but essential—honesty and integrity. These are difficult to define, but we are convinced that a venture cannot be successful unless they exist.

Honesty and integrity show up in a variety of ways . . . how the men evaluate the worth of their contributions to the venture, the realism of their objectives, what they think is a reasonable objective. How does management speak of their suppliers and customers? Do they feel a sense of accomplishment in giving the customer a good product at a good price? How do they handle their personal affairs? What have been their relations with previous investors? What transactions have they undertaken among themselves or with the company? Even the balance sheet is indicative of a management's attitudes and practices in these important areas.

That is our stew. We look for a technical partnership with someone—a management team that offers something unique, sound, realistic and achievable that we hope to share.

A Typical Successful Stew

In 1962, we made an investment with a company called Data Products. We backed a management team who planned to acquire two divisions of Telex and Midwest Instruments at the time those two companies merged. One of the divisions had under development a line printer for the computer industry. The other division had a disk file, a large memory device, which had been developed and was in limited production.

Here was a case in which we were backing a team that had most of the ingredients we require. They had successfully formed a company once before—Telemeter Magnetics, which had been sold to Ampex. They wanted to do this again, but this time they wanted to do it in what they believed would be the right way.

The team had business as well as financial management: the president was a good executive and the vice-president a strong, financially-oriented administrator. They made an excellent team; they had confidence, optimism for their industry, ability to compete, they were ambitious and they had incentives.

First, they invested $250 thousand of their own money in the venture. Second, we gave them incentives in the structure of the investment.

The deal was made as part of a group investment. Our participants were Continental Capital and SBIC in San Francisco. They had the advantage of being local, close to the business; they also knew the management. The president of Continental would join the company's board in order to provide a continuing relationship. The second major investor was the Bank of America's SBIC. They had had previous experience with Data Products' management during their Telemeter Magnetics days, and they expressed a willingness to continue to support the company with commercial bank credit, clearly a useful asset. Another useful fact was that the man working on the account for Bank of America was now president of the bank. With Greater Washington joining this group, we had a million dollar investment made up of the three of us.

We did the deal as debentures, convertible at a minimum price of 52 cents and a maximum price of $1.50, depending on performance. The 52 cents was what the management had paid for their stock. The $1.50 was an agreed-upon, negotiated figure.

As it developed, Data Products made good progress. They had inevitable setbacks, but moved along quite well. A couple of years later when they needed additional capital, they went through a rights offering. To facilitate that offering, although our debentures were not due, we agreed to convert half of the debentures at the $1.50 price, with the understanding that the company would repay the other half of the debentures out of the proceeds of the rights issue, and issue warrents instead. In addition, we exercised our rights to put up more money to help make it go through.

Data Products' public market hung in the doldrums for almost four years; it then started to move and has continued to appreciate greatly. It is listed on the American Exchange, doing in excess of $60 million a year. We have sold approximately half our holdings for an excess of $1.5 million in capital gains. We still hold half our stock, which costs us $175 thousand. As of December 31, 1969, we valued it at about $3 million on the open market. This is an example of successful venturing . . . and applying the stew formula to it.

What about companies in which we decide not to invest? We try to be of some help. It is easy enough to say we are not interested in their situation, but we go on to offer our reasons for not investing. We try to explain why the venture is not suitable for us, and suggest a couple of other sources they might try. We often suggest that, in our opinion, they probably need a merger, rather than a venture investment, and we even suggest some people who might be interested. There is no fee for this; we feel it is in a sense our responsibility, and that it helps keep the door open for future prospective deals.

ACTIVE PARTICIPATION: A KEY TO VENTURE CAPITAL SUCCESS

Active participation between the venture capital organization and the venture itself is exceedingly important.

In a venture capital relationship, the venturer has undertaken a marriage with a small company for better or for worse, and not just until the stock goes up two points. We think this is the fundamental difference between the venture capitalist and many of the people who are oriented toward mutual fund operation and other investment activities. Mutual funds have flexibility so that if the participants do not like what is happening, they can sell. This is not true of the venture capitalist . . . he is locked into a "for better or worse" situation. Furthermore, the typical venture capitalist is a minority investor who lacks the ability to enforce his wishes.

We offer advice and, in order to be effective, we have to be heard. We believe we make a significant contribution to the company, but it has to be done by persuasion. Our contributions are primarily in the financial area. We can be of great assistance in helping to structure the basic capitalization of the company. Typically, we will help to establish normal banking relationships, to set up other credit sources, and to educate management as to where the money is and how to meet the needs of the various sources.

An important aspect of technological venturing often involves a second level private placement. A year or more after the first investment, it will probably be necessary to raise additional funds. Usually, existing venture capitalists are able to bring in some of their associates or other sources to provide additional capital before the company goes public.

Finally, the venture capitalist has valuable experience in helping to take his company public, or to merge—if this is the path management would prefer to take to realize their gains. In cases of going public, we have become very effective in acting as a middleman between the management of a company and the underwriter. Each has different and strong objectives, and we, as an interested investor, are able to smooth out the differing points of view and bring the two together to complete a successful underwriting quickly.

Besides working in the financial area, we actively provide knowledge and business contracts to our portfolio companies. We also help them with personnel requirements, as well as assisting to establish policies, strategies and tactics that appear to be essential to success.

COMBATING THE LONELINESS OF COMMAND

Finally, two other important areas must be considered. First, we feel it is incumbent upon us to bring to our portfolio companies a sense of perspective, to identify problem areas and to give as much push as we can so that they act on those problems before they become overpowering.

Second, a venture capitalist can make an important contribution by helping to "keep the faith." For the young businessman on his own, trying to form a company is a lonely business. He must live with the problems, the obstacles and the difficulties on a day-to-day basis. But he can turn to the venture capitalist for help and counsel.

General Doriot commented on this problem most eloquently:

> "What does the venture capitalist do for companies? Our answer is along the following lines: if sometimes or possibly often, one feels lonely or wonders what to do or feels the need of knowledge, advice, help or friendship, if one wished he had experience in handling certain types of problems and situations, if one wishes to have someone to talk to even though sometimes it's not clear what to ask and talk about, then probably the venture capitalist can be of help."

One of the big questions we have not been able to answer, however, is—who is there to cope with the loneliness of the venture capitalist?

3
TYPES OF VENTURES FINANCED

G. Stanton Geary

It is important to clarify the definition of a venture capital investment, because the various categories of investments have a profound effect on the structure and the investment philosophy of an organization—ours, in any case.

THE THREE CATEGORIES OF VENTURE CAPITAL INVESTMENTS

The first category is "seed capital" or "startup" situations. These involve the financing of a business from its embryonic state, where front money is used to substantiate the validity of a concept, idea, new product or service. Because the service, product, idea or concept has not been tried in the marketplace and management has not been tested under the heat of fire, a compounded problem is created which represents 100 percent downside risk on the venturer's capital. For this reason, seed capital and startup situations receive a jaundiced reception from most venture capital firms.

The second type of venture capital investment is a classic situation involving investments in companies which have been in business from one to five years. Their product or service has been tested in the marketplace, and the firm, by virtue of its

Mr. Geary is president of Inverness Capital Corporation, in New York City.

rapidly rising sales curve, has demonstrated that demand is greater than the supply. Also, the product or service has been in the field long enough to ascertain its quality, performance and consumer acceptance. Furthermore, while the company is still young, there has been sufficient time to evaluate management's business judgments. In many instances, these companies are on the verge of getting into the black, and some may be profitable already. Generally, they involve an investment of from $150 thousand to $600 thousand; the average investment is approximately $300 thousand.

The third type of venture capital investment is a buy-out or acquisition. Due to its limited size, such a company can be classified as a venture capital investment, even though the firm has a long record of earnings operating performance. In spite of this success, the companies may suffer from poor marketing or management porblems; thus the firm could have excellent growth prospects. Because their products or services are in demand, many such companies have been successful in spite of serious problems.

INVERNESS INDUSTRIES

When we formed Inverness Industries, a private venture capital firm, we decided to focus our attention on classic venture capital investments and buy-outs. It was determined that the best way to handle this was to isolate these activities under separate corporate entities. We established two subsidiaries: an operating group to handle all the acquisition activities of under-marketed or under-managed companies, and an SBIC—Inverness Capital Corporation—which is responsible for all classic venture capital investments. On rare occasions, we do a seed capital deal.

In the operating company, we buy 100 percent of the businesses. In the venture capital end, we are precluded by federal law from owning more than 50 percent of the equity. As a matter of policy, our SBIC does not take more than 49 percent of any business because we want the owner to enjoy the psychological effect of feeling that he is the controlling stockholder. Also as a matter of policy, we will not take less than 20 percent of a company and we prefer to have at least one-third of the equity. There are several reasons for this:

If the company is a success, we must own enough of it to profit sufficiently to justify the risks . . .

We are concerned about the psychological factors and the rapport that develops between the principals of the company and us . . .

If we take less than 25 to 33 percent of the business, management tends to think of us not so much as a partner in the enterprise, but as an outside financing group to whom they gave a sweetener in order to get money when they needed it. We are vitally concerned that management respect us as full partners in the enterprise. Before they build a plant in Europe or begin development of a new product program, we would like to have them call us. We find that if we own 33 to 49 percent of a business, management will develop the habit of discussing it with us first.

BUY-OUT VENTURES

Spaghetti Sauce and Fish

Many buy-out ventures are the same in size as the companies we finance in the venture capital subsidiary. Generally speaking, the age of the owners would preclude considering a classic venture capital-type investment. The businesses may have sales as low as $50 thousand or as high as $3 million, but the owner is usually sixty- to seventy-years old. We are not interested in becoming a partner on a minority interest basis, and the owner is looking for liquidity. In view of his age, he no longer has the desire to make the kind of capital investment needed by the business in order to fully exploit its market potential. This is why we refer to these investments as undermarketed situations. The condition may exist by design rather than from ignorance. In any event, the resultant problem is the same—a business which is not fully exploiting its opportunities in the marketplace. If those opportunities are not exploited within a reasonably short time, the company will begin to deteriorate.

Marketing Expertise Guide to Inverness Investments

Our firm is primarily marketing-oriented. All our operating people have been with marketing companies, and we favor either service-oriented or consumer product-type businesses.

In the operating company, we have made six acquisitions, including a spaghetti sauce business in the New York market. This venture brings us into the grocery products field where our management has extensive experience. We have made five acquisitions in the fish business, but none of these has any consumer products at this time. To further emphasize the marketing approach that we apply to these situations, we can foresee four or five branded products with grocery market distribution emanating from our fish acquisitions.

CLASSIC VENTURE CAPITALISM

From Burglary to Correspondence Courses

The SBIC subsidiary has a capital base of $1 million. Under federal regulations, we are precluded from making investments in excess of $200 thousand, which is 20 percent of our capital. Unfortunately, this eliminates our participation in bigger deals.

A company which requires only $200 thousand usually does not have a management team; it is dominated by one man who has a particular skill. He may be an inventor who has virtually no administrative ability, or a salesman with only a cursory appreciation of the problems of production, finance and product development. In essence, the venture capitalist would be dealing with someone who has a number of key business weaknesses. If the product is successful by virtue of the man's inventive or innovative capabilities, he spends less time in R&D and more time in selling, financing and production where he has limited abilities. Our function is to try to compensate for his limitations. When we make an investment judgment on a prospective venture capital deal, we try to match our capabilities with his weaknesses. If both of us are weak in the same areas, we pass up the deal.

Occasionally, we become beguiled by the romance of some industries which have captured investor attention. This can lead to a serious mistake. For example, we have an investment in the burglary protection equipment field. The company also licenses franchises in metropolitan markets to operate central station monitoring facilities using its equipment. We feel that this particular company's products have a pre-eminent position in sound-oriented protection equipment. At the present time, there is an opportunity to build a substantial and significant enterprise in the security field.

In order to take advantage of this, we must make up for grave limitations of the management, whose basic skills are in the R&D end of the business. This company's future is strictly a function of marketing, because, although the company's technology is superior to anything in the field, the product could be made in anyone's cellar and does not lend itself to patents or other forms of product protection. The marketing of it is not any different than that of a new soap detergent. The "firstest with the mostest" will win the market; yet here we have invested in a company with a serious marketing problem and virtually no in-house marketing or sales capabilities.

We made the investment in the burglary protection device company because we felt that our own people could perform the critical functions which management could not. We hoped to become the marketing arm of the business—and we have. At our own expense, we printed a sales brochure for soliciting prospective franchise investors, and we are in the process of printing another to help the franchisees solicit commercial accounts in the field. If we had not undertaken the function of providing this management service, we would have been left holding a sophisticated line of equipment along with some very mundane and unsophisticated literature. It would have seriously inhibited selling activities, as well as our ability to attract the kind of salesmen we needed to boost our market share within the next six to eight months.

We also instituted cost control systems, established and supervised by our firm's partner, an experienced certified public accountant (with Price Waterhouse for eight years, and comptroller of an electronics instrument company for six years). This service—establishing these systems and financial monitoring of the businesses—is provided free of charge because we feel that it is the only way we can effectively protect our investment.

In addition to taking over the marketing and financial guidance of the business, we have instituted a franchise program to entice capable sales people away from major corporations in order to operate a facility in a major metropolitan market on an entrepreneurial basis. It takes about $50 thousand to operate in a city such as San Francisco. We will put up 90 percent of the money for 49 percent of the equity. To date, we have financed twelve major metropolitan markets directly. This program enables us to attract ambitious people. Generally, a franchise program attracts people in the community with capital; but they are not necessarily the kind of people who do the best entrepreneurial job, particularly when it involves a great deal of door-to-door selling and heavy campaigning. Our financing program helps to overcome this problem.

We also have a company in the correspondence course field. It offers a series of courses on seamanship and navigation, primarily for boating enthusiasts. The firm has a pre-eminent position in its field and capable management with extraordinary marketing abilities. Management is a successful husband-and-wife team—most unusual in this business. The last such team we financed was a disaster of no small proportions. We had to buy out the wife to resolve their divorce, and subsequent events proved we had bought out the brains of the business.

The correspondence school company retained a few local electronics wizards to make a prototype of a new product idea that had been conceived. We received the prototype, but the wizards were incapable of producing it. In the meantime, the company had sent out 35,000 mailing pieces and had received orders for 360 units at $200 apiece; but they had no source of supply. Our other investment interests, however, were able to save the venture. We assigned the burglary alarm company to a crash program to design and build the unit. Although the unit was of slightly different design on completion, ninety of them were shipped before Christmas—just in time to save us much embarrassment. Soon after, we searched around and found a reliable supplier at a much lower price.

We also have an investment in the water pollution field, but we cannot boast about our activities in assisting the company. Owing to the nature of the business, we have not been able to give this entrepreneur the kind of support and help that we were able to give the burglary detection company. This is due mainly to our own limitations. The company has an industrial product. Inasmuch as our background does not lend itself to meeting people socially for the purpose of inducing them to buy a $25 thousand sewage treatment plant, all we could really do here was to help with the internal cost control, planning and general administrative policy decisions. We do not consider this level of assistance to be adequate. Portfolio companies need direct assistance in many vital areas of business, including marketing and new product development.

THE VALUE OF CONSUMER AND SERVICE-ORIENTED BUSINESSES

We favor consumer and service-oriented businesses because they are not "capital-intensive" industries. In view of the limitations of our resources, we must seek businesses that will be self-sustaining after a first or second infusion of capital. Through their own internal economics, they must be able to generate enough capital for efficient operation and growth without any further help from private sources; otherwise, we would be in the position of having to go to other venture capital sources, perhaps at an unfavorable point in the company's development. This could result in a heavy dilution of our own equity position. Primarily for this reason, we avoid high-technology businesses and industrial companies that require heavy plant and equipment investment.

We also favor service and consumer-oriented businesses because they are not tied to the business cycle, a war economy, or the price-earnings cycle. We do not like industries which have already been blessed with the attention of the financial community. When Wall Street money begins to flow into an industry, the investment opportunities within it are desecrated in an appallingly short period. We like businesses with which we can live for long periods of time; therefore, we are not interested in the fashionable businesses recently in vogue in the investment community. In such stocks, there are sharp swings in the P/E cycle, and the venture capitalist can be left in an embarrassing, long-term operating position.

For example, if a stock goes public at fifteen times earnings and someone suddenly decides that it is the greatest thing since sliced bread, the stock goes to 100 times earnings; acquisitions for stock soon follow. The business undoubtedly winds up with subsidiaries whose managers thought they had sold their business for $20 million; then one morning they read in the newspaper that the stock is only worth $2 million. This does not promote good internal corporate morale.

We tend to favor businesses with stable P/E multiples—food industry and consumer products companies, for example—which flourish even in poor economies.

OBJECTIVES: IMPLEMENTATION

In this business, everyone's corporate objectives are fairly similar; but we believe we differ significantly in our manner of implementing these objectives. Our overall objective is to make seven times our money in five to seven years. In order to do this, we try to see a potential gain of over ten times our capital in each investment in three to five years. One rarely ever realizes this potential, but if at least ten times potential cannot be seen at the beginning, the investment had better not be made.

It is remarkable how often people come to us with well-conceived projections which substantiate (inadvertently) our own conclusion that we should not go into the investment. If they would stop to analyze the numbers, they would see that if everything happened as indicated, even under the most favorable conditions, the investor could make only three or four times his capital in four or five years.

A Look at the Weak Side

The weaknesses of our company are not uncommon. We are understaffed, particularly in view of our heavy workload when taking on major capital investments. We are also undercapitalized, which tends to force us into some marginal investments. Although currently, we have no in-house capability for evaluating certain types of industries, in time we expect to correct this problem. One reason we avoid high-technology businesses is that we do not really know what makes a good one go. We are not totally ignorant in this area, but we know enough to know just how little we do know about technology.

One of the most critical weaknesses of many of today's venture firms is that they are far removed from the new generation of businessmen who are in the twenty-three to twenty-nine age group. This group will create the great venture capital opportunities of the 1970's. We must bring someone into our organizations who is at that age level and in rapport with the young entrepreneurs emerging from today's business schools. Also in this decade, we will see many chief executive officers of major corporations, and certainly of smaller and middle-sized corporations, who are thirty to forty years old. The age level of responsibility is rapidly descending.

. . . and the Strengths

Inverness is a small organization and, by virtue of being understaffed, each of us has considerable responsibility. If an entrepreneur gets a "yes" or "no" from one of our key people, he does not have to see the boss, because he would receive the same answer.

Our modest size enables us to do certain things that other venture capital firms cannot do. For example, we run about three-fourths of the burglary detection business (other than production and product development).

We are able to make quick decisions and take action just as rapidly. We also are extremely flexible and have no rules simply for the sake of organization. Our greatest strength, perhaps, lies in the fact that we are a small company.

4

APPROACHING THE VENTURE CAPITALIST

John H. Lamothe

There is a distressing situation in the world of venture capital. In spite of the influx of money, the entrepreneur does not seem to know how to get his hands on it. How can he gain this education?

TIMING

A basic requirement when dealing with a venture capitalist is a sense of timing. This may seem mundane, but many problems can be traced to poor timing. Too many entrepreneurs wait until they are in desperate need of capital before approaching a venture capitalist. They will request capital when it is needed immediately—in thirty to sixty days. Because of the necessary investigation time required, this is an impossible target. Worse still, it casts a poor light upon the small businessman and his organizational abilities; he is not able to plan his work or his financial requirements.

Mr. Lamothe is president of Federal Street Capital Corporation, in Boston, Mass.

CONCESSIONS

Whenever a small businessman waits too long to approach the venture capitalist, it is inevitable that he will be forced to make some costly concessions. Venture capitalists are as human as the next man, especially when someone with a good deal to offer is desperately looking for money.

The entrepreneur must plan his timing—line up his money at least six months before he needs it so that he can deal from a strong position on an intelligent level with venture capitalists.

SELECTION

How does the entrepreneur select a venture capitalist?

This is a very important factor. Quite often the best deal from a venture capitalist in financial terms will not be best for the businessman. The entrepreneur gains the capital that is needed without giving up too much equity; but, usually, the problems of small business are not solved by money alone. Money can bring growth—and growth can bring great headaches. Practically ten out of ten entrepreneurs are not qualified to cope with these problems.

Before a businessman seeks out a venture capitalist for his money needs, he should figure out everything his business needs in order to grow. Can he live in a close business relationship with these venture capitalists for the next five, seven or ten years? Is his marketing organization weak? Does he need a scientifically-oriented venture capitalist? All of these qualifications should be investigated carefully before beginning to consider a venture capitalist.

Where can this information be found?

Ours is a privately-owned company that does not publish statements or a list of our investments; but we are changing, and in the not so far-off future this information will be available. In the venture capital industry alone, there are approximately forty publicly-owned SBIC's which publish statements. This is a good starting point.

INITIAL CONTACTS

The first contact the businessman will probably make is with his broker. Here is the person who undoubtedly has said, "Look, Howard, I've taken you as far as I can. Right now you need some equity capital." Obviously, the next question is, "Fine, but where do I find it?" He will supply some names, many of whom are bankers. We, for example, are owned by twenty-six banks and we receive many referrals. It is a typical "scratch-my-back" deal. We invest on an unsubordinated and unsecured basis so that we can help build a better borrower for the banker. A banker is an excellent starting-point for locating a good venture capitalist. The businessman should check with his auditor and his attorney, and learn about their experiences with various venture capital organizations in the area.

UNIQUE "MARRIAGE"

It is important to comment on the "marriage"—sometimes referred to as a "common-law marriage"—entered into by the small entrepreneur and the venture capitalist. Customarily in such an agreement, the documents are written for a minimum of five years or a maximum of twenty. Our deals currently are averaging seven or eight years. Once that marriage is made, the partners cannot hop a plane to Las Vegas and get a quick divorce. There are forty or fifty pages of documents in typical venture capital contracts—all of them "Thou shalt nots." These are protective clauses for both parties.

It is important to stress that the choice of a venture capitalist should be carefully considered. Avoid the person who says, "I only want 20 percent of your action and my competition wants 30, so come with me." Based on our experience, the businessman will wind up in trouble if he allows percentage alone to determine his choice of venture capitalists.

VENTURE CAPITAL—"THE PEOPLE BUSINESS"

Our business is people; and we always bet on people. We do not care as much about the product or the industry as we do about the quality, the talent of the entrepreneur. The entrepreneur should have the same attitude toward the venture capitalist.

"Peddlers, Beware!"

How many people should be approached in looking for money?

Many businessmen prostitute their deals by peddling them around town. This can be disastrous. In Boston, we usually know the deals that other venture capitalists are currently studying. This does not mean that people are not discreet; they are. But we are not going to spend $3 thousand worth of our time looking at a man's deal while he is working with another venture capitalist. Future entrepreneurs and the people who bring deals to venture capitalists should be aware that this is a poor approach to raising capital.

On the other hand, the entrepreneur has certain reasonable expectations of the venture capitalist. He might legitimately say:

"Norman, you could tie me up for thirty or sixty days during your investigation and turn me down at the end—I cannot afford to lose the time."

Today's venture capitalist is more sophisticated than the venturer of the past. He will answer questions directly early in the initial meeting as to the amount of time he will devote to investigation. He will also caution the entrepreneur about approaching other people. In addition, he will get to the heart of the equity matter early in the discussion. If a small businessman comes to our office and states that he wants $1½ million for 10 percent of his equity . . . and if we like the company but feel the deal should entail 25 percent of the equity—unless we can arrive at a compromise, our secretary is usually called in to serve coffee while we simply chat.

PREPARING THE PRESENTATION . . .

Once the selection is made, how does the entrepreneur prepare for his presentation to the venture capitalist?

Basically, he must develop the attitude that this is the biggest and toughest selling job of his life. The preparation should be outstanding. In principle, we disagree with the letter approach to a venture capitalist. We are solicited with over 400 deals a year, including telephone calls. Last year we looked at 250 of these situations. In many cases, some people never get beyond a five-minute interview.

Most venture capital firms have either an Investment or Executive Committee of the Board of Directors to pass on investments. Our firm has an Investment Committee of five people. When the committee meets to consider a recommendation of one of us, for example, that one is the only person who has met the entrepreneur. The other four members are cold-bloodedly looking at the deal based only upon the written presentation; they have never met the individual concerned.

The national average indicates that out of every 100 deals that a venture capitalist considers, he enters into only approximately 2.8 percent of them. Considering the competition, these odds make a well-planned, written presentation worth the effort.

We prefer to receive written presentations at least a week before we meet with people. We like to educate ourselves, do a preliminary investigation, and make a few telephone calls to investment prospects. If one of our banks has a company like this, for example, we can obtain information on a parallel situation. Much can be accomplished in the week before the oral presentation is made. There is no magic to these presentations, yet some of the proposals that come across our desks are completely inadequate.

The Contents

Basically, a good presentation should include the history of the company, as well as developments in the company for the last three or five years. It should provide a rundown of the key people, indicate their backgrounds, and state how long they have been with the firm. It should provide a thorough discussion of the product, including all available company literature. The venture capitalist wants to know about the track record and growth of competition. A few references should be included because investigation will lead to them eventually. There should also be an in-depth market report. The more information provided here, the less time will be required to investigate the entrepreneur and his industry.

Our description of an "ideal" written presentation would be

one that presented information on people only. We do not believe that companies fail or succeed—only that management fails or succeeds.

The venture capitalist also needs a company's stockholder list. In the financial area, we need not only the complete financial history of a firm, but realistic and detailed profit-and-loss pro forma projections, and cash flows by month for the first year and, hopefully, by the quarter for the second year. These may be "blue sky," but we put more weight on forecasts and projections than we put on the historical past. We are not so much interested in how much money was made or lost last year, as in why and how the company made and lost money.

The presentation should be brief—fewer than fifty pages. No venture capitalist is going to read more material than that. If the presentation can be condensed into twenty-two to twenty-five pages, it will be far more effective and better-received. Above all, the written and oral presentation should point out the weaknesses in an organization. This cannot be stressed too heavily. The venture capitalist is going to make a thorough investigation. If he finds a weakness that has not been pinpointed for him, the presenter will end up with black marks against him. Doubts are created when someone does not point out very obvious weaknesses in such areas as marketing, finance or production. When we become suspicious of an individual, it convinces us that there must be dirt under the rug and we begin checking deeper into the company's operations to find out what else has been hidden.

BRINGING THE TEAM

In making a personal presentation, the entrepreneur should bring along his team. We particularly like to see the person who heads the financial end. If a company does not have a strong treasurer, controller or vice-president of finance, at least the auditor should be on hand. If this is a weak link, maybe we can help solve the problem after consummating "the marriage." If a company has good marketing and production men, they should come along. We will spend a good deal of time at an applicant's plant, so we appreciate help in this guessing area. Everything that we ask for in the seasoned company would be required for a written presentation by a startup situation. In the financial section of the startup company, there should be more concentration on forecasting and substantiation of forecasts. We also place great importance on candor in a projection from a startup company.

If help is needed on the necessary materials, there are specialized consultants who can be retained to prepare the documentation necessary for an initial presentation. Some accounting firm also will provide this type of help on a straight fee basis.

The candid approach to the venture capitalist is becoming increasingly essential in today's business world. Competition for venture capital will also increase. Currently, we see far more seasoned companies because they are unable to turn to banks and/or the public market for financing. Tight money markets can only sharpen a keen edge; and one of the major factors in a successful placement will be close attention to the all-important approach to venture capitalists.

5

THE INVESTMENT BANKER AND VENTURE CAPITAL

Richard B. Fitzpatrick

There is an important question in the minds of entrepreneurs: how to raise capital and run a business at the same time. The answer concerns the investment banker, and many people have a strange and nebulous concept of what this person does.

An investment banker is essentially a guide through the labyrinth of potential capital sources. Investment banking is merely a link between sources of capital and investment opportunities.

On one end is a broad spectrum of investment opportunities and ideas; on the other are men with money to risk. The investment banker is paid for bringing these two together.

BACKGROUND OF OUR FIRM

Our firm entered the venture capital business in the traditional manner. Two of us in the institutional department of an investment banking firm decided to branch out on our own. We had built up a substantial business and felt that we could translate these efforts to our own enterprise if we could find the right corporate vehicle.

Mr. Fitzpatrick is a partner in the venture capital firm of Goldwater, Valente, Fitzpatrick & Schall, in New York City.

We finally found other people who were like-minded, and hung out our shingle in the beginning of 1968. The keystone of our operation was institutional business, and we recognized the changes that were occurring in the field. We reasoned that performance was a way of life with all institutional money-managers: to stay in the game, we constantly had to seek more investments of higher quality at an earlier stage.

Before reaching our second birthday, we had managed six public offerings, ranging from $500 thousand to $6.5 million. We also completed over a dozen private placements. We have handled deals for $50 thousand in seed capital, and two recent closings were in the $2-million bracket in equity and debt.

Our recognition of this special appetite among the institutions was the factor that propelled us into the business we are now in permanently as full-time competitors. One reason we like our position as investment banker for small firms is that there is a great gap between the old, established major firms and the "bucket shop" operators who will do a deal for the pay only, and have absolutely no interest in staying with the company.

For young, emerging companies, there is need for responsible investment banking along traditional lines. The investment banker must have a long-term concern in the development of the company, and must also be dedicated to protecting the interests of its investors. This does not mean that we do not operate in the commission business. We also act as brokers, and we have salesmen who generate income which funds the overall operation and enables us to maintain a reasonable fee schedule.

SEED CAPITAL AND VENTURE CAPITAL

Let us explore here the areas of seed capital, which is front-end money of the wildest sort—and venture capital, which we define as any major financing which precedes a public offering.

We do not think we are unusual in our attitudes toward seed capital, an area of investment in which we have been rather unsuccessful. Bankers or brokers will put together a group of private investors, or use some of their own money to finance a seed deal with particularly unusual characteristics. Most Wall Street firms, however, are afraid of seed capital situations.

A Wall Street house can usually exert its most effective role when the company seeks a second round of financing. An investment banker can call on his full resources to examine a proposal, and shape the presentation to available capital sources to market the issue effectively.

We do seed deals for our own accounts and occasionally for others, but only when we have a thorough knowledge of the industry concerned. If we have or can gain extensive knowledge of a particular type of business and the people who are trying to get the company off the ground, we will take on a startup deal. But the company must have great promise. Our greatest mistakes have been made when we strayed out of the areas in which we had most intimate knowledge. We are extremely cautious in becoming involved in capital deals.

Despite the fact that this is the age of the giant corporation and the conglomerate, there are excellent financing opportunities available to young and emerging small businesses. Key management personnel continue to leave the giant corporations to form their own firms . . . and they need financing.

ADVANTAGES OF THE PUBLIC MARKET

Sometimes an entrepreneur can launch an enterprise with his own resources. Another entrepreneur may have the ability to locate individual investors. In the proper environment (1960-61 or 1968-69), he also can have ready access to public funds. By providing a balance sheet that reveals adequate support of the early business plan, he can sell stock to the public well before his profit-and-loss sheet or his revenues justify it. The company is usually better off with an investment banker or an underwriter in this case, although some firms have successfully gone public on their own. This can be a dangerous route.

Although technology is the business area in which most public spider-webs have been spun, we have not limited our investments to this area. Basically, we are interested in fast-growing companies with good management. The "seed capital-public issue route," as we refer to it, can be utilized only in excellent new-issue market environments with imaginative well-managed growth companies that have unique stories to tell. These elements do not come together often. We feel it will be some time before we again see a marketplace such as we witnessed in late 1968, early 1969, and the early part of 1970, when it seemed as though ice cream could have been sold in Alaska at a premium.

There are, however, many advantages to a public offering. Rapid establishment of a public market is a powerful inducement to seed capital investors even though they remain locked into it for some time. Dilution of the equity base is minimized because the public will pay higher prices than the private investor.

Public status is an asset, of course, to customer and supplier relations, banking support and key employee motivation. Seasoning of the stock with a public offering relatively early in the company's history serves to condition the climate for additional financing when needed, assuming the investor has a winner.

. . . AND THE DISADVANTAGES

The disadvantages are obvious. If the issue fails to come to market after the costly and time-consuming effort put into it, a financial crisis may be imminent. Sometimes, a company must come to market at the wrong time, at less than desired equity prices because the funding need and the cost of preparations to go public burden the company's ability to continue operations.

If the issue goes public and the after-market environment does not treat the company well, it takes a long time to regain investor interest. Of course, it is more difficult to sell additional funding if the stock came out at ten dollars and is currently trading at three dollars.

Particularly in the case of a young company in highly competitive areas, public scrutiny of operations can ruthlessly expose mistakes made in the normal course of corporate growth. While the young public company must be extremely careful to avoid such mistakes, a bear market can shake out dozens of other firms that have not been as cautious.

A variant of the venture capital-public offering route is an approach that has been successful for some technically-oriented companies using a significant portion of overall funding for speculative research and development (R & D). A limited partnership, with the company as a general partner, can be created with capital contributed by individual investors. To the extent that the partnership funds are expended on R & D, the individual investor has a write-off—a tax shelter against ordinary income. If the company chooses to exploit the R & D effort, it can exchange shares of the parent company stock on a pro rata basis among the limited partners. The effect is a tax shelter plus cheap stock for the seed capital investors. The advantages are similar to those in the first approach, with the added incentive of special tax treatments for the investor. The marked disadvantage is the substantial additional costs and complexity in organizing and qualifying such an investment vehicle.

ANALYZING THE PRIVATE PLACEMENT

The third approach is to privately place the company's securities with sophisticated investors. Here, the investment banker can be an effective guide. Private placement is merely the sale of securities unregistered with the Securities and Exchange Commission directly to one or a small number of knowledgeable capital sources.

The Advantages

What are the advantages of private placement? First, the time involved is considerably shorter than that involved in preparing and filing a registration statement with the SEC, waiting for the comment letter, answering it and praying that the market does not change considerably in the meantime. The typical time, from initiation to closing a private placement, is approximately sixty to ninety days.

Second, the type of investor involved in a private placement is generally able to give more help than simply to purchase the securties. This includes valuable business advice, entrée to new customers, additional financing, and sponsorship.

Third, the cost of a private placement is considerably lower than a public offering. This includes fees, legal and accounting and printing expenses.

. . . And Disadvantages

There are disadvantages, of course. The obvious one is that the professional investor is going to look at the proposal carefully and will place a lower price on the equity than the public would. Therefore, the entrepreneur must sell more equity in the company to realize the same amount of money. In the placement of debt, higher interest costs must be borne by the company. The investor is likely to demand a debt instrument because he has no market for the equity. With optional equity "sweeteners," he can become a partner of the business.

Few companies have the insight to ferret out the best private sources of capital, and the money market is a terrifying maze to the uninitiated. We believe the rational decision is for companies to use responsible investment bankers who are knowledgeable in private placement and can spearhead the money-raising effort.

SELECTION OF THE INVESTMENT BANKER

The selection of the proper investment banker is critical. There are all kinds of investments bankers, but the key lies in finding someone who understands the particular business involved. If he understands, he is going to enhance considerably the chances of financing.

In the negotiations, the entrepreneur must lay all his cards on the table. There is an old expression: if there are snakes and alligators under the rug, the rug may start to move at the wrong time. There should be a seal of confession between company and investment banker.

It is essential that the company document its history, full financials, and future business plans. The financial data should include at least a three-year detailed projection of cash flow, with complete profit-and-loss and balance sheets.

Analysis of this data by the investment banking firm will reveal whether adequate return on investment can be reasonably expected for the investors. If study indicates a superior proposal, the investment banker will suggest appropriate procedures including the type of security, size of placement, and a myriad of other details. This process entails extensive financial planning and marketing of the particular issue at hand. It forces the company to carefully plot the future course of action.

The process of verifying the attractiveness of the investment proposal includes both investigation and negotiation of terms of the placement with the issuer. This step is carried out by independent checks of the business by the investment banker. If he has a solid grasp of the industry, this does not take long.

It is important for the company that it check thoroughly on the investment firm with whom it contemplates becoming involved. There are many wolves running around in investment bankers' clothing.

Our firm is in business for the long haul, not the short ride. On a private placement, we like to take a cash fee to cover out-of-pocket expenses, overhead and moderate profit. We always acquire an equity position as part of our compensation. The amount of cash depends on the size of the deal and the maturity of the company. We rarely charge more than a five percent fee, and this percentage is subject to negotiation. The percentage charge is total compensation on a deal, normally scaled down after the first million: five percent for the first million; four percent for the second; three percent for the third; two percent for the fourth; and one percent for all sums raised in excess of $4 million.

THE PRIVATE PLACEMENT MEMORANDUM

With all these facts, the company and its investment banker prepare a memorandum that details, in logical form, the company's structure and the investment proposal. Formats differ among the various investment bankers, but each proposal includes the same essential elements: a clear statement of what the particular business is and where it is headed; qualitative justification of the investment proposal; description of the securities offered and capitalization; the financials and projections to show quantitatively how the funds will generate revenues to obtain the return on the investment desired.

EMPHASIS ON MANAGEMENT

Venture capital financing is a business concerned mainly with people. The management section of the memorandum should reveal the leadership that will be provided to guide the venture to its goals and attain the investor's objectives.

The memorandum should be a well-edited, properly presented and realistic picture of the investment potential that can be readily understood by the prospective investor. While it is being prepared, the marketing people should be working out their plan. We try to stay close to the sources of capital with which we deal so we know what they are looking at, what they are currently doing, the parameters of their interests in various forms of deals, and other such factors.

NEGOTIATING FACTORS

There is little to negotiate in a venture capital stock placement if a deal is well-presented and the fundamentals are understood. When considering equity, there is only one area of negotiation as far as we are concerned: right of registration . . . when does the investor get it, in what form, and how soon is he going to see himself out of the investment.

Attitudes of company principals, investment bankers and investors are important because they help sell the securities. A flexible attitude about the specifics of the placement is essential;

no deals are concluded unless all parties are happy. A good investment proposal can easily flounder on the rocks of rigidity.

A corollary of rigid attitude is greed. All venture capital seekers should remember that half of something is worth infinitely more than all of nothing. After all, the venture capital source whose funds are at risk looks for the same potential gains as those that motivate the company's entrepreneur.

The opportunities for venture capital are outstanding if properly approached. With the right guide and an assistance on all the homely virtues including total commitment, absolute candor and a recognition that everybody must fare well—success is inevitable.

6

WHAT THE VENTURE CAPITALIST SEEKS

Philip A. Fisher

Fisher & Company operates differently from many other venture capital firms. Most of the activities in which we engage are not concerned with providing capital for startup ventures for people who have a unique idea and would like to form a company to sell their new product or service. The investment funds under our management are deliberately diversified in "growth capital" among enterprises that have proven their ability to produce profits; they range from older, large corporations to medium-sized companies and young, small businesses. We believe that this is the best balance of the risk-profit ratio for the investors. These funds are concentrated in two major areas, on the theory that enough mistakes can be made in one's own backyard without getting into someone else's.

HIGH-TECHNOLOGY, LONG-TERM INVESTMENTS

For the last ten years, our investments have been confined solely to high-technology manufacturing companies on the frontiers of science, and to service companies that range from moderately-to highly technological.

Mr. Fisher is president of the investment advisory firm, Fisher & Company, in San Francisco, Calif.

Our time reference is also considerably longer. We are not interested in making money quickly and do not invest in venture capital situations to retrieve our money with the first public offering. We prefer to grow with a company over a period of several years.

The most distinct characteristic of our firm is that we are not interested in obtaining numerous "good" investments for our portfolio. We want only a few outstanding investments in small companies that will grow into medium-sized firms, and medium-sized companies that will eventually become blue-chip growth-oriented corporations.

The overall growth schedule for each is ten years. This long-range policy has returned handsome profits for us over the years.

THREE KEY FACTORS IN A VENTURE CAPITAL INVESTMENT

There are three factors that we consider to be vitally important in making a venture capital investment. Trying to decide which is more important is like attempting to choose the relative importance of good heart, good lungs or a good digestive system. If any one of them is bad, you are in trouble. All these factors are equally important:

Sound Management

We want management that will innumerate the firm's problems with full details, reflecting realism and accuracy. Every business has problems, but management that does not accept this fact falls into one of two groups: either they are dishonest or they lack a clear view of their business. These groups will never succeed, and we do not want to be associated with them.

We also dislike the entrepreneur who comes to us for an investment and attempts to oversell his position. If he thinks we do not have enough intelligence to see the strengths of his company, he should not be dealing with us.

A Sense of Responsibility

We want to be associated with people who have a sense of responsibility to us as their partners, and who are not overwhelmingly selfish about the rewards of success.

Entrepreneurs must have a real stake in and commitment to their business. These men could be drawing high salaries and attractive fringe benefits as employees of a large corporation. They must have a sense of responsibility and willingness to put their commitment on the line along with ours; otherwise they could simply walk away from the situation, accept a salaried position and leave us holding the bag.

This would not be a fair division of the risks. We are not concerned about the amount of money a man puts up, but we want his investment to represent a major percentage of his funds so that he has a total commitment in the venture.

Business Acumen

Finally, we will only invest in management with demonstrated business ability.

In our judgment, the reason that the average investor does not make more money from technological companies is that he does not understand the technology; nor does he understand that he can easily hire experts to explain the technology quickly and clearly. Rather, both venture capital and general investors become so bemused by the wonders of technology that they fail to give proper weight to the business ability of the people who will run the company.

The computer industry, for example, is the heart of the growth industries. Most of the leaders who came out of the computer industry were in the original Sperry-Rand group. Sperry-Rand and Remington-Rand computer divisions, staffed with a majority of the great original computer minds of the country, were not outstanding investments and only recently have become profitable.

Another young computer company, IBM, lacked extensive staff capability, but excelled in business ability. Utilizing these skills, they were able to find the necessary staff and go on to make millions of dollars and become a world leader in computer technology.

There are many examples of entrepreneurs with this business ability who, consequently, built up their companies. The entrepreneur who has engineering ability but lacks business ability loses his lead in the long run and fails in the race with his competition.

But contrary to Ralph Waldo Emerson's premise, the world does *not* beat a path to the door of the man who has built a better mousetrap. Moreover, very few of these companies know how to sell. The man who can build up a marketing team, as well as engineering and production, is the man who will go forward.

If the marketing team creates a success, however, trouble often arises in production. The same techniques that work on small quantities will not work when larger scale production is demanded.

For corporate growth, two kinds of skill are required: manufacturing know-how, and internal acumen such as that provided by a controller who knows finance and can give an early warning when costs get out-of-line.

The company president must be able to select and train people while securing their loyalty. He must understand the rapidly-changing markets and be able to adjust his business to fluctuations in the economy. Investments in new product development must reflect careful analysis.

These are the people with whom we seek to develop close relationships. We do not ally ourselves with the man who is going to stumble around and not recognize a major opportunity, who is afraid to say "no" or afraid to take a risk.

One of the large companies in which our firm is proud to have had an interest for many years is Dow Chemical. Of the major chemical companies, this is the only one on the muddy track of the 1960's that showed a steady increase in earnings. The founder, Dr. Dow, once remarked: "Do not promote an employee who has not made some mistakes. If you do, you promote a man who has never done anything—and probably never will." This is also an integral part of our philosophy.

THE OTHER SIDE OF THE COIN

What do we give in return for outstanding performance as an entrepreneur? Why should such an entrepreneur deal with us instead of others?

The answers lie in the realm of our investment philosophy. We prefer not to get involved in the small company that, in our judgment, has already eliminated its capitalization opportunities. Many able men want to raise a little money, but they have no idea how much they really need. They go to their dentist, a personal friend or neighbor, and raise $5 thousand from one and $15 thousand from another. These new stockholders become quite excited as normal business problems develop; they constantly interfere, and an unhappy situation develops. It would take a great deal of interest before we would get involved in this sort of situation. When someone comes to us, we want to handle his investment problems while he devotes himself to operating the business and making it profitable.

We rarely handle investments under $400 thousand; but we have invested as little as $100 thousand if the situation becomes extremely attractive, and the appeal of the situation has to increase on a logarithmic basis to make it profitable. It takes just as long to follow a small investment as a large one.

VENTURE CAPITAL VERSUS INVESTMENT BANKING

The basis of our investment philosophy is to take our profits out of the investment in capital gains. We do not want interest income, dividends, fees or salaries. We want to do everything we can to make that business profitable to generate major capital gains.

We are paid a fee to manage the affairs of our investors and do not need fees from the company in which we invest. This is most important for small companies because they will soon need more money, with or without success. If the company is unsuccessful, additional funds will be needed to shore it up; if successful, the company will need more money to expand. As companies grow, capital drain takes its toll—more inventory, receivables, additional space, new plants. The young president must also decide whether to reinvest profits in more research and development or to use the funds to build up working capital.

When a good investment is found and the company is financed with notes and warrants or convertible debentures, the taking out of dividends or fees drains blood from a business that needs every drop in order to produce spectacular results.

For a public offering of stock, many companies turn to investment bankers, who charge fairly high fees. In order to avoid the high fees for additional offerings over the next two to three years, many firms double the amount they actually need so that they do not have to make repeated trips to the bank.

This is an expensive and wasteful way of raising capital for small companies. Moreover, it is impossible to see far enough ahead to be certain how much capital will be needed. Since we control the funds placed in companies, the only expense involved is for a permit which costs relatively little and can be renewed. We can put in the moderate amount needed now, then add whatever is needed as the company grows. This complies with our philosophy that every additional share of stock outstanding is one more mouth to feed as long as the corporation lives. It is also unfair to those who have built the company to issue one additional share more than is absolutely needed. In this way, we do not need 100 percent foresight; we can adjust as the situation requires.

When the time comes for the company to decrease the cost of private placements, if we like the company we are apt to lower our equity requirements. If not, we can find other associates who would be interested in investing at the higher price. We also have several large investment bankers in the country, as well as some leading local investment bankers for smaller deals. As a result, we are able to handle small financing at no charge to the company.

There is another consideration which most people who are starting or are associated with small companies do not fully appreciate. If one has a six-month-old baby and watches that child every day, it is difficult to see the youngster grow. Yet there is the knowledge that twenty years from now that baby will be radically changed and the growth will be fantastic. A young and promising company is no different.

GROWTH RATE POTENTIAL: SOME FASCINATING ARITHMETIC

In the case of companies like this—and they are hard but not impossible to find—phenomenal growth is possible. Our firm is not primarily involved in startup deals nor are we interested in getting in on the ground floor. We would much rather invest on the "third floor" at three times the startup price. At this point there will be several years of operation to indicate that a twenty- to sixty-story skyscraper is going up.

This is the arithmetic of what can happen if an investor finds a success-oriented company:

> In the first five years an investment might appreciate as much as seven times. On a $10,000 investment, he would have earned $60,000.
>
> In the second five years it will not increase as quickly, but might appreciate three times–from $70,000 to $210,000. Although this is a smaller percentage return on his investment, it is $140,000 more than the original $60,000 invested.
>
> In the next five years his investment might increase two-and-one-half times. The $210,000 would become $525,000. The increase in dollars is spectacular, even though the percentage decreases.
>
> The next time, if his growing investment only doubles, his original $10,000 becomes a million dollars.

Why would an investor not take the $60,000 after the first five years and invest in another firm that may also appreciate seven times? It is not wise to take this risk. We have found it is safer to stay with a growing company that is doing a great job. We only want to get rich with a minimum of risk and with people whom we can trust.

In several cases we have found management that has grown beyond our greatest expectation. This is the kind of investment we like.

With time, we have made millions with the funds we have invested, and have created fortunes for the owners of those companies. Currently, we are in the midst of doing this with several other companies, and we hope to find new deals with more people with whom we can develop this close—and profitable—relationship.

7

PACKAGING THE DEAL

Gilbert Kennedy

Clearly one of the most important on-going factors in the association of the venture investor with his portfolio company begins when the investment is packaged to meet the combined needs of the company, the entrepreneurs, and the venture investors.

There are numerous sources of money—institutions, and individuals—who are perennially interested in venture investments. The entrepreneur must decide which of these he will contact for money, as well as the best format in which to package his presentation. It is a continuous process and difficult to segment because different investors require different formats.

DIEBOLD COMPUTER LEASING: STARTING UP—WITH $85 MILLION

One of our favorite ventures involved a startup situation known as Diebold Automation, which later became Diebold Computer Leasing. This $85 million startup venture was, in the summer of 1966, not as well-known and analyzed a business as it has since become.

It was a major deal involving a large amount of financial leverage—a $75 million revolving line of credit, about $6 million in mezzanine money, plus straight common stock.

Mr. Kennedy is president of Diversified Technologies Inc., in New York City, the venture capital division of Singer Corporation.

It was a complicated deal. Even though it was a startup, the new venture utilized a nationwide leasing company as a marketing arm, a commercial finance company as the principal lender, and the Diebold group were consultants smack in the middle of it all. Although theoretically a startup, the firm was a going business from the day they opened the door. As a special type of startup, the project, therefore, required a different kind of presentation to raise $85 million, compared to the needs of a small startup such as a "garage factory."

Another type of startup example is a small company called Computel Systems Limited—a time-sharing concern with a small service bureau. We became involved with this company through friends—one of the ways venture capitalists become involved in many good deals.

The entrepreneurs came to New York from Ottowa. They needed $50 thousand for a down payment to obtain a Univac Computer in nine months. There was no traditional format for this deal inasmuch as the company had been formed at this time.

Nevertheless, a group of intrepid investors put up money and an investment banking firm in Toronto committed to undertake a larger private placement. The placement required a "Blue Book," a thorough analysis of the company, which also was used later as the basis for a prospectus.

The crux of the story is that traditional presentation was needed for Diebold Computer Leasing, while Computer Systems required only a down payment to get in the waiting-line for the Univac 1108—an extreme contrast in packaging requirements. Not every investor would be interested in both of these deals. Nevertheless, at the time they were originally financed, they were both valid venture capital deals. It is important to be selective in finding the people who are going to raise the down payment money, or finding a special kind of investor who is going to invest in a deal such as Diebold Computer Leasing.

The process can be more efficient if the entrepreneur uses a professional middleman who knows where the sources of capital are located, and who understands what turns these people on—and how to avoid turning them off the deal.

Many people who are looking for capital go to Wall Street, which is like buying an apartment guide for the city of New York. A large share of the business on Wall Street during the last five years has been private placements. Wall Street is quite competent in analyzing, dissecting and writing up the essential aspects of going concerns, as well as startups.

SELECTING A GUIDE FOR YOUR QUEST

In the quest for investors, a "guide" may save the capital-seeker months or years of looking through the maze of possibilities. The guide, whether a consultant, an investment banking firm or an attorney, helps the venture capital investor because he can focus on exactly what the investor is seeking. However, it is essential to be selective in the choice of such a guide, as well as the investor firms.

THE APPROACH: SELECTIVE—BUT DIRECT

Once the right-sounding venture capitalists have been found, it is best to use a simple and direct approach: just telephone or write.

The venture capitalist cannot spend hours talking to sixty entrepreneurs a week if he is to get anything accomplished. This is why the packaging of a proposal is critical to the entrepreneur.

The necessity of processing a large number of deals is a problem faced by everyone who manages a significant amount of capital. There is no way to do it without extensive reading. A venture capitalist is not buying concepts or memoranda—he is buying business propositions. If a project cannot be reduced to a business plan and expressed on paper, there is something wrong with it. At least ten times a week, the venture capitalist will receive a call from someone with a high-pressure pitch. If he replies, "I'm too busy, would you send me a memorandum of it?"—the caller will usually declare, "No memorandum will do it justice—but I'll write up one and send it anyway." In almost every case, the proposal never arrives. The man does not have a business plan. He does not know what he wants.

We also receive many hard-sell, promotion letters. In late 1966, when I arrived at my present job, I found many old letters which had been lying about unanswered for weeks. Soon, identical letters began to come in—retyped this time with a different addressee. Some people shop their deals all over the country. It is absolutely incredible for them to think that venture capital investors are crap-shooters or concept buyers, like some performance funds during stages of the last bull market.

Basically, a sophisticated investor wants to see a three-dimensional picture of a deal without a lot of fluff and precautionary, registration-oriented statements tossed in for effect.

Apparently, some people feel that a good proposal follows the outline of an S-1 form. Much of the content of an S-1, however, is not very relevant. We want to know the good as well as the bad things about the project. We want comparisons, if they are available—anything that can be written in ten to twenty pages. Length is not necessarily strength; but if a deal is complicated, it should be spelled out, even if it means using a lot of paper. All pertinent facts should be included.

THE MIDDLEMAN: SOME INSIGHT

A word to the middleman: If an entrepreneur has asked a venture investor to help him raise money, that investor is being paid to help package the project and present it to selected venture capitalists who have a particular interest in such situations; he is not being paid for owning a small black book of phone numbers.

Nothing aggravates us venture investors more than a finder or middleman, investment banker or attorney who believes he is doing a job and deserves his percentage for giving the entrepreneur our telephone number. This is a ridiculous assumption, and one which the entrepreneur catches on to quickly.

Too many middlemen, too many percentages to be paid for no service, make the deal that much harder to finance. The more cheap stock there is in a company, the more that company has to earn before the hard-money people start seeing daylight.

A TYPICAL VENTURE CAPITAL PLACEMENT MEMO: THE "BLUE BOOK"

The "blue book" on a particular company is a typical private placement memorandum. A venture capital deal is different from the private placement of shares of an established and/or listed company. A "selling" memo can be written for Singer, Esso or General Motors, but such a memo cannot be expected to do the job for a typical venture deal. The venture capital deal should contain an explanatory memo, which clearly spells out all the qualities of the company—the good, the bad, the indifferent—but not the irrelevant.

Write-ups should be no longer than necessary; descriptive essays kept to a minimum. If the situation appears to demand a vast amount of data, it is best to use exhibits—putting the critical material in front and the background at the end—so that venture investors are given a chance to choose between exhibits. We have had more experience in raising venture money than in spending it, and these have been sound guidelines for us.

For example, the memorandum for the Diebold "blue book" involved about a year's preparation. The actual writing of the proposal did not take long, but it took a full year to answer key questions and spell out the deal in sensible terms. A year sounds like a long time, and perhaps it could have been done more quickly, but if a business is worth devoting one's life to, it is certainly worth a few months' investing in preparation for the necessary probing by prospective investors. For some reason, the art of writing startup blue books is deteriorating rather than improving.

A Typical Proposal: The Diebold "Blue Book"

The Diebold Computer Leasing proposal was organized as follows:

The first page contained the deal—so-much money in return for so-many types of securities.

The next page contained the pro forma of capitalization. Although it can appear anywhere in the proposal, it is better to show who gets what as early as possible in the memo; after all the convertibles are converted, warrants and options exercised, the Class B and C securities converted, who ends up with what? And what will it cost them? It should be spelled out because if the investor's search is too hard, the capital search begins with two strikes towards the dugout.

Next should come a brief description of the company and its intended business.

This should be followed by a description of the industry as a whole, then a detailed business plan. The Diebold business plan answered questions about competition, obsolescence, and changes in the money market that would normally arise in the operation of the business. An extensive section described the joint venturers who were forming the company. One section also discussed foreign operations; another cautioned the investor and pointed out "Areas of Risk." (These sections required twelve pages.)

There were also six different financial projections, pro forma financial statements and three pages of assumptions and extensive footnotes with the projections. With any startup, assumptions are quite important and become the biggest job. The financials flow from the assumptions, and the assumptions are obviously the key components of at least the top-line figures.

The appendices included: a marketing agreement between Bankers Leasing Corporation and Diebold Computer Leasing (actual contract included); a consulting agreement between the Diebold group and the company (actual contract also included here); a more extensive description of proposed foreign operations; and a six-page summary of the principal terms of the proposed loan agreement between Commercial Credit Corporation and the company. One appendix included a twenty-five-page memorandum on residual values of IBM 360s and the relationship of residual values to technological obsolescence. This was followed by a description of Bankers Leasing Corporation.

The complete proposal totaled about 100 pages; but the ownership picture could be reviewed in the first two pages, and it took only ten pages to learn what the business was all about. If he were interested in the deal, the venture capitalist could then complete the entire report.

This is only stage one of the venture deal. The next stage requires days, weeks, maybe months to dig into the facts covered in the memorandum. No memo can completely cover every base, but it must touch upon the important ones.

The Diebold "blue book" lacked one thing—a comparison with the competition. The investment bankers apparently ran out of graphs, and had none to do a comparison. We would certainly include one in any report we wrote today.

NEXT STEP: NOW THAT THEY'RE INTERESTED . . .

At this point, the interest of the venture capitalist has been piqued. If he is an investment banker, he may have outlined some terms. Terms are the beginning of the guts of the package—who gets what and for how much.

Some businesses may dictate the form that financing should take. A leasing company that plans to borrow a lot of money must have equity. There cannot be too much quasi-equity or mezzanine money or free stock which destroys the leverage for the people who paid heavily for main floor seats.

The investment banker would probably suggest a mix of securities in such a large deal. The entrepreneur knows what he wants out of the deal, but may be modest enough to ask the banker how much he will have to give up—not the best strategy by any means.

In most situations, the entrepreneur should tell the banker what he wants. The banker will then make suggestions or tell the entrepreneur that he is asking for too much. For example, if the entrepreneur wants 80 percent of the company, and does not put up a cent but wants to raise $10 million, he will have a hard time finding an investment banker.

This is where the first discussion ends if the entrepreneur goes the route of the consultant or banker. At this point he has to face reality because the bankers have a good feel for what will and will not sell. If the entrepreneur is sharp, he, too, may have a good idea of what will sell; if not, he may not be a good entrepreneur.

ROUND TWO IN THE GLAMOROUS XYZ COMPANY?

The entrepreneur also runs a great risk of jeopardizing second-stage financing by using people who will strike an easier initial deal than a competent investment banker will. The entrepreneurs who did that in 1967 through 1969 later returned to New York, Boston and other capital centers in an attempt to raise more capital. There are not many dentists, doctors and stockbrokers around these days who have the cast to go for "Round Two in the XYZ Company," which was originally financed at a phenomenal ratio of price to prospective earnings. The XYZ Company, desperately in need of funds, is now coming to institutions. Many times we are faced with a situation where the first price was so high that the entrepreneur does not want to sell the next round to investors at only a third of the mutual financing price. This poor fellow is really in a bind.

Many people paint themselves into a corner by packaging and pricing their deals too early, while others simply price themselves out of the venture capital market. It is wise not to assume a greedy stance when approaching sophisticated investors.

RULES OF SELF-DEFENSE

How do the company and the investors protect themselves in a deal? Fifty-one percent in non-cumulative voting stock for directors is one answer; but if the deal gets down to the point where fighting is this hard, it is probably dead or on its last legs.

The best way a venture capitalist can protect himself is to avoid getting into an investment where he does not trust the people with whom he is associated. This is also true for entrepreneurs. The minority-majority ownership problem is more a function of the economics of the deal than it is of control of the company. Generally, a venture capital investor is not looking for a leading role in the operating management; he simply wants to be in the investment business. He must take an active interest in his portfolio companies, if only to protect his investments. Even if he is a majority investor, he is probably not the chief executive officer and does not want to be. If he does, he is in the wrong business or has invested in a problem company.

If we, as venture capitalists, liked everything about a new deal except the terms, we would negotiate to get the price lowered. If terms other than price relate to improving the security or protection for the investment, we would do the same. We would explain our reasons for thinking the price was too high or whatever, and that this was the wrong kind of security, then try to get the group to follow our suggestion. If agreement cannot be reached after these discussions, we pass up the investment.

PACKAGING AS THE KEY TO SUCCESS

In summary, packaging is a difficult task for the company as well as the investor. It can kill good deals. To get locked into a company with a capital structure that does not relate to the dynamics of the business is a bad situation. Anyone who wants to raise money must remain flexible as he ventures forth on the quest for capital in today's money market.

8

THE TAILORING OF VENTURE FINANCING

Edward Glassmeyer

In negotiations between the entrepreneur and the investor, so much energy is expended on the question of valuation that one or both of the parties tend to overlook the critical issue of the amount and quality of securities to be issued for the dollars invested.

The following kinds of questions should be asked (and answered) as part of the investment process:

What is the best stimulus for a company's growth? . . . the lowest financing cost?

Which instrument represents the most secure form of financing for investors, or will give an entrepreneur greatest control of his own firm?

THE INSTRUMENTS

First, to define the "instruments" or financing vehicles. . . . There are four instruments commonly used to finance venture capital investments; they can be used alone or in combination:

Mr. Glassmeyer is general partner in the Sprout Capital Group, Donaldson, Lufkin & Jenrette, Inc., in New York City.

1. Senior Debt. These include bank guarantees, short-term notes (secured as well as unsecured), and long-term debt as provided by banks or insurance companies. Senior obligations are normally associated with fixed maturities and high interest costs.

In venture capital situations, senior debt can be used to bridge a merger, acquisition, or additional equity financing, as well as to finance time gaps in the working capital cycle for ventures that cannot attract bank debt. A venture capitalist who views such a senior obligation as a risky investment will usually take warrants as the traditional approach to provide this credit.

2. Subordinated Debt. This is, as a rule, junior to bank and insurance company loans and other senior obligations. It is treated by senior lenders as equity if it does not dominate the balance sheet. Normally, it has lower interest costs and is a longer-term security than a senior obligation. The equity feature of convertible debt makes it attractive as a financing instrument in venture capital financings.

It is important to differentiate between convertible subordinated debt and subordinated debt with warrants. If the warrants are not detachable the instrument is, in essence, a convertible security. If the warrants are detachable, the investor can defer his investment decision until after the loan is repaid. Customarily, the warrant expiration date follows the last installment due on the debt by as much as two years. Convertible debt, on the other hand, forces the investor to make his investment decision simultaneously with the maturity of the obligation which, in some cases, could be premature. Investors, therefore, often take the option of debt with warrants; entrepreneurs would rather finance with convertibles.

3. Preferred Stock. In venture capital financings, preferred stock is used almost exclusively with a conversion feature. Preferred stock has these attributes:

It adds to the net worth of the company.

It has preference over common stock in liquidation.

With call provisions, it has many of the same features as a subordinated debt instrument.

It can be written as an agreement with many of the covenants of a debt instrument, but cannot accelerate repayment as in the case of a debt obligation.

4. Common Stock. The most commonly used instrument in venture capital financings is common stock. Stock is the most junior of all securities and has no preference in liquidation. In most venture situations, holding stock allows the investor little chance to recoup his investment in the event the company should fail. On the other hand, the purchase of stock should provide the greatest absolute return because a larger portion of the company can be reasonably negotiated if the venture capitalist is providing pure equity.

In many circumstances, the highest return on investment can be achieved by reducing the investment base through debt repayment, release of a guarantee, redemption of stock, or holding optional warrants to purchase stock at a later date.

The stock purchase warrant is simply an option to purchase common stock during a specified period of time at a predetermined price.

How can these instruments be most effectively utilized by the company and by the venture capitalist?

THE COMPANY'S PERSPECTIVE

Let us begin with a look at alternative instruments, from the entrepreneur's point of view. It may be helpful to visualize this in terms of a matrix with a row of the four instruments across the top of the page, and a list of variables describing the costs and benefits of each instrument along the left-hand column.

Valuation

The first variable to compare among the instruments is valuation. Which instrument will provide the entrepreneur with the highest valuation for his company, and minimize the dilution of his ownership interest?

The entrepreneur normally will be able to achieve the highest valuation for his company by issuing the most senior instrument for his needs. For example, if the financier need only guarantee bank debt, the equity offered in order to obtain such a guarantee will be less than that sold to investors for the purchase of preferred or common stock. With debt, the money invested buys yield, some controls, and repayment, in lieu of a larger portion of equity.

For the entrepreneur, the trade-off matches a permanent investment upon which to build his company against a limited life investment which he is obligated to service with interest and principal payments. He also must give up certain controls to the money source, but—even more important—less of his company. As a rule, the more senior the instrument used, the higher the valuation. And normally, the higher valuation comes at the expense of building a strong capital structure.

Control

The next important feature is control. Most entrepreneurs do not want to give up control of their company either by selling 51 percent or more of the equity, or through the provisions of negative and affirmative covenants in a securities purchase agreement. If the entrepreneur can raise the required dollars without issuing 50 percent or more of his common stock, then he can maintain greatest control through the sale of common stock. If he must give up control in order to raise the funds required through the sale of stock, he can offer the investors a more senior instrument and trade the senior position for ownership.

Provisions such as maintaining a given working capital ratio, a level of net worth, restrictions with respect to additional sales of stock, or bank borrowings, will seem onerous to management—but certainly not as severe as majority ownership of his company by the investors. Therefore, from the standpoint of management control, an entrepreneur would choose common stock first, preferred stock next, then subordinated debt, and finally senior debt, unless his financing requirements would force the sale of over 50 percent of his company if common stock were used.

Flexibility

Management will have its greatest flexibility with the issuance of common stock, owing to the lack of restrictions on its financial and operational decisions. Also, for stimulating growth, the sale of common stock will enable the company to show lenders, suppliers and customers a stronger capital structure and a greater borrowing base for leverage. A company can remove many barriers to growth by issuing common stock and resisting the use of debt.

Profit and Cash Flow Maximization

Another important consideration is profit and cash flow maximization. Both subordinated debt and senior debt require interest payments throughout the life of the obligation, as well as principal repayments, which are usually ballooned toward the maturity date in venture capital financing. Therefore, common stock, with no claim on the corporate treasury other than dividends—which are usually paid only after an extended period of profitable operations—represents the best financing instrument to conserve dollars and maximize earnings.

The evaluation of alternative instruments should include a calculation of forecasted per-share earnings comparing debt, preferred and common stock. The instrument which maximizes earnings will depend on each negotiation. It is possible that the trade-off between ownership and yield to the investor would produce very similar results with either debt or equity. In this calculation, it should be remembered that preferred dividends are deducted from after-tax earnings to determine earnings per share. The entrepreneur should keep in mind that the marketplace will capitalize his earnings at a higher rate. He will normally achieve a higher multiple of earnings in his stock price if his balance sheet is weighted toward equity versus debt.

Also important to the entrepreneur are the administrative details of a financing: how quickly will he receive proceeds? How simple is it? What will his closing costs be? The more junior the instrument, the quicker the closing; the shorter the documents, the cheaper the cost of closing.

THE INVESTOR'S PERSPECTIVE

From the standpoint of the venture capitalist, in order to *maximize returns* he will have to trade off the larger equity interest represented by junior securities against the debt features of senior securities.

With respect to *valuation,* the investor should achieve the greatest percentage of ownership of a company seeking venture capital through the use of common stock owing to its junior position in the capital structure and the irrevocable commitment of funds to the company.

The venture capitalist must also be concerned with his *return on investment*, as well as the absolute percentage of the company he owns. In the calculation of returns, the investor must factor in the reduction of his investment base at the time a debt is repaid. If the investor has negotiated for the purchase of a short-term instrument with an option to purchase stock at some future date, his return may be substantially greater than if he had purchased a larger equity interest through a direct common stock investment.

Customarily, in a successful venture, a debt/warrant package will produce a higher return on investment, and common stock a greater absolute return.

As far as maximizing *yield, security, repayment, control* and *flexibility* are concerned—all of these variables favor the use of the most senior debt instrument and become weaker as one moves to more junior instruments.

Looking at the continuum from senior debt to common stock, there is a very clear trade-off between minimizing risk and maximizing return:

. . . Minimizing the risk through the use of a more senior obligation where protective covenants, early maturity of the obligation, and other controls greatly reduce the risk of losing one's investment.

. . . Maximizing returns by accepting greater risk of a common stock investment for a compensating increase in the percentage of the company acquired.

Probably as important as the level of return expectations is the investor's ability to liquidate his investment. With the advent of the proposed Wheat Amendment to the Securities Act,[1] a paradox has arisen: the vehicle that provides the least control may provide the greatest escape for the investor. The Wheat Amendment, if passed into law as it is now written, will allow an investor to begin to liquidate his investment—if it is held in the form of common stock—eighteen months after the date of his investment.

If his securities are convertible securities or warrants, for example, the investor must wait until eighteen months after the convertibles are converted or the warrants exercised.

The venture capitalist cannot underestimate the importance of choosing a financing instrument that will allow him to realize his investment or to get out alive and in one piece if the investment should decline substantially in value. From the standpoint of realizing gains in a successful venture, the common stock instrument appears attractive. When liquidating a poor or moderately successful venture, a debt instrument with a fixed maturity is preferable. In either case, registration rights should be as much a part of a purchase agreement as the exchange of securities for dollars. Even with the proposed Amendment to the Securities and Exchange Act, an investor, as well as an entrepreneur, should always focus on how he will best realize the goals of the investment.

APPLICATION

Inasmuch as we have defined the major instruments used in venture financings and discussed some of the trade-offs between them, the best possible summary of this venture capital finance package would be some illustrations of the use of these instruments.

For startup ventures, service companies, research and development companies, and ventures that require a long lead-time before a saleable product is born, the most junior security should be utilized. Generally, these companies do not have the assets to secure a senior lender's investment and, as a practical matter, should not inhibit their ability to layer senior rounds of financing on an equity base by burning up debt capacity prematurely.

In these instances, common stock should be preferable for both the investor and the company. If these companies were to go out of business there would be little advantage to holding a debt security because there would be few assets to move against; if the venture succeeded, the larger ownership interest purchased in exchange for stock would provide a greater return to the investor. Moreover, such a company would benefit from better customer relations—such as credit from lenders and suppliers—with a stronger capital structure resulting.

If a company has working assets and is a going concern, then a tight agreement can be written spelling out how the firm will be operated and how assets will be employed. If the company's cash flow can support debt service, an investor can achieve yield, security and control through a debt instrument and a venture capital return through the use of a conversion feature or warrants.

When investing in strong people, the investor will want to maximize his return and minimize his control. In such a situation, common stock is useful.

When investing in patents or a product, the investor will want very much to control the development of the product and the manufacture and marketing of it. In this case, the investor is not backing an entrepreneur and his business judgment; therefore, a more senior obligation with restrictions is in order. Once a management team can be found, it may be appropriate to convert the debt into a more junior instrument and build a vehicle that has the capacity for explosive growth.

THE OVERALL VIEW

The financing instrument is the modulator that allows an investor in a high-risk project to hedge his bet; but it also allows the investor in a low-risk project to increase his return potential. The clever application of a financing instrument can add substantially to the value of an investment; a sloppy approach will detract from the value of such an investment.

If the entrepreneur desires to build a company himself and he has the confidence of his investor group to pursue this, the most junior security will work best for him as well as the investor group. If the project is not successful, there would probably be very little to be gained by holding a senior security. However, when making a product investment or a "turn-around" investment, a fairer return on a venture capitalist's money can be achieved through the prudent use of debt with its control provisions and benefits in liquidation.

The theoretical objective of investing in high-return, low-risk projects can be obtained if both the investor and the entrepreneur recognize the strengths and weaknesses of their investment and tailor their financial package accordingly.

9
VENTURE CAPITAL: THE LEGAL ASPECTS

George W. Bermant

After the entrepreneur has read at length about where to go to get money and how such finance can be relatively free from pain, our job is to explain the sobering legal aspects of the transaction according to the federal and state securities laws.

All venture capital—whether it be seed money, investment in a going business, or a private placement after the company has gone public—inevitably involves the use of securities issued by the company to the venture capitalist.

Assume, for instance, that we are consulting with the company that will be issuing the securities and dealing with the venture capitalist. We assume also that although this company has heard the words "Securities Law of 1933," "Investment Company Act of 1940," "California Corporate Securities Laws," and heard about the various securities laws of the individual states, it really does not understand technically how these laws operate or what effect they can have in a venture capital deal.

For a company to understand what it is getting into when dealing with a venture capitalist and issuing securities without a formal registration, it is essential that it knows something about the federal securities laws—what the company can and cannot do.

Mr. Bermant is a partner in the firm of Gibson, Dunn & Crutcher, in Los Angeles, California

THE SECURITIES ACTS: AN OVERALL VIEW

The Federal Securities Act of 1933,[1] usually referred to as the "Securities Act" or the " '33 Act," is of primary importance to anyone who is issuing securities, regardless of what form those securities take or at what period in the development of a company they are issued.

The Securities Exchange Act of 1934[2] regulates the activities of the stock exchanges and of companies whose securities are registered and listed on the exchanges. It also affects the activities of larger companies traded over-the-counter. Typically, registration under the '34 Act is not relevant to the issuing of securities if registration is not required under the '33 Act. However, the recommendations of the Wheat Report[3] (proposed in 1970) call for significant changes in the after-issuance trading of securities.

Other Federal Securities' regulations include: the Public Utilities Holding Companies Act,[4] relevant only to public utility holding companies; the Trust Indenture Act,[5] important to anyone publicly issuing securities of a debt nature for which there will be a trustee acting under a trust indenture; and the Investment Company Act of 1940,[6] which relates to the activities of mutual funds and closed-end investment companies. Most of the larger SBIC's are registered under this act, and are also regulated by the Small Business Administration under the Small Business Investment Act of 1958.[7]

The Investment Company Act of 1940 also has appended to it the Investment Advisors Act, which purports to regulate the activities of people who offer investment advice to individuals.

INSIDE THE '33 ACT

By its terms, the '33 Act provides that all sales of securities are illegal unless a registration statement is in effect and a prospectus is delivered using jurisdictional means (that is, any instrumentality of interstate commerce or the mails). Since in most cases the interstate telephone system, the mails or the airlines are used, this act is almost always applicable.

Many people think that the '33 Act is applicable only to public companies or to public issuances unless an available exception or exemption from applicability can be found. Fortunately, numerous exemptions and exclusions from the coverage of the broad range of regulations are available.

Almost all meaningful exemptions are contained in Section 4 of the Act of '33. The one most often claimed states that "a transaction by an issuer not involving any public offering" is exempt from the provisions of Section 5 of the Act. Though it says nothing about private placements, it does say ". . . not involving any public offering."

The other exemptions contained in Section 4 are, taking them in order:

Section 4 (1) exempts persons other than an issuer, underwriter or dealer from the registration and prospectus delivery requirements. This is why securities of a listed or an over-the-counter company may be sold without concern as to whether or not a registration statement is in effect. When someone buys or sells one hundred shares of American Telephone on the New York Stock Exchange, he need not worry whether a registration statement is in effect, because he is a person other than an issuer, underwriter or dealer in American Telephone. This is probably not true with respect to the securities of his own company. He is probably either an issuer or an underwriter of his own company, as those terms are defined in the '33 Act. The definitions in this Act are not exactly comparable to the usual meaning of the words "issuer" and "underwriter."

Section 4 (2) of the '33 Act also provides that a transaction by an issuer not involving any public offering is exempt from Section 5 prospectus delivery and registration requirements.

Section 4 (3) says that dealers are exempt, but provides some limited qualifications of the exemption. This is the forty- or ninety-day period following the effective date of a registration statement. (The prospect of a company's going public would entail a greater discussion of this exemption, but it is not relevant to a venture capital discussion.) This section augments and modifies 4 (1), which says dealers are not exempt.

Section 4 (4) provides that a transaction by a broker is exempt. The law differentiates, without saying it in so many words, between dealers and brokers. Generally, a dealer is one who is acting as principal; a broker is one who is acting as an agent. This is the only known difference in the securities laws context between broker and dealer.

Section 4 does not exempt companies from the sections of the Act which provide civil remedies for fraud or for failure to make full disclosures.

These are the principal transaction exemptions in the '33 Act.

There are sections of the Act which are referred to as *securities* exemptions, but look more like transaction exemptions.

Section 3(a)(9) is an unusual securities/transaction exemption. It says that securities issued by an issuer to its shareholders solely in exchange for other securities are exempt. This section exempts the common stock issued on conversion of a convertible debenture, as long as either the initial sales were registered, or there were other private placement exemptions available. At least, that is the way the SEC reads it.

Section 3(a)(10) of the '33 Act is treated by the SEC as more of a transaction exemption and relates to what most people outside of California believe are bankruptcy-hearing cases. This involves a situation in which a company is coming out of bankruptcy and the court so notifies all such people as stockholders and creditors. If the court, after a hearing, finds the issuance of shares is converted in a fair, just and equitable manner, the issuances are exempt from the Federal Securities Law.

In essence, Section 3(a)(11) provides that securities of an issuer offered on an intrastate basis are exempt from the '33 Act. However, the issuer must be incorporated under the laws of, and doing business in, the state in which the offer is made, and all persons to whom the offer is made must be bona fide residents of the state. They must live there—have a home there—not just reside there temporarily. The channels of interstate commerce and the mails may be used in an intrastate offering, as long as the issuer and all offerees reside in and are incorporated under the laws of the state.

The issue of domicile as against residence is raised here because in Hawaii many people involved in intrastate offerings feel that a serviceman who is stationed there, or passing through on his way to someplace else, is a resident of the state for purposes of the intrastate exemption. As far as we know, the courts have not ruled on this circumstance specifically, but the Securities and Exchange Commission regularly brings civil and criminal suit against people who take advantage of this rather relaxed reading of the word "residence" for the intrastate offering.

TRANSACTIONS WITHOUT PUBLIC OFFERING

The exemption most clearly available to the issuer in this case is contained in Section 4(2), which covers transactions by an issuer not involving any public offering. It is necessary for an issuer of securities to venture capitalists to understand the availability of that exemption, and how a public offering can be accomplished accidentally when the issuer made what he believed was a private placement.

Section 2(11) of the '33 Act defines "underwriter" in a way which can be a trap for anyone not aware of the ramifications of the language. In the common parlance of the Street, everyone thinks of an underwriter as an investment banking house such as Lehman Brothers, Blyth & Co. or Merrill Lynch—firms that underwrite the company going public, prepare new registration statements and have their names at the bottom of a prospectus.

It is important to understand the exact language of the law relating to underwriters as stated in the '33 Act: an underwriter is "any person who has purchased from an issuer with a view to, or offers or sells for an issuer in connection with, the distribution of any security."

Clearly, the professional underwriter who puts his name at the bottom of the prospectus and is working with an issuer on disclosure matters for the prospectus is an "underwriter." But, so is a non-professional who purchases a security from a company and then sells it to someone else—*unless there is an exemption available for the resale.*

If stock is sold in a transaction not involving a public offering, the sale might be exempt because the person involved may be a knowledgeable person who is not a member of the public. In the event that the stockholder wishes to sell to a third person, that sale requires an exemption of its own, in that the '33 Act says that all sales must be registered and a prospectus delivered unless an exemption is available.

What exemption is available on the resale?

If the person who purchased the shares from the company resells the security, then it is not an exemption transaction with regard to him and, therefore, it is a violation of the law.

This problem has created the concept of the investment letter, by which the venture capitalist declares: "I am purchasing these securities for my own account, for investment, and without a view to further sale or distribution." This statement comes directly from the definition of an underwriter in the '33 Act. It is designed as evidence to the issuer that the person buying stock is not an underwriter.

These concepts have been developed over the years since 1933, but major revisions were recommended in the Wheat Report. The new proposals were contained in the "Securities Act, Release 4997."[8]

THE REQUISITE INVESTMENT INTENT

The Wheat Report recommendations had not been adopted by this printing, requiring that we continue to live within the confines of the Securities Act of 1933. The Act says that a person who buys for investment without a view to further sale or distribution of the shares, must establish proof to the issuer prior to the sale of stock, or to the courts or the SEC staff after the sale of the stock, that he was not in fact an underwriter.

It is generally believed that the intent of the purchaser when buying unregistered securities is the controlling factor. If the buyer had a requisite investment intent at the time of purchase, then irrespective of when or why he sells, he is not an underwriter because he did not purchase with a view to distribution. He purchased with a view to putting the shares in a safe-deposit box and forgetting about them.

If taken literally, this implies that there could be a closing at the corporation's offices at 10:00 A. M., a change of decision at 10:05 A. M., and a subsequent sale—without the seller's being construed as an underwriter. But the fact is that if such action were taken, there is no court, lawyer, or administrative agency that is likely to believe that the seller had the requisite investment intent at the time of the purchase. If the buyer were to decide to sell the security twenty years later, it would generally be agreed that the seller had requisite investment intent. Thus, somewhere between five minutes and twenty years, there is a time when the buyer can rely upon the fact that he had the requisite investment intent.

Years ago, it was suggested that the proper time period for

holding these securities was six months, which conveniently coincided with the long-term capital gain holding period. However, because it corresponded to this holding period, it was not difficult for the SEC or the courts to decide that an investor did not acquire the securities for investment. The court held, instead, that the buyer acquired the securities for another reason, the long-term capital gains holding period. Thus, the six-month holding period was not evidence of investment intent.

For reasons which are not clear to us, thirteen months became the magic number for holding unregistered securities. (The only instance we know where thirteen months is relevant is in one of the rules surrounding Regulation A offerings. There is a provision that if underwriters receive options or cheap stock, they must agree not to sell or distribute the shares they receive within a thirteen-month period in order to hold the size of the issue under $300 thousand.)

The SEC has historically taken the position that there is no specific holding period required for investment letter stock. As a practical matter, though, a long period of holding will evidence that the proper investment intent existed at the time of the acquisition. Subsequent to the thirteen-month period, attorneys in the field held the opinion that the buyer had the requisite investment intent if the letter stock was held for two years. Owing to the natural conservatism of lawyers, the two-year period has gradually lengthened. As of this writing, most sophisticated securities attorneys probably will not give an opinion letter, except in unusual circumstances, if the holding period is less than two and one-half years—preferably three years. We do not know why three years indicates any greater investment intent than two years. However, this problem typically does not arise in the case of venture capitalists because, for various reasons, venture capitalists typically want a more specific understanding in their initial investment documents.

The SEC has said that broker-dealers and investment companies—open-end mutual funds in particular, but also closed-end companies—never buy for investment. The SEC states that it is not in the nature of these businesses to make long-term investments. Uppermost in the minds of these types of investors is the disposition of the securities acquired. Consequently, irrespective of how long a fund—such as the Fund of Letters—holds a stock in its portfolio, the fund will always be deemed to have taken the security with a view to subsequent distribution. Thus, they will forever be underwriters and required to deliver a prospectus under valid and effective registration statements at the time of the sale of these securities.

It is not our intention to single out the Fund of Letters. At the time the Fund went public, the question of letter stock was foremost in the minds of the SEC. Fund of Letters said frankly that they were out to buy letter stock of public companies and were going to realize their profit by selling such stock. By virtue of its power, the SEC made the Fund say that they would always obtain registration coverage. This is the way the venture capitalist can always get out of a company in which he invests.

The venture capitalist expects entrepreneurs to agree to register stock for him at some point downstream when he is ready to get out of a deal. These registrations take many forms. Our experience in representing the issuer, or occasionally the venture capitalist, is that the current trend is to expand the requirements of the entrepreneur's registration covenant.

Going Piggyback

Years ago, it was characteristic for the venture capitalist to ask for the right to be able to sell as part of a firm's public offering. This right to registration was all that he asked for, and it became known as a "piggy back registration." The timing of the registration is left in the hands of the issuing company. Typically, according to this plan, the venture capitalist and/or the investor has the right to have the shares registered only once—at the time the company is registering shares for itself or for any other shareholder.

The piggyback, however, has a number of pitfalls for the company as well as the venture capitalist. The latter may feel that the company's initial public offering price is below the amount he wants for his position in the stock. Typically, the first public offering price will be at a multiple of earnings, a multiple of sales (in case the company does not have earnings) or some dividend figure if sales and earnings multiples are not attractive.

HOW TO CREATE A HOT ISSUE

The way to create a hot issue is to underprice it. The degree of "warmth" will depend to some extent on the degree of underpricing. In initial public offerings, particularly high-technology companies, it is considered smart to "leave something on the table for the public investors," to give the person who is a regular customer of the brokerage house a small free ride for his money. The public also thinks highly of the company that comes out, for instance, at fourteen dollars and opens at twenty-two dollars.

THE ENTREPRENEUR AND THE VENTURE CAPITALIST: A SPECIAL RELATIONSHIP

The venture capitalist is part of the inside of the company. He knows what is going to happen to the stock (assuming that everything goes as planned). He has no desire to sell the stock he bought at fifty cents for a mere fourteen dollars. He wants to sell it for twenty-two, twenty-three or thirty dollars—the expected price of the stock two weeks after the public offering.

At this point there is a conflict between the venture capitalist, who knows that the issue is underpriced, and the underwriter, who wants to price the issue sufficiently low to be sure the issue will be sold. Also, the underwriter does not want to distribute stock of the venture capitalist at brokerage rates when he can do it on an underwriting basis which will result in an 8 to 9½ percent commission.

In the first round of piggyback registrations, an entrepreneur must decide whether to allow or require the venture capitalist to sell in the same registration prospectus in which the issuer is selling.

Several important facts become apparent. If the venture capitalist is required to sell because of his registration rights, he can still refuse because he believes the stock is going to be underpriced. He might then take his chances with the holding period. Conversely, it does not make the company look good if the venture capitalist, as one of the principal investors, is bailing out of it. What is wrong with the company if the venture capitalist wants to get his money out before the company has really established its long-term growth? The typical technology company may still be losing money or be in a period in which profits have just begun to develop. The venture capitalist wants to be able to sell in the after-market at a higher price, but the underwriter is against this action because of the problems in controlling the distribution mechanism through which the stock is placed.

To solve this problem, the venture capitalist can be told that he cannot sell in the first offering. If he feels that he wants his money and must be able to sell at the first public offering, the entrepreneur can agree—if the venture capitalist joins in the underwriting. If he does not agree, then it must be pointed out that the underwriter states that the venture capitalist will have to wait ninety days after the first public offering before he can begin selling stock in the market.

This is a typical compromise on an underwritten public offering by way of a piggyback registration. The investor is given the right to bail out through a "shelf registration," a registration for which the issuer does not have an investment banker underwriter as such; but the investor (in this case, the venture capitalist) receives the right to call his broker and sell shares promising to deliver prospectuses.

In a shelf registration on the over-the-counter market, securities are sold through brokers on a principal or agency basis. On a listed security, the broker can be telephoned and told that the caller has the particular stock, and the prospectus is on file with the exchange.

As a rule, if the entrepreneur is not going to require the venture capitalist to join the offering or underwriting upon which he piggybacks, the issuer can require that the venturer stand by for a period of time until the market settles down. Alternatively, he may also require that the venture capitalist not join in the first public offering, but wait until the second or subsequent public offerings before his piggyback rights are effective.

The venture capitalist usually feels that as long as he has any stock, he is entitled to piggyback regardless of what type of registration is made. He may note that his participation costs nothing, that the filing fee is negligible, the legal fees are not large, the accounting fees are zero, the printing cost is negligible—so why should the entrepreneur not allow it?

The only argument against this is that it is a nuisance to have to worry about giving notice of piggyback rights, including the shares in the offering, if no response is received; it is also a nuisance to make arrangements with the underwriters to include them in the offering.

Must the venture capitalist be included in a debenture offering if he holds common stock? This is a negotiable point and it affects the prospectus. If the venture capitalist is selling a security different from the one the company is offering, the issuer needs a far more complex prospectus and underwriting documents.

Usually, if the venture capitalist or investor is required to join in the underwriting under his piggyback rights, the question arises as to what happens if the underwriter will not include the venturer in the offering. The underwriter may feel that he has enough shares, or that he does not want the particular investor in his offering. This is also a bargaining point.

In this situation, the venture capitalist might suggest—as part of his bargaining position—that if the underwriter will not take him in, then he (the venture capitalist) will have thirty days in which to find an underwriter who will underwrite shares of both the investing group and the enterprise. The underwriter is now on notice that if he excludes the venture capitalist from his offering, he could lose the company as a client. The entrepreneur can tell the underwriter that he has a contractual commitment; therefore, if the investor is not to be allowed into the offering, the entrepreneur may be required by contract to let the venture capitalist find another underwriter.

The venture capitalist also will often insist that if all the shares he wants to sell are not included, the management of the company cannot sell any shares. The venture capitalist does not have to share his rights to sell with anyone else, but has the right to all of the secondary position. This is another bargaining point for management which can cause problems in the sale of the stock.

CAN MANAGEMENT SELL WITHOUT REGISTRATION?

The management of the company is locked in, as is indicated in the last sentence of Section 2(11) of the Securities Act, which defines an underwriter as one who buys from a controlling stockholder with a view toward the distribution of securities.

The management of the company is an issuer for this purpose, and people who buy shares from them are underwriters, as though they had bought the stock directly from the company. Thus, if management relinquishes the right to have any of its shares included in the registration statement unless the venture capitalist is able to sell all of the shares he wants to sell, a very valuable right may be lost to management. The entrepreneur would be much better off selling his stock, along with that of the venture capitalist, on some type of pro rata basis.

At this point, the venture capitalist may again state that he wants the entrepreneur to be rich and be willing for both to join in the offering. Therefore, the venture capitalist will not sell as many of the shares as he may want to sell in order to leave room for the entrepreneur in the offering.

THE DEMAND REGISTRATION

As the problems of the piggyback have multiplied, venture capitalists have consistently stated, rather justifiably, that they want more than a piggyback registration. If the entrepreneur does not initiate the registration, the venture capitalist is locked in and may be concerned about getting squeezed. (This discussion is irrelevant if the venture capitalist owns over 50 percent of the company, because the entrepreneur is then working for him. We are assuming this is not the circumstance.)

Usually, the venture capitalist will state that he wants a right to call for a registration of the stock whether the issuer wants one or not. If the investment is in a startup situation or is a pre-public venture capital situation, the entrepreneur can reply that he wants the venture capitalist to have piggyback rights, but only based on some target period. This period typically will be related to management projections for the company.

When is the public offering contemplated? When can the venture capitalist get out? These are issues to be resolved in negotiations regarding the demand for registration rights.

The management plan, for example, may state that based upon September 30, 1972 projections, the firm will be in a position to go public; therefore registration will be filed sometime in the fall of 1972. The venture capitalist, however, is worried about his investment in the company and what could happen if management failed to follow through on their plans. In the event the venture capitalist wants the right to make the company go public at some "window period," an opening perhaps between January 1 of one year and January 1 of the following year, he has this right if management has not done so prior to that time. The question of how long the window is open will depend to some extent upon the experience of the venture capitalist, and the difficulty his attorney has had in the past (or believes he will have in the future) in convincing the SEC that the venture capitalist originally invested without a view to selling or distributing the shares.

If he can prove that he took the securities for investment, or did not act like an underwriter for a period of four or five years, the likelihood is that the venture capitalist will be able to sell the stock whenever there is a public market. If there is no public market, he has little ability to sell the stock anyway. If the company continues to be privately-held because projections have not been fulfilled, probably it is not a viable public vehicle.

The combinations and permutations of demand or piggyback registration rights are as infinite as is the ingenuity of the venture capitalists, investment bankers, management of the issuer, and the attorneys for all sides. Management can provide two free registration rights, with the venture capitalists receiving unlimited additional registration rights at their own cost—or unlimited piggybacks and provisions whereby a demand can become a piggyback if the company elects to make it such. All of these result from the experience gained through participation in other deals.

A typical problem in the demand registration might involve a public company with a demand right outstanding on letter stock by a venture capitalist. Because the stock is depressed, a public offering may not be appropriate. Management can ask the venture capitalist for the money by offering letter stock with a registration statement in a year. The only problem is that a year later the company may have made four acquisitions, and three of them may not have audited financial statements. There is no way of filing a registration statement, and yet everybody was in favor of the acquisitions.

Now what happens? The issuer is in default of its contract. The venture capitalist makes his demand for a registration statement and gets no action. If the market goes up, he profits by the delay. It is a heads-he-wins, tails-you-lose type of deal.

Consequently, the issuer may ask for more time. A provision for reasonable delay may be put into the agreement. This is protection for the issuer against a venture capitalist who decides to force its hand. Some will do so, especially if there has been a falling-out among the parties involved.

ISSUE WARRANTS

What are the problems in issuing warrants or options to venture capitalists or other investors? In this instance, we are referring to the venture capitalist as the buyer of whatever the issuer is selling; but the same rules would apply to any purchase of an unregistered security relying on the private placement exemption of the '33 Act. As indicated earlier, we are also referring to the venture capitalist who is not the majority partner in a venture, and does not have the board of directors on his side.

There is nothing wrong with the idea of issuing warrants. As an economic matter, it may be the best deal for management and the best investment the venture capitalist can make, as long as management does not have to register the warrants for him. Various problems are created when management registers the warrants, rather than require the venture capitalist to exercise his options, buy the shares and register the stock himself. When a warrant is in the hands of the public, before stock can be sold to a holder of the warrant, there must be a registration statement in effect concerning those shares. If the warrants run five years beyond the time when offered to the public, management must go through the complexities of registration every year until every warrant is exercised or has lapsed. Management, therefore, is not only undertaking to file a registration statement on the warrants, but they are also undertaking to keep this registration alive. They must always be ready to accept the money of the public and to submit a prospectus for the conversion to stock.

LETTER STOCK AND REGISTERED STOCK: SOME CLARIFICATION

"Letter stock" is a term that has come into use recently to indicate stock issued on an investment letter. The letter is nothing more than evidence that the holder understands that he cannot sell the stock, and it gives the company the right to sue the holder if he sells it. Letter stock is merely unregistered stock.

However, the term "registered stock" is a misnomer. What is really registered is the sale. The law says that no person shall sell a security unless it is registered and he delivers a prospectus, unless he utilizes a number of available exemptions. Merely having stock that was registered means nothing unless at the time of stock sale one of the exemptions was available.

SEC RELEASE 4997—THE "WHEAT REPORT" RECOMMENDATIONS

The SEC produced Release 4997 (based on the "Wheat Report") and several other related releases under the '33 Act, to change some of the ground rules and to make a more objective test by which a person can determine whether or not he can sell lettered stock.

If adopted, these regulations would eliminate the concept of "fungibility." Fungibility, which we describe as the "hottest-in, first-out rule," means that if an individual owns investment letter stock for which he can find no exemption under which to sell it, then the first stock sold is the hottest stock owned, even though he may also have owned stock issued by the company twenty years before.

This is how the SEC uses the law of fungibility. Stock cannot be sold without its being deemed to be the stock that is the most restricted. If an individual has ten thousand shares of stock acquired from his grandfather in 1925, the one thousand shares sold will be deemed to be the stock that was acquired in the private placement three months ago. On the other hand, if a private placement of a thousand shares is made and the shares purchased in 1925 are delivered as part of the private placement, the stock that the individual purchased last week is free stock because the taint of fungibility is eliminated.

The rule makes no sense. It is designed to prevent fraud of a special nature, but it strikes across the board at everyone, and enforcement and interpretation has become a religion at the SEC. As long as the rules stay as they are, the concept of fungibility is going to run rampant. This concept will be eliminated if the new regulations are adopted.

Further, the new regulations will eliminate the concept of intent as a factor in stock negotiations. By this concept, a man's intent is studied in an attempt to determine whether or not he has purchased stock with a view to distribution. The new rule says that a distribution does not exist if a person limits his sale to approximately one percent of the outstanding securities of the class being sold within any six-month period. No matter what is done, as long as the stock is sold in certain defined kinds of transactions, and the holder has been at risk for a year and has not purchased any restricted securities for that year, at the end of that year one percent of the outstanding issue may be sold to the public in regular, ordinary, unsolicited brokerage transactions. The issuer must be registered under the 1934 Act, however, which means that he has to file the annual and current reports.

Under the new regulations there will be just two reports—Form 10K annually and Form 10Q quarterly—but they must be current. A security listed on any national securities exchange, or a security of one of the so-called larger, over-the-counter companies must register under Section 12(g). These are the only requirements for the public non-distribution of letter stock after the one-year holding period. The proposed rule is clear that every six months, up to one percent of the outstanding issue can be sold. If it is listed, there is a lower limit of one percent or a week's trading volume.

Under those circumstances, if the stock is publicly-traded, venture capitalists can plan on making limited offerings of up to 2 percent of the company per year without a registration. This gives them limited flexibility to realize on their investments without the burden of a registration every time they wish to do so. However, inasmuch as most venture capitalists will own 20 percent or more of a given issue, the 2 percent limitation is only of moderate value.

If the company is not registered under Section 12(g) or listed on an exchange, then there is an arbitrary five-year holding period under the proposed regulations. This means that stock is restricted in the hands of a noncontrolling person until the end of five years, when it becomes unrestricted.

Every time a restricted stock is issued, a five-year holding period for the release of the letter restrictions begins. However, if the company is qualified under Section 12(g) or listed on an exchange, the limited one-percent-per-six-month-selling provisions are applicable. This is what the Wheat Report recommends as interpreted by the Commission's first proposed rule. If adopted in the original form, we will be rid of the concept of change of circumstances and many other problems.

Further considerations by the SEC lengthened the holding period for security sales; other wording changes have convinced many attorneys that the entire area may become even more complicated and restricted. Under the proposed rules, if three months after a private purchase is made, the entrepreneur has a disastrous family consequence, he must still wait a year. He can sell privately only if an exemption can be found so that he is not an issuer, underwriter or a dealer.

Section 12(g) has certain statutory requirements. The company must register under Section 12(g) if at the end of any fiscal year it has five hundred shareholders and $1 million in gross assets. But in order to take advantage of the Rule 160 provisions, it is possible to voluntarily register a company, even if the company does not meet the statutory requirements.

Varadyne, Inc., for example, is a case in point: our firm set up an undertaking with the California Corporation Commissioner before taking that company public through a shell acquisition. We made a commitment with the Commissioner voluntarily to file a Section 12(g) application so that the Commissioner could determine if the transaction was fair, just and equitable. Varadyne did, in fact, register under Section 12(g) even though it did not have to do so. At the time of registration the firm did not have $1 million in assets.

Some of the most successful large companies in Southern California were listed on the New York Stock Exchange *before* they had a registered public offering. Litton is an example, filing its first registration statement with the SEC under the '33 Act at about the same time it became listed on the Exchange. Teledyne, one of the hot stocks in Southern California, was sizzling prior to the time that it filed its first registration statement.

These are companies that grew essentially by acquisition, but also through an exemption from registration contained in Rule 133, which permits public distribution of securities without registration. This loophole will be closed by adoption of the Wheat Report. If revised Rule 133 is adopted, the "no-sale" theory that has permitted vast public companies to be created without a registration statement will disappear. The alternative will be to have a private placement consisting of twenty-five persons or less, or a registered public offering.

AN ALTERNATIVE: THE SHELL GAME

Shell corporations offer the entrepreneur a possible alternative source of doing what he wants with his private enterprise other than going to a venture capitalist. It may also be a part of his venture capital deal. A shell corporation has no assets other than a list of public shareholders. It may have some liabilities, but if it has assets it is not considered a shell.

There are two kinds of shell corporations. One is the company which was public, then went bankrupt; this is the historic shell. As the shell concept has become more popular, most of these have disappeared. Someone then came up with the idea of manufacturing shell corporations. Any public company can create a shell corporation—a publicly-held, zero-asset, zero-liability company —as easily as a popcorn machine can create popcorn. The public company merely creates a wholly-owned subsidiary. Suppose that "X" Company creates a subsidiary, "X-1" Company, by issuing one million shares for a thousand dollars in cash. It then spins off that company to its shareholders on a share-for-share basis. Inasmuch as the company has no value at the time of the spin-off, there should be no material, taxable transaction in connection with the spin-off; thus, a publicly-held shell with 100,000 or one million, or whatever, shares outstanding is created.

The people who control the "X-1" shell (the management or those who control the "X" Company) then find out if the entrepreneur's company would like to go public by the shell route for a modest consideration, which is designed to compensate the company for its efforts, legal fees and the like. They offer to sell control of the shell. The entrepreneur then dumps his assets into the shell in exchange for, say, 900,000 shares of the stock. At that point, the shell ceases to be a shell and becomes a publicly-held company.

The only problem with this fascinating arrangement is that it is illegal—or at least the SEC says it is illegal. The SEC claims, in such a case, that the company made a public offering of the stock of the shell to its shareholders. There is a sufficient thread of logic to their position so that they would probably win the case in court. But instead of bringing a court case, the SEC issues a release stating that it is illegal,[9] which terrifies people. Therefore, the entrepreneur's publicly-held company does not have a market. High on the list of things that have little value is a publicly-held company with stock that cannot be traded.

After issuing the release and telling people that this would be illegal, the SEC took action in early December 1969 and issued stop orders on transactions by brokers who were trading stock in those shells that the SEC has said should not be traded. The SEC said it would hold hearings. This effectively stopped brokers from dealing in such transactions.

There are not many shells in existence that were created in ways other than by spin-offs. There are a few that have liabilities which would be horrendous after an entrepreneur puts his assets into the shell, and thus do not look very attractive. A few others that are controlled by people with questionable backgrounds are also available, but do not look very attractive. Thus, the shell game, to a large extent, has been eliminated.

In some ways, this is too bad. If an entrepreneur has a venture which is in relatively early stages of development and has some potential, but he cannot find a good investment banker to handle a public offering, the shell game might create a public market and price the company's stock at a respectable multiple. If that can be accomplished, the entrepreneur can use the stock of the company to make acquisitions and to further the growth of his company. Under those circumstances, it seems to us that the shell has some marginal utility. It should be remembered, however, that to get the use of the shell, an entrepreneur must give up 7 to 12 percent of his company for nothing but a stockholders' list—and, with fingers crossed, no liabilities.

10

LETTER STOCK: THE LAW AND VENTURE CAPITAL*

Edward G. Novotny

"I represent and warrant to you that I am acquiring the shares of your company for purposes of investment and not with the view to distribution within the meaning of the Securities Act of 1933. Yours truly, John Smith, Purchaser."

With these few simple words, a typical form of the popular restricted security commonly referred to as "letter stock" is created.

A COMPLEX RESTRICTED SECURITY

"Letter-stock" is a term that covers a variety of special restricted securities. It can take the form of common stock, warrants or debt securities that can be exchanged for or converted into common stock. Letter stock transactions are covered by the exemption provided in Section 4(2) of the Securities Act of 1933.[1] In general, this Act requires securities registration whenever there is a direct

* The author wishes to gratefully acknowledge the cooperation of Messrs. M. J. Epley, John Howard, George Bermant, and Charles M. Noone. These leading attorneys were kind enough to help interpret and review the various legalities of letter stock as discussed in the course of this material.

Mr. Novotny is senior vice-president and manager, eastern operations, of Martin E. Janis & Company, Inc., a public relations counseling firm with offices in New York City and Chicago.

or indirect public offering of securities by an issuer or, with certain limited exceptions, by persons controlling an issuer.

Letter stock can be a complex security. In some cases, for example, considerable time and expense may be required "to work out of" letter stock. The brief words of the typical letter stock agreement described above may suffice, but the issuer may have more complicated ideas in mind. In most instances, he will extend the agreement a page or two; he will make some reference to civil and criminal liabilities under the 1933 Securities Act; he will stipulate that the stock may never be transferred without first satisfying numerous requirements.

Adding to the Complexity . . .

A basic principle of the Act is that the burden lies with the issuer to establish the facts that justify an exemption from the Act. An unsuccessful attempt at exemption can result in serious trouble. Any person who sells stock in a transaction which does not fall within the exemption is exposed to civil liability for recision of the transaction, or damages in the amount of any loss suffered by the purchaser. *The recision remedy is available against the issuer and—in the case of a non-exempt resale by the purchaser in a private placement—against the purchaser as well.* And if that does not serve as a deterrent, *there is also a possibility of criminal liability if such a situation occurs.*

A TYPICAL LETTER STOCK OFFERING

Plans for a private offering of stock usually begin with a resolution at a meeting of the company's board of directors. After discussion, the directors decide that it is in the best interest of the company to seek a specified sum of money for particular goals, such as product development, market expansion or new plants. The board then delegates to its chairman or the company treasurer, vice-president of finance, or president, the task of seeking funds by selling company securities to professional investors or to a group (numbering not more than a fixed number of persons); and such effort is to be terminated no later than a predetermined date, all to be coordinated through the company's legal counsel.

The board's resolutions are clear and precise, because a company does not want other people attempting to sell the project throughout the financial community. Legal problems may arise if an offer is made to the "wrong" people; therefore, the company must know to whom the offer is made, and this can best be accomplished when only one or two people are involved. Also, when too many people are involved, the offering can easily get out of control, with everyone in town asking for a piece of the company. This situation can make for more enemies than friends, in view of the restricted nature of the offering.

WHAT CONSTITUTES A PUBLIC OFFERING

According to law, there are two key factors in establishing a valid private placement exemption from the provisions of the 1933 Act:

1. The offerees (as distinguished from ultimate purchasers) must be persons who, by reason of their position with the issuer (senior executives, for example), or because of their inherent sophistication (as in the case of institutional investors such as insurance companies and mutual funds), do not re-

quire the protection afforded by the registration provisions of the Act.

2. The issuer must not only establish the qualifications of the offerees (including those who accept the offer and become purchasers), but it is his duty also to determine that the otherwise-qualified purchaser does not intend to re-offer or resell the securities to others in a manner that would result in a total of offerees who would not be entitled to an exemption under the Act in the first instance. The issurer must also ascertain whether any purchaser is acting as a nominee for others; if he is, the persons for whom he is acting must fall within the permitted category of offerees.

Thus, states the law, the burden is upon the issuer to establish the facts upon which an exemption from the registration requirements of the Act is based.

Violating the Law: the Offense

The securities laws can be violated—even though not a share of stock was ever sold. Some authorities may claim, for example, that an offeree can have a valid private offering to eighty or ninety insurance companies, but could run headlong into a legal problem if the sale is made to a handful of widows and orphans. The character of the offeree is a very important guideline.

It is important, therefore, to work closely with experienced legal counsel. Such counsel will be even more appreciated in a year or two when the company may have to represent before the SEC that "on said date, pursuant to authority from the board of directors, twenty thousand shares of company stock were sold to five persons of a group of not more than ten offerees . . ."

. . . Another Disadvantage Or Two

It should also be noted that although the expenses of formal registration are avoided through privately-placed securities, the restrictions of letter stock result in the issuer's receiving a lower price for these securities. The discount attributable to the private placement restrictions may be quite substantial (usually a minimum of 15 percent below the price had it been registered); but there are legal fees, as well as fees to the broker or investment banker for placing the securities. The savings in the cost of registration may constitute only a deferral of the expense, since the purchaser of privately-placed securities will ordinarily insist upon a right to require their eventual registration; and this would require almost the identical out-of-pocket expense and effort that would have resulted from a formal registration. *The major advantage to the issuer, however, is that he has the use of capital in the interim.*

In weighing relative costs, it should be noted that a formal registration involves an underwriting discount which may range well over 5 percent and may offset the consideration to be given to the private placement discount.

Sufficient Warning to the Investor—or Fraud

The private offering exemption is contained in the registration provisions of the 1933 Act, but there are other provisions forbidding fraud in the sale of securities.

A company, for example, can bring in a small group of professionals, show them the facility and the financials, have them interview employees, and have an accountant and attorneys carefully examine all aspects of the business, including sales backlog and competitors. At this point, the company could make the mistake of believing that because the group had learned "the full story" before making the decision to invest, anything that happens after is legal. This is not so; it is not a "caveat emptor" situation wherein the buyer buys at his own risk.

The proper circumstances are spelled out in clearly-defined federal laws and administrative practices. Violations of these circumstances, for example, might be: an officer of the company sells stock based on the knowledge that the company was about to be sued by the former employer of their top engineer for misuse of confidential information; or the leading competitor, through soon-to-be-released technological advances, has rendered the company's product obsolete; or the highly-acclaimed R & D chief was just told by his physician that he has six months to live. If it can be proved that the company's management withheld pertinent information of this sort that could have affected the investor's decision, a simple—and probably successful—case can be made by the investors under the anti-fraud provisions of the Act.

WHY USE LETTER STOCK?

The principal function of letter stock is to avoid the necessity of complying with the rigorous and time-consuming registration requirements of the 1933 Securities Act. There are three major problems in complying with standard SEC registration requirements:

1. There is considerable cost in out-of-pocket expense and in time and energy of company personnel in preparing a registration statement.
2. The extensive disclosures required in a registration statement

under the Act may be considered by management to be highly detrimental, especially with regard to competition.

3. The time involved in complying with registration standards is a major deterrent–sometimes several months of paperwork, then a lengthy wait while the SEC reviews the material. For a company with a pressing need for cash, the timing factor may be conclusive in favor of a private placement, which often can be completed in one-half to one-third the time.

THE INVESTMENT PROPOSAL—AND VENTURE CAPITALISTS

A typical private placement involves a private company with a maximum of three to five stockholders. On the average, the venture capitalists will provide from $100 thousand to $500 thousand of initial capital, hopefully to be followed in one to three years by a public offering. Eventually this offering may be followed in two to as-long-as seven years later—depending on the particular situation—by a secondary offering for the benefit of the venture capitalist and the insiders. Thus the make-up of the investment package is very important. The material should be carefully prepared by management, utilizing the advice of company legal counsel and members of the venture capital staff. It is important for a company to be frank with its venture capital backers when assisting them in the preparation of the investment memorandum as the foundation for the letter stock agreement. It should be complete, with all key bases adequately covered.

The creation of the stock purchase agreement can be a critical phase, with divergence of interest developing between the company and the venture capitalist. A small business, for instance, may agree to prepare a registration statement any time it is requested by the venture capital investors. This could create practical problems for the small firm in the form of high costs and the time-consuming business of preparing an unlimited number of registrations. Most venture capitalists, however, will be motivated by the portfolio company's best interests. Professionals realize that the company can produce a great deal of profit for all concerned if major roadblocks—requirements which will divert management from its primary functions—are avoided.

THE PURCHASE AGREEMENT: PRIME CONSIDERATIONS

The specifications of the stock purchase agreement will depend upon the relative bargaining power of both parties. The following points may prove to be a useful checklist in preparing for and negotiating the agreement:

1. Obviously, one of the most significant factors is the extent of the discount required by the purchaser to offset the delay in immediate transferability of the securities that are being purchased.

2. Another basic factor to be negotiated is the character of the securities or the package of securities to be sold. A principal advantage of the private placement is that the area for adapting the security to the particular needs of the issuer and the purchaser is almost unlimited. They may choose to utilize ordinary stock, or to tailor some combination of debt obligations with equity participation on a convertible basis or in conjunction with warrants.

3. Another key point is the requirement for eventual registration of securities. Under the structure of the 1933 Securities Act, only the issuer can file a registration statement; and a purchaser, in order to protect himself, must obtain contractual

provisions if he wishes to be in a position to cause a registration permitting resale of his securities at a later date.

Registration Provisions

The extent of the registration provisions varies widely and the following areas are to be considered:

Piggyback. Perhaps the most frequent provision is the so-called "piggyback" under which, if the issuer proposes to file a registration statement covering other securities, he must notify the holder of the privately-placed securities of his intent and, if requested, he must include the privately-placed securities or a portion of them in the registration statement. The purchase agreement may provide for one or more piggybacks. It may further require that in order to participate on a piggyback basis, the holder of the privately-placed securities must agree in the case of an underwritten offering by the issuer to sell on terms agreed upon between the issuer and its underwriter; or, in the alternative, the holder must agree to withhold the privately-placed securities from the market for a stated period following the effective date of the registration statement by the issuer.

A more extreme provision is one which permits a prospective underwriter to block the inclusion of privately-placed securities when an offering by the issuer is being registered. Ordinarily, the additional expense caused by a piggyback is minimal, since the legal and accounting work is unchanged, and the expense is paid by the issuer.

Obviously, the greatest weakness in a piggyback provision is that it does not come into play unless and until the issuer determines that he is going to file a registration statement. It is customary, therefore, to include a provision allowing the issuer to file a registration statement for those securities even though he did not otherwise propose to file one on his own behalf. Again, the purchase agreement may provide for one or more such registrations.

A very important factor here is the question of who is to bear the expense of a registration, particularly in a case where the issuer did not otherwise propose to file one. There are two obvious alternatives: the issuer or the holder of the securities, or some allocation of expenses between the two. Another provision which may be inserted is a so-called "trigger figure" requiring a request for the registration of a certain amount of the privately-placed securities in order to require the issuer to file a registration statement.

Permissibility of Transfer. Once the securities have been privately placed with appropriate safeguards, the purchase agreement must provide mechanics for determining the permissibility of transfers at a later date. The ordinary provision in this context states that in the event of a proposed transfer of privately-placed securities, the holder will notify the issuer and indicate the details of the proposed disposition. The issuer then is to consult with his counsel and within a specified period of time determine whether the transfer can be made without registration under the Act. If that determination is made in the negative, the agreement may provide that the transfer is not permitted, or that the issuer proceed with the necessary registration.

Shelf-Registration. The purchase agreement should also contain a provision specifying the period during which the registration statement relating to the privately-placed securities must be kept effective. If the holder of the privately-placed securities does not propose to employ an underwriter and dispose of the securities in a "one-shot" manner, the prospectus must be kept current throughout the period of distribution. This is the so-called "shelf-registration."

Ordinarily, the prospectus contained in a registration statement can be used for a period of at least nine months following the effective date. However, should material events occur affecting the issuer or his business, it is necessary to amend or supplement the prospectus to reflect those events. An example of such an event would be an agreement to make a significant acquisition. Accordingly, an obligation to keep a registration statement in effect or to keep a prospectus current for any extended period of time may prove burdensome upon an issuer. Moreover, during a period when a distribution of his securities is continuing, even though the offering is by the purchaser in the private placement and not by the issuer himself, the issuer is significantly restricted in certain areas—such as purchases of his own stock which may be made for stock option plans or other reasons, and in publicity where press releases may have an effect upon the price of the stock.

The question as to how long a registration statement should be kept in effect usually involves intensive negotiations. There are substantial additional problems in this area when dealing with privately-placed warrants or convertibles which may require a so-called "evergreen" prospectus for the full term of the conversion privilege or warrant exercisability.

Indemnification. A final factor to be considered in the registration provisions of the purchase agreement is the matter of indemnification. Ordinarily, it is appropriate for the issuer to agree to indemnify the holder of the privately-placed securities against any claims or liabilities arising from an untrue statement of a material fact or from an omission in stating a material fact in the prospectus relating to resale by the private purchaser—except to the extent that information in the prospectus is furnished by the purchaser (ordinarily limited to his name, address and security holdings). The purchaser will also usually require that the issuer agree to give similar indemnification to any underwriter of a re-offering of the securities by the purchaser.

Generally, each purchase agreement in a letter stock transaction must be custom-tailored according to the needs of the issuer and purchaser and their relative bargaining strengths.

Some experts in the field believe that if a person buys private placement stock and obtains a provision to have the stock registered for his benefit, the mere event will prevent a valid private placement from occurring. This is based on the assumption that he did not indicate the proper investment intention, but merely wanted to sell the stock. For many years, however, the practice has been that private placements are made with provisions for registration. Many attorneys feel that a court would never turn its back upon this custom of the industry.

On the other hand, a company could consider the right to piggyback, joining in other registration statements which will be prepared and filed for the benefit of the company.

IS THE TRANSACTION EXEMPT?

A Threefold Legal Safeguard Test

In negotiating a private placement, the issuer's major interest must be to assure that the offering and sale of the securities constitutes a valid and an exempt private placement. The burden is upon the issuer and the company's legal counsel. A minimum of three basic steps can be taken to ensure compliance with the private placement provisions:

First, the individuals who will be approaching prospective purchasers, whether they are company personnel or outside brokers, should be clearly instructed as to the limitations imposed by the Act and should keep detailed records of the people they approach. There should be a written record in the files of the issuer with their names and, if necessary, identifying information with respect to each offeree, and a clear indication (with copies, if possible) of all information furnished.

Second, prior to delivery of the securities to the purchasers, the issuers must try to ascertain that the purchasers do not contemplate any re-offering or resale of the securities in a manner which would destroy the validity of the private placement exemption. This involves more than the mere obtaining of an investment letter. The issuer should have sufficient information with respect to each purchaser to be satisfied that there is no reasonable basis for doubting the validity of the investment representation. The issuer's final judgment, if challenged, will be evaluated with 20-20 hindsight and possibly with knowledge of factors unknown to him at the time of the placement.

The third, and perhaps the most effective, safeguard is to place a legend on the securities being issued indicating the existence of the restrictions upon re-offering or resale, thereby preventing the original purchaser from deliberately or inadvertently re-offering the securities in a manner that would invalidate the exemption. In connection with the clarifications to be effected by the Wheat Report[2] (currently awaiting action by the SEC), the SEC has strongly recommended the use of a legend on the face of privately-placed securities, and has indicated that it will regard the presence of such a legend as a significant indication of whether the circumstances surrounding an offering are consistent with the private placement exemption. To supplement the protection afforded by a legal legend, the issuer may also enter a stop-transfer order with the transfer agent for the securities involved. Although the agent would ordinarily question the transfer based upon the legend, the stop-transfer order provides useful additional protection.

If an issuer complies with these three key standards, he can be reasonably certain that he is in a position to establish the validity of the private placement exemption.

The Best-Laid Plans . . .

With all the work completed, checked and double-checked, a variety of contingencies may arise between the time the documents are signed and the day they come to pass. The company and the investors should be aware of certain areas that must be carefully negotiated. In some cases, the company may want to go back to the marketplace soon after the first offering, and the venture capitalist may want to join the offering. The investors may be unhappy that the company's monthly, quarterly or semiannual reports are always late, sales never meet projections, or the cost of sales are too high. "Why not do things differently?" asks someone in the group—and there is a sudden break in the relationship.

What if the company wants to go back to the marketplace, or to its own stockholders for a rights offering again? The venture capitalist now stands firm and points to the registration provision, demanding that the company immediately register the venture capitalist's securities.

From the issuer's standpoint, timing of the piggyback registration should probably be conditioned upon approval of the underwriter—not thirty days later, but perhaps as long as six months or a year or some other reasonable time.

HOLDING FOR INVESTMENT

The concept of "holding for investment" brings us back to the original representation of purchasing for investment. There was a time when a six-month holding period was considered reasonable, rather than the currently agreed-upon "not less than two years, three years is best" holding period. The rationale was taken from the tax law on capital gains to show that the investment had been held for a sufficient period of time.

Assume that a period of time has passed and the holder believes he has firmly established the fact that he has "held for investment" and he would now like to sell his stock. This can lead to questionable situations. The basic concern is proving the investment intent. To go through the ritual of getting an investment letter, the company and experienced counsel can place a huge stamp dipped in bright red ink on the stock certificate stating: "These securities have not been purchased pursuant to an exemption under Section 4(2) of the Securities Act of 1933 and may not be sold, transferred . . . except under certain circumstances." Some attorneys suggest adding an extra fang or two: ". . . upon receipt of legal opinion acceptable to counsel for the company."

Even though the company places the necessary terminology on the certificate, stock could be transferred in ways other than through the corporate books. Many people, for example, sell securities after faithfully representing that it is not for purpose of distribution or resale between members of their syndicate, group, partners, friends or clients. They simply transfer it by assignment.

The Holding Period: Guiding Principles and Rules-of-Thumb

The guiding principle for the length of time that letter stock must be legally held before sale is that the privately-placed securities ". . . may not be resold to the public unless there occurs an unforeseen change of circumstances which establishes that the resale is not inconsistent with the investment intent evidenced at the time of the original sale. . . ."

Overall, there seems to be no definite answer as to a generally agreed-upon period that furnishes sufficient investment intent. The necessary time varies with the circumstances of each case, although most attorneys would probably agree that the longer the period of retention, the more persuasive the argument that the resale is not at variance with the original investment intent. Examples of this are an advance or decline in the market price of the issuer's securities or a change in the results of the operations. These are normal investment risks which should be anticipated when securities are purchased. Also, the purchaser's inability to repay loans incurred in connection with the purchase of the securities would not ordinarily be deemed to be unforeseeable, thus would not ordinarily justify a resale of the securities by the purchaser or by his creditor.

The rule-of-thumb is that holding privately-placed securities for a period of not less than two years (and it appears that the SEC looks more favorably upon three years) satisfies a statement of investment intent at the time of the original purchase of the securities. This "rule" has not been codified, nor has it been concurred in by the SEC or the Commission staff. In fact, under the concepts embodied in the 1933 Act, it is at least arguable that a purchase with a specific intent to sell after a period of, say, five years, is inconsistent with the investment intent required to establish the exemption. There is no question, however, that in determining the validity of an expressed investment intent, the longer the holding period, the better.

The holding period problem is as much a headache to the SEC as it is to issuers and legal counsel. The Wheat Report is a constructive attempt to substitute objective holding periods. According to some legalists, there will still be many transactions in which the establishment of investment intent is necessary and in which the question will arise as to how long securities must be held in order to permit a resale which does not contradict the intent. Attorneys feel it is unnerving to have to rely upon subjective questions of investment intent as distinguished from an objective holding period. An awareness of the problems in this area, however, is essential in order to develop intelligent negotiations for private placements. An issuer cannot assume, for example, that once the securities have been held for two years, he no longer has to worry about the costs and effort involved in effecting a registration of the securities.

Timing . . . and the Change of Circumstances Factor

It is difficult for an attorney to try to justify to his client a three-year holding period after the client has heard of a one-year or two-year rule, or that a "change of circumstances" could affect the holding period. (The SEC recognizes that after stock is received there could be a significant "change of circumstances" which could affect the duration of the holding period, since it was necessary or reasonable to sell the stock under the circumstances despite the fact that the original purchase was made without intent to sell).

As one experienced practitioner recently put it: "As a practical matter, the shares may be sold in any manner after a sufficient amount of time, which is rather indefinite but probably two to three years."

The current official dogma is that if stock is acquired for investment, a lapse of time does not automatically free the stock from restrictions on resale. Thus the SEC creates a specific period of time as the holding period. A general guide appears to be that the holder should not agree to sell for a specific period of time. If this appears to be illogical, it is because this area of the law does not seem to be based on logic. One answer to this puzzling problem is a statement by the investor that his intentions are pure, and that he is buying for investment and has no present intention of selling.

No one, of course, buys stock with the intention of being buried with it; but there do not appear to be any practical remedies for the problem in the near future.

MANY SHARES, LITTLE PAPER

How many stock certificates should an investor receive for his ten thousand shares?

Usually, regardless of the number of shares, only one certificate is issued. In some cases, an attorney might request that relative to estate planning, it would be advantageous to have several certificates because there are certain courses of action that might be taken in the event of death. In this case, the investor would prefer a dozen certificates, a majority of which could end up in the safety-deposit boxes of friends. Under these circumstances, the company can do very little, even though it stamps the original certificates and has the investment letter. The securities laws may have been violated by the purchasers, but not by the company.

The Controlling Stockholder

A controlling stockholder who has held his stock for a sufficient period of time or has experienced a sufficient change of circumstances to eliminate any limitations upon his resale by reason of an originally expressed investment intent is generally subject to the same statutory requirements as is an issuer when he sells. There is one exception to this principle, however—set forth in Rule 154 under the 1933 Act—which provides in effect that a controlling person may sell during a six-month period a number of shares of the class outstanding. If the stock involved is listed, there is a double test and the controlling person is limited to the lesser of the one percent rule or a number of shares equal to the highest trading volume during any one of the four calendar weeks preceding his order for sale.

The purpose of this rule is to permit limited trading activities by controlling persons to satisfy personal financial needs where, on the basis of the number of shares involved, the SEC does not believe that the protections of registration are necessary for the public. Shares held by a controlling stockholder constitute letter stock only when taken in a private placement and prior to the expiration of the necessary investment period. Thereafter, the shares remain subject to the limitation of the Act and may only be disposed of within the rather restricted limits of Rule 154.

In order to avail himself of the opportunity to make limited sales under this Rule, a controlling stockholder must comply with the specific provisions of the Rule as to the nature of the transactions in which his securities are sold. In brief: the broker may act only as a broker and may not purchase as a principal; he must receive no more than the customary broker's commission; he must not solicit, or arrange for the solicitation of orders to buy in connection with the transactions; and he must not be aware that his controlling personal customer is violating any of the provisions of Rule 154 regarding the amount of securities sold or the nature of transactions involved in such sales.

Rule 133 Transactions

With regard to securities that are issued in corporate combinations—so-called "Rule 133 transactions" the SEC takes the position that if the action of the disappearing or non-surviving corporation is taken at a stockholder's meeting (as distinguished from action resulting from individual stockholder judgment), a sale of the securities of the surviving corporation to the stockholders of the disappearing corporation will not be deemed to exist. In effect, a corporation wishing to distribute its securities could locate another corporation controlled by persons willing to merge or sell its assets, and the pure "no sale" principle would allow the stockholders of the disappearing corporation to make a free unregistered distribution of the securities of the surviving corporation.

In order to plug this legal loophole, the SEC added a provision to the Rule to the effect that "controlling persons of the non-surviving corporation in a Rule 133 transaction are subject to substantially the same limitations which exist upon controlling persons of the surviving corporation by reason of Rule 154." These include the limitation of either one percent or the highest weekly trading volume on the amount of securities that can be sold as well as the limitation to pure brokerage transactions in connection with the disposition. Also, stockholders of the non-surviving corporation who were not in a position to control the company receive free stock upon consummation of the transaction. Dispute exists, however, as to whether or not investment restrictions apply. The SEC says they do.

THE REGULATIONS ICEBERG

The Securities Act of 1933 can be likened to an iceberg—a small percentage of general provisions above and an unseen massive body of vague and changing interpretations below. Like common law, it is not the law as written, but the interpretations have created "the living law" as it now lives—or somehow survives in spirit. Some of the securities laws defy logic, but legal counsel has somehow learned to live and practice with them.

Consider a situation in which the interests of both issuer and venture capitalist suddenly merge. If the private offering is successful and business is good, the company probably will have a substantial number of stockholders. At this point, some of the investors want to withdraw from the deal. Or, there may be a merger or acquisition of the company by another firm, in which case, the investors receive stock in the other company. This problem is covered by Rule 133 of the 1933 Act. The rule stipulates, generally, that in a situation in which an individual stockholder cannot be held to individual action because the action was on the part of all the stockholders, the new shares received are not taken pursuant to the investor's personal investment representation, but the old "letter" may survive.

What if there is a public offering and some of the investors in the company wish to sell their stock? Investors who are not in covert gain no relief from the "one percent rule" (Rule 154), which permits the sale of less than a substantial amount of stock through brokers' transactions. The stock, as explained in the Rule, may be validly sold by the broker and, by implication, by the seller. "If a security is admitted to trading on a security exchange," the Rule points out, "an investor can sell an amount equal to the lesser of one percent of the shares outstanding at the time of the receipt by the broker of the order, or the larger aggregate reported volume of trading on security exchanges during any one week within the four weeks preceding the receipt of such order." But the Rule does not apply specifically to letter stock.

Following a private offering to the venture capitalist and a subsequent public offering, this Rule also permits the president of the company to sell shares held in limited amounts from time to time.

If the stock is not traded on the securities exchange, the one percent rule then applies every six months, as there is no way to compute trading volume.

There is also a possibility of "back-dooring," a private offering put on top of a private offering. "Back-dooring" can develop when someone buys stock under a proper private offering and begins to distribute it to other people. If this is done at a time when the company knows or should have known about the transaction, the number of offerees includes those to whom the company has offered the stock as well as those to whom the purchasers offered the stock. If the company offers stock to a dozen people and one of them says he plans to place half of what he has purchased, the company can create an impropriety without realizing all of the ramifications. Furthermore, the eighteen or so investors to whom the private purchaser has offered the shares may not be the sophisticated kind of investors to whom the exemption is restricted.

The investor must be wary of these situations. It is very important for him to investigate the people to whom he sells stock. This becomes critical in "intrastate" offerings. Intrastate exemptions can apply to an unlimited number of offerees, as long as they are bona fide residents of the state in which the issuer is incorporated. The company must make a detailed investigation at this point to make sure the representation of address is valid, an identical move when stock is sold in private offering to someone who represents to the seller that he is a sophisticated investor.

THE LAW, THE ATTORNEY GENERAL—AND WALL STREET

There are other groups to worry about besides the SEC. Some states, through the Attorney General's office, have begun a much more active program in policing private offerings in their states. In New York, for one, if a private offering is made to ten or more people, regardless of who they are, the offering must be filed in the state.

If stock is sold to a Wall Street house, the terms of a loan agreement or stock purchase agreement will probably require that the company supply such details as monthly profit-and-loss reports and new product reports, among others. With a successful public offering, the Wall Street house will find itself privy to a large amount of inside information that could be useful to its customers. Assuming that the house knows the law, it will not divulge this data to customers. However, in such a situation, the company should provide that the information to be supplied as part of the private placement will terminate either upon the filing of the registration statement or its effective date, in order to anticipate the company's responsibilities to the investing public.

LETTER STOCK IN A NUTSHELL

Facing the Problems of Limitations and Disposal versus Formal Registration

In the final consideration of letter stock, depending upon the particular placement involved, there are two major questions to face:

1. What sorts of limitations exist?
2. When, and in what sorts of transactions, may the securities be disposed of?

Letter Stock . . . and the Venture Capitalist

The fact that there are many problem areas involved in owning letter stock (among them, lack of liquidity, uncertainty of knowing exactly when a sale can be made, problems in dealing with the SEC) raises the question, "Why buy a private deal when so many opportunities are available in the public market?"

For the majority of the investing public, the traditional stock exchanges and the over-the-counter market are preferred courses. However, buying registered stock in the public marketplace has disadvantages of its own:

1. The investor rarely has the opportunity to conduct extensive research before making an investment.
2. The majority of publicly-held shares in high-growth-type companies are valued at high multiples in the public market.
3. The investor in a publicly-held company rarely can become involved in the operation of the business, or maintain any significant flow of information about the true progress of the firm.

Although the venture capital investor pays a price in terms of liquidity, properly arranged private financings enable him to overcome the inherent limitations. The long-term venture capital investor feels that this type of investing can be done on the basis of fundamental analysis and that the probability of success is enhanced by his direct involvement in the affairs of the business; that is, he feels that the benefits resulting from this type of activity will overcome the myriad problems created by owning letter stock. In the long run, the venture capitalist hopes to be rewarded by better investment performance and greater personal satisfaction as a result of serving as a constructive force in the success of the venture.

11

How To Monitor Venture Capital Investments

Walter A. Forbes

This discussion is concerned with what the venture capitalist should do between the time the investment is made and the time that gains or losses are realized. We are ignoring the many other facets of venture capital—looking for investment opportunities, screening them, the excitement of the new investment's potential growth and the uniqueness of the portfolio company's products, plus all the interesting aspects of the early stages of making an investment.

We are concerned here with the period starting after the check is handed over, a period of let-down for some venture capitalists. All too soon the excitement of the chase is over, and the enthusiastic projections showing immense capital gains become necessary concerns.

It takes more than money to insure a good—and successful—venture capital deal. The quality of the monitoring program between the placing of money and the realizing of gains or losses is often the reason for the success or failure of an investment. A well-conceived monitoring and investment management program can make the venture capitalist's work more predictable and also can improve the overall return on his portfolio.

Mr. Forbes is a principal in the venture analysis firm of Forbes, Chinn & Britt Inc.

GENERAL PURPOSES OF MONITORING

There are six general reasons for establishing a monitoring and management program for venture capital investments.

First, a monitoring program allows the venture capitalist to follow the progress of the business. It protects him against surprises—such as the bank's noting that the business is overdrawn, suppliers cancelling contracts, lawsuits, and many other irritating problems.

Second, company management can be efficiently backstopped. If management turns to the venture capitalist for help and he has not done any monitoring, he will lack an understanding of the particular problem; consequently, he will not be a useful resource for the struggling portfolio firm. A key part of the backstopping process is an understanding of the people and market requirements of the business. Assume, for instance, that an important man leaves the company. . . . Who will know the full qualifications of the position, the details of the job, and what to look for in a replacement? Further, an immediate "catch-up" program is likely to be time-consuming and costly. Monitoring can prevent the need for precipitous change, sometimes so disruptive that it can destroy the company.

Third, a monitoring program allows the evaluation of the financial and management needs of a company on a continuing basis. For example, the venture capitalist, when asked for more money, will not have to make a judgment based on static information, but can make a decision in tune with the company's changing situation. A key factor here is that an informed investor will be able to react very quickly.

Fourth, a monitoring program enables the venture capitalist to make a better judgment about when to get out with a profit. All too often, he is not quite sure what the right time is.

Fifth, such a system will help the venture capitalist stay in touch with what the downside risk is. He may believe he can always get his money out without an adequate monitoring program; but a healthy investment can deteriorate as quickly as the sun sets.

Finally, a monitoring and management support program helps the venture capitalist and the entrepreneur work toward a common goal. Initially, they are usually in complete agreement about the company's goals, products, employee-hiring practices, and all the variables necessary for running a business and planning its long-term growth. After the investment, however, the entrepreneur and the venture capitalist can drift apart. Subtle changes sometimes take place in the company. In many cases, without really knowing it, the entrepreneur may slowly shift his plans. He may try to sell the firm's product to a slightly different market segment, or he may implement modifications in the product which then lends itself to a different customer appeal.

The venture capitalist who does not use a monitoring or management program can come to a rude awakening that a combination of many small changes have, in fact, changed the focus of his portfolio company. One of the principal purposes of a sound monitoring and management program is to maintain effective interaction between the entrepreneur and the venture capitalist. This, in turn, improves the ability to keep talented people in the company and insures the fact that the investment is on the right track.

Thus, the main purpose of monitoring is to help control venture investments so that they will not be permitted to rule by forcing reactions without the understanding and knowledge necessary for sound decisions.

BASIC ALTERNATIVES

Strictly Passive . . .

There are two types of monitoring programs. At one end of the spectrum is the strictly passive role—negotiating a minority position, turning over the check and then waiting for whatever announcements may come from the company. A passive role has these advantages:

- A venture capital firm with a passive philosophy requires only a small staff and minimal overhead, in that its business is essentially to screen and evaluate the initial concept of an enterprise, and then make an investment decision after doing some further detailed investigation. Once the check is written, the deal is put into a portfolio. In many cases, that can be the end of a particular venture unless something very good—or very bad—happens.
- Using this philosophy, a small staff can make a large number of investments; therefore, the odds are good that the venture capital firm will come out ahead of the game.
- A strictly passive role gives the entrepreneur his head, allows him to feel unencumbered and, theoretically, provides the greatest opportunity for him to express his creativity and energy. This particular point is often argued by an entrepreneur when he comes back for more money, saying that he did not have the freedom to do what he wanted.
- It takes little time to manage this type of venture capital portfolio because of the lack of commitment to any one deal. Therefore, if a new industry becomes very popular, the firm has the flexibility of changing focus quickly to new markets.

The disadvantages of the passive approach reflect some of the obvious purposes of monitoring. In short, it is almost impossible to know where the money went and how it was used. It is difficult to react to problems quickly—except by gut feel. Also, when additional information is needed, a hostile atmosphere may be encountered at a company that has been left on its own and merely received a check.

. . . Or Rolling up Your Sleeves

At the other end of the spectrum is the active role, the full- or part-time involvement of the venture capitalist's staff in the operational affairs of the company. In our firm's case, if the venture situation required it, one of our partners would devote his energies full-time, live on-site and work on a day-to-day basis with the portfolio company. The obvious advantage here is that the venture capitalist plays a role in the success of the firm. He knows the people, and knows the bad news as soon as anyone else knows it. Also, he can help develop solutions before problems become too serious. Essentially, he is free to make his own mistakes as the master of his own fate. This type of program also allows the entrepreneur to learn to delegate authority and to rely on other people. Active involvement by the venture capital staff often helps the entrepreneur to develop these skills at the very beginning.

The primary disadvantage of this type of program is the expense. The cost of allocating a staff member to a venture is often too high. Most venture capitalist firms use staff men for investigating new projects and assign them to work with a number of portfolio concerns.

PASSIVE VENTURING—AND HOW IT CAN GO WRONG

We were recently contacted by a group of private investors who had invested over half-a-million dollars in a small electronics firm with one proprietary product. They had made their investment almost a year before contacting our firm. During this twelve-month period, the investors had taken a passive role, avoiding any active involvement in the day-to-day operations of the business. They had a seat on the board of directors but attended meetings infrequently. The investors were looking for a group of venture capitalists to invest additional money and, consequently, they wanted a quick assessment of the condition of the company. They had "a feeling" that things were not going as well as planned. The company's president was vague about sales and earnings, and about how the product was being accepted in the marketplace.

In cases like this, our firm conducts a reconnaissance of the company. We spend five to ten days evaluating the general status of the business, spot-checking certain areas and completing a thorough analysis of the company's cash position. In the case of the electronics company, we found little more than a beautiful physical plant: a secretary (and sometimes more than one) for every executive; fully paneled offices; a xerox machine in almost every room; and new company cars for all the officers. Upon further investigation, it was discovered that several principals of the company were taking kickbacks from suppliers and draining the company's cash for personal expenses. In addition, there were a few illegal agreements with suppliers.

Admittedly, this is a particularly dramatic—and, hopefully, unusual—situation. Our firm wrote a report for the group explaining our understanding of the company's main problems, and illustrating how they could be solved and at what cost. Our report was controversial. Unfortunately, it became difficult for the original investors to interest other groups. Prospective investors coming out to the plant for the first time could not understand why the original investors had not been aware that their money was being squandered on unnecessary overhead expenses and a fancy physical plant.

Although it has certain advantages, when the passive strategy goes wrong it is difficult to explain obvious problems which a small exercise of curiosity would have uncovered. More importantly, when other investor groups are approached for additional money, it is difficult to explain why there was no awareness of these problems.

ACTIVE VENTURING

There are also disadvantages to the full-time role. Our firm was involved with a company in which a venture capital firm's staff man had assumed a full-time role. A considerable amount of money had been invested. The man on the scene quickly became close to the principals on the management team, became caught up in affairs of the company and began to believe inflated projections of performance to the extent that his reports did not reflect the actual condition of the company. In becoming caught up with the enthusiasm of the venture, he had lost his professional objectivity.

Because the staff man's lack of objectivity had allowed the company to fall into serious financial problems, the venture capital group needed to raise additional funds. They faced a difficult problem; the company had been mismanaged—an extremely difficult thing for them to explain, in that one of their own people had been on the scene. In this case, it can be seen that neither role is necessarily a guaranteed solution to monitoring and management problems.

There are certainly many alternatives. The most obvious would be active board membership, or membership on the executive committee of the company. Additional monitoring activities include such checks as frequent trips to the company, an active system of reports, and others. The important factor in a monitoring program is not whether it is active or passive or somewhere in-between, but rather the results of the program and what it is worth in terms of staff time, expense, and all the other factors important to managing a business in a professional fashion.

KEY ASPECTS OF GOOD MONITORING

A major aspect of good monitoring is the structure of reports. The problem is to devise a structure that puts weight on the important variables of the business that need to be monitored. When some investors set up a monitoring program, they usually rely on standard variables (sales, income, budgets) and sometimes lose sight of the unique characteristics of the portfolio company. However, it is essential to determine the critical variables of the business. To be sure, sales and earnings growth is a fine thing, but it may be much more important to know *where* sales and earnings are coming from; in some cases, for example, monitoring a major customer may be the answer.

Also, when implementing a monitoring program, it is particularly important to insist that the structure of reports be followed explicitly. Our firm has a policy that if a report is late, we call and request an explanation. If we have not received the information we want within the next day or two, we go right to the company. In almost every case where there is a delay and excuses begin to pile up, there is invariably a real problem.

Perhaps money has been invested in inventory that is not selling, or personnel problems have arisen. A report structure is a mandatory part of any monitoring program; and it is just as important that people live by it and report on time. It is a management responsibility that can easily be tested: the report either is or is not there.

There are seven variables that usually reveal key facts about a company:

- We pay close attention to a company's *rate of growth*. When we see a slowdown suggesting that projections will not be reached, we investigate. Often, the entrepreneur indicates that he will reach his company's projections by the end of the year due to heavy sales in the last few months of the year. While this may be true, if a slowdown in the rate of growth is indicated, we demand a full explanation of why it has occurred.

- *Cash management* is a critical aspect of any business. We want to know the entrepreneur's attitude toward cash management, what cash procedures he plans to employ, the status of his banking relations, plus his program for implementing successful fiscal controls.

- We closely watch a company's *working capital position*, paying particular attention to the aging of accounts payable as well as receivables. One interesting aspect of accounts payable is that by checking who is paid, who is not, and how old the debt is, an investor is able to feel the general health of the business.

- Checking *relationships with key customers* is an excellent way to find out exactly how the company is doing. Such checking often requires discussion with customers (a kind of probing that requires much care and discretion). Nevertheless, it is often possible to learn more from customers, and in some cases suppliers, in a few short minutes than can be learned at the company itself in a week.

- The company's *order backlog* is checked frequently to determine whether it is increasing or decreasing. The age and quality of the orders is also important. It is easy in many industries—housing, for example—to build a large but unsubstantiated order backlog. A schedule of cancelled orders can also be revealing.
- *Personnel turnover* at all levels within a company is important. This factor is frequently an early indication of serious problems.
- It is always useful to check the *aging of inventory*. Even a spot check of certain items will often indicate that a problem is developing.

Another key aspect of any monitoring program is the prudent use of outside opinion. Major corporations have only insiders on their boards. This tendency can lead to ingrown judgments about running a business. Some investors also tend to allow only insiders to have a voice in the company, to understand the business and, in some cases, to determine policy. A weak board is sometimes cited as the reason a venture enterprise is not working. Our firm insists that someone who is uninvolved, such as an outsider who has not invested in the situation, sit on the board. The outsider functions as an "anchor to windward"—someone who can call insiders back to reality and can blunt enthusiasm or optimism when neither is warranted.

One way to use outsiders is to ask outside consultants to look at a particular aspect of the business, talk to key executives in order to provide another opinion of what is happening. Another approach is to test a strategic plan that the board is considering by analyzing it to determine if the company has the wherewithal to implement it. A third alternative is to elect a strong individual to the board—someone who understands the company's market—with the understanding that he does not have to answer to anyone and can always speak his mind.

If those companies used as examples earlier had relied on this type of individual, or had they called in an outside consulting group early in their development, many problems could have been avoided. In both these cases, the product and the concept were good. The problem was that management was neither supported enough nor called upon sufficiently to explain their actions.

A good time to use outsiders, incidentally, is during the period of transition between promotional and operational stages of a new business. Often entrepreneurs are very capable promoters, but cannot effectively deliver the product or provide the service they have promoted. It is essential to catch this problem early or the business may not survive the transitional period.

Timing is another critical aspect of a good monitoring program. At the beginning, it is essential that the venture capitalists have an active role in the company. Businesses change when they receive large sums of money. An entrepreneur will invariably react to a new-found fortune in unexpected ways. There is a tendency to start spending quickly on things that did not seem essential when the business was just getting by; also, pressures tend to mount very quickly because return-on-investment projections must be met. In addition, people often get greedy and spend most of their time worrying about the company's stock price.

In general, venture capitalists ask a great deal of an entrepreneur. It is the rare man who is capable of personally handling an active business effectively. Thus, it is usually appropriate that the venture capitalist assume an active posture at the beginning. As soon as the business achieves some stability—when problems are assessed and plans to correct them are formulated—the venture capitalist should begin withdrawing to a more passive role. The first six to twelve months of a venture are particularly sensitive, and it is not good business to invest money without taking the time to develop a monitoring and management program during this period.

At the same time, it is possible for investors who wish to remain primarily passive to work out a compromise. Although they may not want to invest the time necessary to monitor their own investments, they should at least seek out these services from others in the field. Such services can be expensive, but the cost is quite low when compared with what is at stake in the success or failure of a venture.

MONITORING PROGRAMS—IN DOLLARS

Few investors carefully consider the cost of a monitoring program. For example, an investment banking firm in New York earned fees of slightly more than $50 thousand by raising money for a private placement in a new venture. Since then, the venture has had a very spotty record. Four years after the initial investment, the partner in charge at the investment firm sat down and figured out the hours that he and his associates had spent in trying to make the venture successful. Based on their annual salaries, he determined that in four years they had spent time worth about a quarter of a million dollars. This calculation did not include the time of clerical and staff people, or basic overhead expenses absorbed by the firm. While the firm did receive a few warrants in the deal, the imputed value of the warrants was only $10 thousand. Thus, for a total fee of $60 thousand, the investment bankers incurred a real cost of over a quarter of a million dollars—not to mention the cost of their time in terms of lost opportunities.

If they had analyzed the nature of the business at the outset, established a responsive monitoring program, carefully structured a system of reports, and decided on some "go" and "no-go" decision points, they probably would have withdrawn from the company about three years sooner in the realization that the business was likely to hover at a slightly less than profitable level for a long time to come.

Monitoring a venture capital investment properly has a major impact on the economics of the venturer, as well as on the success or failure of the investment. Time spent in thinking about the requirements of a business and a basic monitoring program, whether it is essentially passive or active, will save a great deal of time and money in the long run and, in many cases, be vital to the success of the venture.

The best monitoring programs are reasonably rigid. A venture capitalist should be active, at least at the start. He should demand a series of reports and carefully watch the critical factors of the business. The entrepreneur or management team should answer questions quickly and completely. They must live up to their responsibility to produce the reports required, and to follow the agreed-upon strategy. In these early stages, the venture capitalist should require that he be treated as part of the company.

Using hindsight, we and the investment banker estimated the cost to establish a proper monitoring program for the venture discussed. We decided it might have cost about $10 thousand for the time necessary to develop a system of reports. We also determined that to call in outsiders to check on some of the problems turned up by the reports during the first six months would have cost another $15 thousand.

Thus, at a cost of perhaps $25 thousand, the firm could have avoided spending a quarter of a million dollars of time, plus related overhead expenses. Using the time saved, the group might have made three or four other investments, any of which could have worked out better than this one.

Investing time and money to take an active monitoring and management position in a venture capital situation is the most productive money an investor can spend.

12
A Checklist For Monitoring

Emanuel Batler

Venture capital is commonly stated to be a risky but rewarding financial activity. In the mythology of the field, the idea has grown that the high rewards-risk ratio makes venture capital an exciting and worthwhile investment area. Perhaps this is the reason that many venture capital pools have been established in the United States in the last several years.

In order to succeed at venture capital investing, the venturer must approach the risks with the same precautionary attitude as an insurance company would. Although the insurance companies have available actual statistics to allow them to establish premium income sufficient to cover the total risks, they work continually at improving the statistics by careful medical examination of their clients. In effect, they try to improve the statistics by screening their risks. Only in this way can they increase their return on investment.

The venture capitalist's problem is much more difficult. Of course, it is standard operating procedure for him to analyze carefully the business plans and the entrepreneur-founder's background and references. This kind of pre-screening is somewhat comparable to the medical examination required by insurance

Mr. Batler is President of Glentech Instruments Ltd., in Toronto, Ontario, Canada.

companies; but the analogy ends here. Once the contract is signed, the insurance company can safely depend upon the averaging power of statistics; the number of risks is so large that the bad ones are compensated. In venture capital, the number of risks is relatively small so that there is no averaging effect which can be relied upon to produce a predictable spread of winners and losers.

The relatively small number of investments (risks) leads to the establishment of a new principle based on the totalitarian law of physics, which states that anything that is not expressly forbidden by scientific principle is compulsory. (The rule was originally advanced by a British novelist as the governing principle for a colony of ants.) From the venture capitalist's standpoint, this means that any contingency that cannot be expressly anticipated is certain to happen.

From this law, the principle of the turn-around index emerges. The success of a venture capital pool is directly correlated with its turn-around index—the ratio of investment situations that can be turned around from sick-to-healthy, against the total number of investments. The total number of investments is part of the turn-around index because the totalitarian law establishes that every investment is going to have some troubles. The really rewarding investments are those in which the troubles are minor and relatively easy to fix, or which tend to fix themselves.

TEN WAYS AN INVESTMENT CAN GO WRONG

What are some of the most common of these inevitable troubles? The following list of the most frequently occurring problems is based on material compiled by Alan Grieve, president of *Gdn.* Venture Limited of Toronto, Ontario:

1. Basic business concept
2. Insufficient funds
3. Poor financial management
4. Unforeseen contingencies with major effect on cash flow
5. Management cannot supply balanced total management
6. Management "plays" to the stock market or gets rich too soon
7. Business concept is premature or ages prematurely
8. Weak board of directors
9. Personality conflicts between founders
10. Critical change in marketplace

A closer look at each of these key problems is in order . . .

1. Basic Business Concept

Possibly the most common problem is that the investment was made in a business concept that simply was not right. The history of American business is rich in stories of major companies that were once on the brink of bankruptcy. With few exceptions, most of the companies listed on the New York Stock Exchange survived key crises in their history. The fact that they are listed indicates that management met the challenge of crisis and altered the main thrust of the company in the new directions required for success.

One of the great venture capital successes, often cited as an example of the possible upside returns, is Digital Equipment Corporation—one of the most successful investments of American

Research & Development, the leading publicly-held (NYSE) venture capital company. The original founding concept of Digital Equipment was to manufacture small, standardized digital circuit modules based on the transistor. The president of DEC conceived a plan to supply a wide spectrum of these modules to circuit designers who could assemble various equipments without the need to design a variety of basic items. In retrospect, this was a limited view with limited horizons. However, the idea of assembling DEC modules into a rudimentary basic mini-computer was conceived in the hope that this would expand the market by consuming some of the output of the company in its own captive proprietary line. The rest is history. DEC has become the IBM of the mini-computer field. As of the end of 1970, it is estimated that DEC had installed over ten thousand mini-computers, and the annual volume of the company was as of this time in the \$100-\$200 million range.

DEC's ultimate success grew from its realization of the potentialities of the mini-computer market. Supported and guided by aggressive DEC and ARD managements, it changed its major thrust from manufacturing digital computers to mini-computers; and by the time major competitors in the computer field reacted to the exploding market for mini-computers, DEC was leading in that market.

In an investment made by the J. H. Whitney Venture Group shortly after World War II, we see another example of successful modification of an original concept. The company was founded to manufacture powdered orange juice based on a process that had been perfected during the war for foreign-based American troops who were homesick for the drink. When the GI's became civilians again, however, they did not want powdered orange-juice. Apparently, what was acceptable on Guadalcanal was not eagerly sought in Wichita, Kansas.

Rather than accept defeat, the company decided to market a product that happened to be an intermediate step in the production of powdered orange-juice. In the process, fresh orange-juice is transformed into a frozen slush just prior to being freeze-dried into a powdered state, very much like instant coffee. It was decided to market this frozen orange slush through frozen food outlets which were just beginning to be established in the United States. The company prospered and ultimately became the Minute Maid Corporation—and frozen orange-juice became a staple of the American diet.

High-technology companies often face the reality that although the newly-developed technology may be innovative and desirable, it is simply too costly in terms of the resultant product; that is, the customers want it but are not prepared to pay the price that the entrepreneur must place on the new product to make it profitable. One remedy, obviously, is to try to develop a lower-cost version of the potentially successful technology.

Here, the venture capitalist is often faced with the need to introduce new management (at least, new technical management) into the company in order to effect a rapid cost reduction. Frequently, it develops that the original inventors and innovators cannot quickly reduce the cost of the product because the process may require entirely new approaches. This proves to be a common route through which competitors enter the market—by spotting ways to bring out a lower-cost version of an attractive original idea. If the possibility appears likely, the venture capitalist must act quickly to introduce new talent, with the mandate for fast cost reduction. The rationale for a new group is that if the original group had been able to see an obvious low-cost route, they would have adopted it in the first place.

In summary, if the basic business concept is wrong, the remedial approach is to see what can be salvaged. If the concept is so basically and fundamentally wrong that nothing can be salvaged, then, of course, the operation must be terminated.

2. Insufficient Funds

If a business is conceptually unsound, there is never enough money to support the operation. If the business is basically sound and the entrepreneurs did not project their requirements adequately (and they always seem to fall short), then it must be realized that the problem of the business is that it needs more money; the venture capitalists then must either provide these additional funds or arrange to bring in other investors. Some venture capital organizations with vast capital pools anticipate that many of their companies will need more money, and that additional funds will most likely be needed when the conventional sources have been exhausted. The timing is never right; therefore, these organizations always carry funds in reserve for situations that look as though they are going to need it.

In October 1970, for example, our firm invested approximately $230 thousand in a scientific instrument company in the Boston area. At the time of the investment, it was believed that an additional $250 thousand would probably be needed to bring the firm to a positive cash flow. Currently, it is hoped that other investors can be attracted to provide these funds because the company appears to be a very promising investment. However, we have set aside the necessary capital in the event that a venture partner cannot be found to come in on equitable terms.

3. Poor Financial Management

There is a saying: "When you are out of cash, you are out of business."

The end result of poor financial management is usually a call from the company on Wednesday afternoon informing the venture capitalist that they will not be able to meet the Friday payroll. Somehow the actuality of the company's experiences did not go according to the original game plan. Receivables which were to generate cash did not come in, while cost for salaries and other overhead expenses continued unabated. Each month that the cash flow is delayed is an expensive matter because the ongoing salaries must be paid, and usually there is no recovery of the extra losses incurred as a result of the time slippage.

Typical factors leading to sudden shortage of cash are:

- An inadequate or inaccurate financial reporting system
- The venture capital group's failure to respond soon enough to deviations from the game plan
- Poor bank relations
- An overly optimistic original cash flow plan, in terms of generation and collection of accounts receivable, adequate contingency provisions, startup budgets, and the like
- Management's failing to react quickly enough to deviations from plans

In many cases, management of the cash flow may turn out to be the key factor in the company's success.

4. Unforeseen Contingencies With Major Effect On Cash Flow

The number of parameters that could have a negative effect on cash flow is almost infinite—a fact which almost guarantees that one of these contingencies will occur (another example of the totalitarian law of physics), and the company's costs will be increased one way or the other.

The most typical contingencies are:

- Unanticipated increases in the price of raw materials
- Marketing and distribution costs exceeding the plan, as it becomes necessary to increase expenditures on promotion, dealer discounts, etc.
- Competition's reacting to the company's new products by price reductions or similar tactics
- Product difficulties increasing warranty and service costs. (Sometimes these arise from engineering defects, at other times from quality control. A good example of quality control problems is a company with sales in excess of $100 million annually, currently listed on the NYSE. Its orginal product consisted of magnetic tape which it introduced at a time when there were already several well-established suppliers with national brand recognition. The firm hoped to obtain a beachhead in this large and growing market by supplying tape of superior quality. It developed that quality control problems in their production processes almost killed the company. Huge quantities of tape had to be withdrawn from the field and replaced at company cost. Fortunately, the company's progressive attitude in connection with tape replacement tended to enhance its reputation with many of its customers. The customers were prepared to live with the quality control problems as long as the company continued to maintain a posture of backing up its products by replacing tapes of defective quality. In a sense, this tactic accidentally had some positive

> consequences. Nonetheless, the effect on the company's cash flow was disastrous and an enormous additional infusion of capital was required from the original venture capitalist. This fresh capital was crucial and the company would not exist today had the venture capitalists not been able to supply the additional financing required during the crisis.)

It seems that the only certain aspect of the problem of unforeseen contingencies is that they are certain to occur, and the venture capitalist must expect that additional cash will be required sooner or later.

5. Management Cannot Supply Balanced Total Management

It is axiomatic that a business, whether it be a new or an old established firm, cannot survive without balanced management that can function with complementary effectiveness in the areas of finance, engineering, production and marketing. In fact, many venture capitalists will not consider proposals if the company does not have a team with talent in each of these areas. In cases where a venture capitalist detects a lack of specific talent in a new venture, he will arrange to recruit additional management to supply the deficient skill. Almost every venturer spends considerable time in the investigative phase prior to investment, carefully checking the ability of the management team.

If the need for a balanced team is so obvious, then how can this become a problem?

The problems may develop in several different ways. A common pitfall, for instance, is the presumption that management experience gained in a large company environment will prove to be a guarantee of success in the small company. That is rarely the case, however; the lack of momentum that characterizes the large company is missing.

The ability of a large company to tolerate mistakes is also lacking in a small company; problems, therefore, surface more quickly, because it is tougher to start up a new operation or expand a young company than it is to maintain the onward thrust of a mature company. Many startup companies, financed by venture capitalists in the era of 1967 to 1969, had management teams that came from IBM and other large companies in the technical and consumer product areas. More than once the venture capitalists were disappointed when they found that these management spin-offs could not make the rapid shifts in approach required by the small company executive, but tended to concentrate on the form that proved to be successful in a large company.

The desire to maintain a completely balanced team throughout the history of the company—from its very inception—can be an expensive procedure. It is not always necessary to have a senior financial man in a company, particularly when the firm is in a development phase and its financial character is simple. Here, the company is only spending money on the development of a product and/or a particular market; much of the investment is in salaries of people creating the product and/or market, and simple monitoring will suffice to insure that there is appropriate adherence to the budget. The extra expense of senior talent in terms of salary and equity cannot be justified in the name of balanced total management.

Problems may also arise as the result of changes in the character of a business, due to changes in the basic business concept or in major unforeseen contingencies or critical changes in marketplace, requiring many corporate changes, including management. Sometimes if the original management is locked in because of their equity position, changes in top management cannot be made easily. Usually, it is up to the venture capitalist to initiate these changes because the founding entrepreneurs will seldom turn against one another and eliminate a comrade who cannot adjust to the new requirements. This can be fatal for investors who take a passive role and do not consider that making major management changes is an integral part of their function.

6. Management "Plays" to the Stock Market—or Gets Rich Too Soon

The most traumatic experience that a young company may undergo can arise from the process of "going public" and becoming a publicly-held company. Consider the case of a company that, after several years of operation, plans to make a public offering. The firm has established an acceptable track record and has proved to be a reasonably successful operation. What can occur is perhaps best described by relating what happened to one portfolio company of a Boston venture capital group:

The company had been in operation for some six years, and in the final three years had demonstrated a considerable expansion in volume and an even higher rate of growth in profits. The incumbent management was a smooth functioning team, and it was felt that they could handle a very substantial increase in growth. It was also believed that the market would support considerable growth if the company could raise sufficient additional capital to finance the larger work-in-process and accounts receivable that would result from greater volume. It appeared that the additional growth would provide more than average profit because the staff would not have to be expanded. Thus, it was decided to raise the additional capital by taking the company public through an S-1 registration.

The troubles began when the actual process of preparing for the underwriting began. Filing an S-1 is a complicated, time-consuming procedure, and the filing statements must be very carefully checked so that no statement can be misinterpreted in any way. The chief executive of the company felt that going public was such an important step in the company's history that he would not delegate any of the tasks involved, and he took on the preparation of the necessary documents as a full-time personal assignment. At the time, this seemed a good idea because he was totally familiar with all aspects of the company's operation. For the next six months, his principal—and almost sole occupation—consisted of negotiations with lawyers, accountants, the underwriter, consultants. Little time was left for running the fledgling business.

When the company finally went public, the president elected to field all of the queries that flowed in from new and prospective stockholders. Subsequently, he insisted on continuing to play the role of the financial public relations representative, and he handled all interviews with security analysts, members of the press, mutual fund managers, and anyone else who was interested in information about the company's affairs.

At the very time that the president was speaking most optimistically of the company's future, its business had, in fact, peaked. But in the interval, while he was enjoying his new role as the head of a company with a public image and neglecting his responsibilities to handle the company's affairs, its affairs began to turn downward. The president had switched roles from an initiator of action to an interpreter of actions that he believed would take place.

Continual contact with the financial media also tended to affect his judgment on company affairs. In discussions with other company management and at directors' meetings, he tended to take the posture that company plans must be drawn up in the light of their effect on the price of its stock and general acceptability from the security analysts' viewpoint.

Obviously, this was an exaggerated reaction—and the negative effects were comparatively severe. The company went into a decline from which it never quite recovered. In retrospect, the investors concluded that it had been a mistake to allow the president to become so heavily involved in the stock market image of the company, and they disposed of their investment to a mutual fund that was willing to buy their unregistered stock at a large discount.

A parallel problem occurs when an entrepreneur realizes his ambition to become rich through the sale of some of his holdings in the company. Many men, of course, are compulsive workers, and making a great deal of money will not cause them to change their compulsive work habits. But experience has shown that many entrepreneurs, once they attain financial independence, lose interest in the company that made them rich. They now look for fulfillment in fields outside the company; having won the money game, they become interested in winning the status game. One such example concerns the president of a software company that in a few years went from a few employees to thousands, and became the leader in the industry. In the process, the young president became wealthy by selling a portion of his holdings; he bought a $500 thousand home in an exclusive area in California, as well as some race horses and other typical trappings of the very rich. This man, aware of his own disinterest in the company, was one of the first to propose to the board of directors that he be replaced as chief operating executive.

It is difficult for an investor to conjure up a quick solution to a problem with such far-reaching consequences. The venture capitalist must adopt a watchful attitude when the original entrepreneur shows the first glimmer of ambition to become wealthy overnight. The obvious option is to try and force a management change if financial status affects the entrepreneur's dedication.

7. Business Concept is Premature or Ages Prematurely

The art of venture capital investing often involves putting money into advanced "state of the art" products or services—but not so advanced that they are premature. Many investors have nursed along a company which appeared to have a major innovative concept, but have become financially wearied and given up waiting for the company to begin growth. It can be a crushing experience to see another investor taking over at bargain prices—and suddenly behold the investment flash into overnight success. This has led some venture capital organizations to follow a policy that they will not invest in companies offering a product that is radically different from anything else in the market, especially when it is obvious that a long indoctrination period will be required to create acceptance. Even products that seem to fill an important need often have a long maturation phase. For example, the tape recorder, based on the German Magnetophon, was developed shortly after World War II, but did not see significant growth for years after its introduction. Fortunately, the venture capitalist who financed the first company in the United States had the stamina and foresight to continue to support the company until acceptance came from professional broadcasters and then the public. The concept of tape recording was so different from the previous methods of recording on shellac discs that it took years for professional broadcasters (who, incidentally, profited greatly from the advantages of tape) to adopt the system.

Sometimes, however, products that are radically different are accepted quickly and their growth is almost immediate. One famous example was Velcro, a new technique for clothing closure. It immediately and successfully challenged the zipper which had been virtually the only other clothing closure since the button. Its advantages were obvious and quickly understood, and so many new uses were established for Velcro that its use in clothing was rapidly augmented by other uses (such as fasteners for various tools and cameras in the Apollo Spacecraft). The Polaroid camera is another example of a product that grew as fast as production capability allowed.

Rapid product acceptance was also evidenced by the snowmobile. The first one—called the "Ski-Doo"—was introduced by Bombardier, a company in Canada. For years, the firm had a history of doubling sales and went from a few hundred units a year to over a hundred thousand in less than a decade. Although many competitors emerged to challenge its market position, Bombardier was still the leader in the field, with over 50 percent of the market in 1970.

Versions of the snowmobile had been available for many years, dating back to World War II, prior to its reintroduction by Bombardier—although they were not as technically successful as the "Ski-Doo." Regardless of the excellence of these early models, it is doubtful that they would have succeeded because the general public was not accustomed to spending significant sums of money on recreation vehicles. It was through their conditioning in later years, in purchasing outboard motors, sports cars and boats, that they became willing to spend several hundred dollars on adult playthings.

Perhaps one of the most notable examples of a product that was too advanced for its time is the laser. When the laser machine was invented and it became possible to manufacture it in quantity, everyone hailed the availability of a device that could provide highly coherent light with incredible intensity and spectral-purity; it captured the Nobel Prize for its inventors. Many companies were quickly established to produce lasers for what everyone expected would be an explosive market. In a remarkably short time, however, the price of the laser went from tens of thousands of dollars to about a hundred dollars; and the hundred-dollar laser was equal in performance to the original ones costing tens of thousands.

After being around for over ten years, the laser is just beginning to find significant applications outside of pure research. Of the many companies that were founded to produce lasers, only a few remained in business—only one or two significantly profitable. The laser has been dubbed as "a solution looking for a problem." Now, evidently, with the advent of solid state lasers, there will be a very rapid expansion of its application in many fields. But for early investors, it was a sad story of a concept far ahead of its time.

Another type of venture capital disappointment is the product line that seems to be a great success, then suddenly encounters a new technology or competitive product which soon renders it obsolete or at best insignificant. There is no way of being sure that some inventor, somewhere in a garage, is not working on a better device. This, after all, is the essence of the American free enterprise system.

One example of this problem was a cosmetic product container made of soft plastic, which enables the product to be sprayed out by squeezing the bottle-sides. A successful advertising campaign was constructed around the ease-of-application factor; but the dreams of profit dissolved abruptly in the ensuing flood of aerosols and roll-on applicators.

8. Weak Board of Directors

The ideal board of directors is one which the management can consult easily and continuously, a group that has a real feel for the problems of the company and can help it along through valuable personal experience. This implies a board of directors all of whom live or are headquartered within a few miles of the new company's headquarters, who know as much about the market as the company's competitors, and have a broad spectrum of experience and wisdom in production, engineering, marketing, finance and, ultimately, stockholder and investment banker relations.

The other side of the coin is a board of directors who live hundreds or thousands of miles away from company headquarters, who have only a superficial knowledge of the company's affairs, and whose collective knowledge generally is in unrelated fields. Obviously, such a board is likely to be weak and ineffective. Meetings tend to be informal sessions, with top management merely reciting its views and receiving superficial reactions to what could be unwise decisions.

9. Personality Conflicts Between Founders

One of the basic tenets of group psychology is that within any group of people, a pecking order will be established. This is particularly true of the kind of people sought for top management. If the pecking order has been based on competence that happens to correspond with the hierarchy within the table of organization, everything can run smoothly for long periods. If, for instance, the president is the strongest member of the team, there should be a minimum of personality conflicts. If, however, it develops that true competence lies with other members of the team, then it often becomes necessary to make a shift. Usually, this means that the president leaves the company and a reorientation between the top executives must take place. Some venture capitalists have expressed the opinion that within three years of the founding of companies, as many as half the number of original presidents may be gone.

Obviously, one of the advantages of venture capital investment in a firm that has been operating for several years, as opposed to a startup, is that the top management team has had time to work out its personality problems; those that would not fit have left, and the survivors have established a smooth working relationship.

10. Critical Change in Marketplace

It is axiomatic that the market for every product will see crucial changes coming from direct or new competitors. This is a classic example of totalitarian law. Because competition cannot be prohibited, it is compulsory that it will seriously affect business sooner or later. If the "later" is sufficiently late, the company may have had enough time to develop sufficient strength to cope with the changed conditions. If it happens sooner, it may cause the company to collapse.

Large companies as well as small ones are affected by this phenomenon. IBM, for example, was a latecomer to the computer field and did not make a major commitment to this effort until 1952—by which time, the UNIVAC Division of Remington Rand had established a five-year lead. When IBM, however, finally decided to act on the potential of the computer market, Remington Rand's domination ended.

In some cases, a significant price reduction by a major supplier has a serious effect on all competitors. For example, in 1970, IBM lowered the prices for peripherals for the 370-series computer system. Until that announcement, the number of manufacturers and leasing companies who were selling peripheral equipment was growing rapidly. Their position in the market was primarily dependent on the price gap between their equipment and IBM's inasmuch as they all offered equipment which was plug-compatible with the IBM 360 and IBM 370 system. When IBM announced its new prices, all of the peripheral manufacturers protested that its pricing was driving them out of business.

Sometimes a critical change in the marketplace takes place because of a change in government policy. For example, the decision of the federal government to cut back on the NASA space program plunged the technological centers in Boston and Palo Alto into a severe depression. Many venture capitalists who had invested in companies offering advanced technology found themselves with investments in companies that could not market their product.

How does the venture capital investor anticipate problems and adopt a defensive posture in time to avoid the catastrophe of critical market changes?

Generally, the answer lies in the definition of the marketplace itself. If the products of a company are destined for a narrow market, that market will be particularly sensitive to changes induced by other organizations, whether they are competitors or the government. A company that manufactures computer peripherals is obviously sensitive to the policies of IBM, in that the latter dominates the computer industry.

A company selling products to a diffuse market is protected from such an eventuality. Thus, it may be that even if a product is unique—and competitive—the venture capitalist must assume the existence of extra risk when the market is narrow.

WHAT TO DO AFTER THINGS GO WRONG

What should the venture capitalist do when things go wrong? Raymond Frankel, president of New York-based Technological Investors Management, Inc., speaking at a seminar on venture capital at the University of Toronto, had this to say on the problem:

> There are three basic attitudes a venture capitalist can take. The first might be typified by the statement, "We are the financiers and we play the percentages." Those venture capitalists who take this approach reason the situation somewhat as follows: the situation has gone wrong, and we made a bad investment either because our judgment was incorrect, certain circumstances changed, or unforeseen matters have occurred. At this point, we will try to sell out and take our loss. We will not get involved in operations because we do not have the personnel or the competence to run a portfolio business. Our job is to make investments and we will not be distracted from our primary job because we have made an error. Venture capital is a game of risk and percentages. Our efforts are best directed toward increasing the percentage of success. Submerging ourselves in a full-time effort to salvage one of our failures is not only wasteful effort, but a poor use of our time and talent, which should be utilized to maximize our overall investment results. The venture, therefore, must stand or fall on its own merits.

An opposite-end approach for the venture capitalist would be: if you can't do the job, we will. Some investors try to set up their deals so that if management fails, they can move in their own people and take control. This presupposes that the investors have the capability, the spare personnel and the desire to run the business, and that they consider the enterprise sufficiently important that they are willing to devote a major part of their resources to its success without detracting from their primary investment goal.

These examples represent the two extreme approaches; there is also a middle ground. In view of the high risk in venture capital investing (between five to eight deals out of ten getting into trouble), some venturers hold that there must be a tendency toward involvement in order to influence the percentages, by doctoring the sick with a potential recovery while ignoring the "living dead" which can drain time and cash resources. On the other hand, judgment is required to devote time only to situations that can be saved.

Anticipate the Problem

Despite the best of judgments and the most strenuous of efforts, the venture capitalist must expect that some ventures will get into trouble and some will fail. Problems are almost certain and it is, therefore, important to try to anticipate them, and gear up sensory apparatus for detecting them at the onset.

Act Early

It should be presumed that every minor symptom is a harbinger of big trouble—and remedial action should be planned early. Money will not be saved by delaying treatment. When trouble really sets in, the entrepreneur, in an effort to correct his own mistakes and turn the situation around, tends to become overwhelmed and his effectiveness diminishes. By acting early, the venture capitalist can assess whether the entrepreneur can function under stress conditions. If not, the venturer must be prepared to join the battle, bring in outside consultants, or bring in new people.

Be Willing to Invest More Funds

If the long-range possibilities that first attracted the venture capitalist are still there when the troubles begin, he must be prepared to back up his convictions with the courage of further investment. The general experience is that most ventures start out with too little money. When additional money is needed for an ailing enterprise, it is sometimes possible to obtain additional financing from other sources. The bargaining position of a troubled company, however, is obviously weak.

The new investors may demand more for their money than the original investor group. Sometimes the original investor has little choice and must choose between being decimated or wiped out completely. The alternative is for the original investor to invest more funds on condition, by mutual agreement, that a way can be worked out to redirect the company toward success.

In the history of venture capital, there are many examples of companies that achieved great success after passing through major crises. But in almost each of these situations the company was reorganized, new managers were brought in, new products emphasized or acquired, or various combinations of these and other traditional remedies utilized. But "what to do" was part of the refinancing plan, and it was worked out before major additional funds were introduced. In some cases, small interim funds were advanced during the reorganization.

An interesting example of the importance of having sufficient capital "stamina" to continue to finance an idea that is apparently basically sound was described recently by Ramond Frankel. He was a member of the J. H. Whitney Venture Capital Group when they invested in a group who planned to take over the publication of *Scientific American,* a magazine that had been in existence for fifty years and had fallen into serious trouble. The new group planned to completely overhaul the format and editorial approach. They believed that with the new editorial policy and a modern format, the fast-rising technological population of the United States would create a strong, new market. *Scientific American* has since become the leading magazine in its field; it enjoys world-wide stature and an elite audience that allows it to command high advertising rates. But back in the early days, the revamped magazine did not take off as expected and four successive injections of capital were necessary before it finally became profitable. It is not difficult to imagine how each successive investment in the magazine required a further escalation of courage on the part of the venture capital group. But their persistence and conviction in the formula ultimately paid off, and *Scientific American* became one of the great magazine successes of the 1950s.

Be Tough—but According to Plan

By the time our firm has invested in a situation, we have learned to like the top management team. Usually, they are intelligent people and, in time, the venture capitalist believes in them, admires them, and finally invests in them. When it has been decided that action is required, it is essential to act quickly and decisively! There is an old Dutch saying which, broadly translated, reads: "Gentle surgeons make terrible incisions."

Organizational Approach

In view of the great probability that each investment will have problems, the venture capital investment organization must be prepared to cope with them. This means that the venturer must be prepared to play an active role in his investments.

One organizational solution is that which was adopted by New Business Resources, a venture capital organization based in Dallas, Texas. They assign a venture manager to each investment; and he maintains close tabs on the organization, becoming much more involved than members of the portfolio company's board of directors. This familiarity and involvement in the organization means that when action is necessary, the venture capital executive can be assigned to the problem on a full-time basis; valuable time is saved in bypassing the learning process. The venture manager stays with the assignment from the time that New Business Resources starts to investigate the potential investment until the firm disposes of it.

Another organizational approach is that used by Data Science Ventures of Princeton, New Jersey. As part of their management teams, they have people with operational and organizational experience who can be resident consultants and can manage investments that get into difficulty. In one case, they made an investment in a company and later found it necessary to remove the president. One of DSV's management people who had operational experience assumed the presidency for a period of six months. (Obviously, this solution has definite limitations because the average organization cannot maintain a staff of people to leap into every investment problem.)

Some consideration must be given, however, to a predesigned disaster plan, in the event an investment gets into serious trouble.

KEY MONITORING INDICES

It is common practice to require each venture investment to furnish regular monthly reports on key aspects of the business; but the interpretation of these reports sometimes requires very subtle skills in order to recognize danger signals. Regular reports, even those which are extensively detailed and presumably touch on every sensitive business factor, will rarely offer the venture capitalist as much information as it will the local management who run the business on a day-to-day basis. Spotting the first signs of difficulty can be an exercise in financial detective work for the remote investor.

One approach in getting management to alert the venture capitalist to potential trouble is that adopted by the Heizer Corporation in Chicago. Their policy requires the comptroller or chief financial officer to circle every major figure with a green, yellow or red pencil to indicate "okay," "pending trouble" or "real trouble," respectively. A corollary approach would be to have the president prepare a summary comment on monthly reports indicating the probability of problems. When these techniques are used, it is an overt reflection on either the president or financial officer if they fail to indicate pending difficulties.

Often the first symptom of trouble in a company is a break or "wobble" in the flow of goods to the customer. Overruns in research, delays in final development, and delays in shipment of final products are early indicators. Research or set-up overruns are obvious problems, but they are not easy to spot because the trouble does not become apparent until the engineers are seen spending as much money to do the last 2 percent of the project as was required to do the first 50 percent.

There are other possible signs of developing trouble—for instance, continual delays in receipt of monthly reports. Usually when trouble begins to surface, the local managers are the first to know; and when they sense trouble, they somehow start taking longer to prepare the reports (which, naturally, do not reflect well on them). Thus, when reports start arriving late each month, it may be a symptom of trouble.

Another indicator is a "puff-up" of work-in-process. A sudden increase in this area may be a signal that something of a fundamental nature has gone wrong—with the product, the production process, the distribution system, market acceptance, or the market.

When the flow of goods begins to encounter significant delay, local management will often issue hold-orders to suppliers to stop the arrival of now-unwanted supplies. By issuing these orders quickly enough to restrict the flow, the "puff-up" in work-in-process may be deferred or suppressed. The only way to detect this problem, if it has occurred, is to learn the "stretch-out" instructions to suppliers. Aside from polling major suppliers, one sure way to ascertain such goings-on is to request that as a matter of policy and good relations with the venture capitalist, the company must inform him of any change in supplier relations, particularly if instructions are issued to stretch out shipments.

The "A," "B," & "C" Plans

The use of short- and long-range plans or budgets are a common management tool—designated, for our purposes, as the "A" plans. Emerson Electric in St. Louis, however, expects its divisional managers to prepare two additional—the "B" and "C"—plans. The "B" plan is based on a sales projection about 10 to 15 percent below the "A" plan; the "C" is a disaster plan based on a serious drop in the market. Obviously, this creates a significant amount of additional paperwork for the managers; but it forces them to consider what size organization they would have to pare down to in the event of a serious setback, and thus forestall the need for emergency sessions when trouble looms. The "B" or "C" plan can be activated immediately when a reduction in activity is certain.

LOOKING FOR TROUBLE

Field Visits. Venture capitalists tend to do their most intensive work during the investigation phase. They will carefully visit field and branch offices, key customers and sometimes even competitors; but once they are in the deal, for reasons that are difficult to understand, these visits seem to become rare. Admittedly, when a venture capitalist has a portfolio to look after, the pressures of time make such visits unfeasible; but the task can be delegated to junior people or external auditors.

Personal visits are not always necessary. The telephone can cover a lot of territory. Sometimes, by a long-distance or transoceanic call, it is easier to get the attention and time of important sources who might be reluctant to book a formal appointment.

Exit Interviews. The middle-management executive who is on his way out is more than willing to relate the shortcomings of a company; and there is no one he would rather give the inside information to than "that dumb investor who got suckered into putting his money into the company."

Cancelled Orders. Cancelled orders or returned goods are tremor-indicators. It is important to make sure that this information is relayed to the venture capitalist. One venture capital organization, for example, has placed the obligation on the manager of administration to inform them of significant cancelled orders.

One-More-Person. When troubles start to surface and the founding management begins to realize that running a successful business is tough, a typical initial reaction of management is to hire a specialist to help doctor the problem area. When a company is growing or getting ready to grow, it is logical and necessary to make additions to the production or sales staff or to certain supporting administrative areas. But when the company is not growing and the president suddenly wants to hire a specialist or consultant, the venture capitalist should be suspicious. Management may be cuing him (unwittingly) to trouble of a fundamental nature, particularly if the original plans did not call for this staff member.

STRUCTURING THE DEAL

The general partner of one of the most successful and famous venture capital partnerships in the United States holds that he makes only equity investments. The rationale here is that the debt will not be repaid unless the enterprise succeeds, and, if it succeeds, an equity position will produce as good or better capital gain. Debt is "near equity"—even if it is termed "debt"—and has all of the jeopardies of equity.

Nonetheless, many venture capital organizations will only make debt investments with equity and warrant, or option bonuses. There are two major reasons for this: first, capital can be repaid without paying income taxes; second, and more important, it is possible to impose a series of conditions in the debt contract that give the investor additional power, perhaps even control in the event these conditions are not met. In some cases, failure to meet the conditions means that the venture capitalist can automatically take complete control of the board or take over the stock of the founding entrepreneurs which has been used to collateralize the debt.

Typical of some conditions that may be embodied in a debt contract are—

- a minimum working capital level
- a minimum "acid-test" ratio
- a minimum cash level
- completion of certain tasks or milestones by a certain date . . . (when setting up such a condition, it is necessary to specify how the acceptability of the task will be measured)
- receipt of a minimum amount of orders
- receipt of a government license or franchise

Any parameter that is peculiar to the business can be introduced as a condition. Failure to meet any one of these conditions, or failure to meet principal and interest payments, can be established as a cause for default. The debt contract also should contain a list of any additional powers which the venture capital organization can assume. These powers may include everything from the right to take complete and total control of the company to liquidation of the company under any terms that are satisfactory to the venture capitalist. Here again, the default program can be worked out to suit the particular investment and the policies of the venture organization. An almost infinite number of options is possible.

Some venture capital organizations, for example, do not have management resources to directly assist a company in difficulties. Therefore, they do not seek to have default clauses giving them managerial power. Rather, they are interested in clauses that enable them to dispose of the company on either an outright sale or "merge-out," with complete power to negotiate the disposition contract. For those venture capital organizations that are interested in managing the troubled organization, the default clauses describe what managerial powers can be assumed immediately and under what terms. The structure and contractual terms of debt instruments are a key element in giving venture capitalists the power to act when things go wrong, and are frequently used when the investor group does not have voting control of the company.

Also one of the key elements in the venture business is "what to do when things go right." These positive elements in improving the growth and strength of a small company contribute greatly to the success of both the company and the venture capitalist. Many successful venturers are inclined to spend more time with their stronger companies that are moving forward than with turn-around attempts on problem investments.

13
The First SBIC

Alan K. Ruvelson

While in the diamond importing business with my father, I learned some things from him which apply to the field of venture capital. One of his premises, for example, was that there was not much money to be made on perfect diamonds. His rationale was that everybody seemed to know all about perfect diamonds, but not too many people knew what could be done with those that were imperfect.

In a sense we were also bankers (although we did not recognize it at that time); we extended large and liberal credit, even though we did not have equity claims.

ENTICING LEGISLATION: THE SMALL BUSINESS INVESTMENT ACT

Early in 1958, we heard about the Small Business Investment Act, which had been passed in late August of the previous year. This Act was partially based on a study by the Federal Reserve Board, which had evaluated the needs of growing industry and concluded that there was a notable lack of venture capital as contrasted with other types of available financing.

Mr. Ruvelson is president of First Midwest Corporation, in Minneapolis, Minnesota, and First Midwest Capital Corp., the first SBIC subsidiary.

FORMING AN SBIC

To make a sound evaluation of the feasibility of forming an SBIC (Small Business Investment Company), we asked our accountant and our attorney whether or not they would put their own money into such an operation. They said they would, so we felt we must be on the right track.

Soon after, we organized a small group consisting of thirty-two individuals and the Northwestern National Bank of Minneapolis. Together we invested $315 thousand and received our license in March 1959—the first SBIC in the country. At the same time, Citizens & Southern Capital, of Atlanta, Georgia, joined us as the first licensees in this new financial community.

Our SBIC is licensed by and subject to regulation by the SBA (Small Business Administration). Because we are a publicly-held company, we also have the SEC looking over our shoulders.

FINANCING FOR THE '70's

In 1969, we reorganized into a holding company, First Midwest Corporation. The SBIC and venture capital activities are conducted by our wholly-owned subsidiary, First Midwest Capital Corporation. While the parent company concentrates primarily on real estate development, the SBIC subsidiary is oriented to achieving capital gains.

SBIC's are unique in the venture capital field. The SBA has laid out certain dicta. SBIC's, individually or as a group, cannot own a majority of the voting stock except to conduct a rescue operation; and then we must negotiate with the SBA on an approved plan of divestiture. SBIC's are carefully regulated so that they cannot be self-serving, or provide sons-in-law with jobs, or directly or indirectly acquire control of the business that is being financed. We function strictly as professional, minority investors to privately-owned companies. In return, the SBA provides leverage to SBIC's, which by law can reach a multiple of three times their net worth. However, budgetary shortages have limited such borrowings in recent years.

GENERALISTS

First Midwest Capital has twelve outside directors on its thirteen-man board. They are "generalists" who are not oriented to any particular high-technology field. Our working staff consists of three full-time men, two of whom are certified public accountants who were previously with national accounting firms.

As far as investments are concerned, all SBIC's like to invest in good people. We are primarily in the people business, but are also interested in proprietary products or services, and try to relate our general experience to the prospective situation. We can offer extensive assistance to our potential portfolio client if we understand his business. We are basically grass-roots investment bankers.

At First Midwest Capital, we do not consciously try to avoid any kind of situation, although we shy away from high-technology investments. Even though we are not directed by policy toward startup situations, one of our most recent portfolio companies fell into this category.

We want to be sure that management is committed both in effort and resources. We do not expect young men in new business to be able to match our dollars and we put up more dollars for less equity than management. However, we expect management to put its available funds on the line and continue alongside us if problems arise.

We shy away from people who, when presenting the deal, rely heavily on far-out protection situations, where we are expected to put up most of the money for only a small percentage of the equity. Promoters of such deals are unrealistic. They may be able to get to the public marketplace, but we look at inflated market quotations for small over-the-counter companies with a jaundiced eye.

CLIENT ASSISTANCE, EXPERTISE

Initially, we thought it would be a good idea if our portfolio companies and other concerns were to pay a nominal retainer to employ our consulting services. After several years, we revised our thinking and concluded that management consulting was an entirely different field; it did not mix well with high-risk investing. We decided, therefore, not to continue in a retainer capacity with client firms, but to concentrate our efforts on portfolio firms and charge fees only for projects where we are called upon to perform a specific function.

Our reasoning is simple: our prime opportunity was capital gains. We can justify anything that will enhance these gains or minimize our downside loss exposure. We charge on a loss basis because we are not in the business to make a profit from consulting, but only to assist our portfolio companies. We have no available time for firms in which we have no investment.

When founding First Midwest, we requested representation on the boards of all portfolio firms. In recent years we have completely reversed that position. We will accept a board position only if we believe we can play a constructive role. We have discovered it is a great luxury to be a "minority of one." We would, however, ask to attend all board meetings and receive minutes.

Overall, we have learned to follow the rule of the successful equestrian: use a firm but light hand on the reins, develop confidence and rapport, and in this way we will receive more cooperation and the best performance.

In 1968, we suggested to four portfolio clients that they might raise funds in the public market through the "hot" new issue market. They agreed and asked us to assist them in making the necessary arrangements, including the discussion of terms with underwriters. The deals we arranged, according to the companies, were considerably better than they would have been able to negotiate. We have also negotiated several loans for portfolio firms from senior lenders on terms which have been advantageous to them.

We also are ready, willing and able to assist in negotiating loans with commercial banks. (Editors Note: see subsequent comments by Dale S. Hanson.) To maintain maximum independence and eliminate the possibility of conflict of interest, we do not have an officer of any bank on our board of directors.

GENERATING INVESTMENTS: EXPOSURE AND REPUTATION

Exposure and reputation have proven to be the best means of generating investment opportunities. We have been in business for over a decade and are well-known in the field. Because of our efforts and those of other leading SBIC's, the term "SBIC" means good business in our area. The major term lenders and banks respect us. We also have worked closely with many attorneys and CPA's in our area, but probably the best source of referrals is the management of satisfied portfolio companies. Corporate finance departments of brokerage firms can be helpful guides, too.

Some of our referrals come from government agencies; we, in

turn, refer many companies to these agencies because companies that do not qualify for equity money may be helped by loans from the various federal agencies, including the SBA. We like to help small firms locate capital because we might develop an equity financing relationship with them later.

INVESTING CRITERIA

We are subject to criteria imposed by law and government agency regulations. The SBA tells us we cannot invest in any company with assets over $5 million, net worth over $2½ million and/or average after-tax profits for two years in excess of $250 thousand. Occasionally, SBA will modify these criteria, and we are permitted to utilize alternative standards relating to the number of employees.

As for our investment size preferences, we will invest as little as $50 thousand, but prefer to invest not less than $100 thousand. Our upper limits are about $500 thousand, although theoretically we have been able to invest as much as $800 thousand in a single company. We have, however, developed larger investments, including a $1,800,000 deal with an investor group consisting of two insurance companies and several SBIC's. We have arranged, for example, participations with banks, insurance companies, pension funds and other venture capital investors.

There are relatively few industries that SBIC's are prohibited from backing, but among those prohibited are finance, agriculture, passive leasing and gambling. The rules do not keep us out of most fields that have explosive growth or major expansion opportunities which can justify outside equity investment, though we intentionally avoid the "papa-and-mama-type" business.

A critical factor in any investment is determining how to get out of it profitably. There is nothing less desirable than being locked into a perpetual minority situation in which investment values cannot be realized or translated.

Some Words of Advice

In deciding whether or not to back a man and his company, we ask the following key questions:

- Is the management directional?
- Is it believable?
- Does management have depth?

One-man businesses are too dangerous, although the principal can be protected with key-man insurance.

We are concerned about how our funds are used. We do not want our money used to bail out someone else. Rather, the funds must be used sensibly to increase working capital, broaden product lines, expand markets, begin new enterprises, increase research and development, undertake plant modernization or site acquisition, purchase new equipment and facilities, or make acquisitions.

The only way we can be successful in this difficult and complex business is to have an opportunity to gain equity. In other words, we require the right to buy a minority position at a predetermined price, inasmuch as we invest disproportionately large amounts and subordinate our investment to bank and financial institution loans. We must be able to buy our equity positions at a reasonable price.

Our simple interest coupon is usually 1-1½ percent over the prime rate, and we cannot profit by requiring compensating balances. We prefer to purchase a debenture with warrants rather than a convertible debenture.

PROFITABILITY: A LESSON

At one time, our firm had rejected a deal because the prospective company did not want to part with sufficient equity. The investment banker who brought the deal to us, however, was persistent and asked that we have lunch with the principal. Having seen the numbers, we did not believe there was too much downside risk in the investment. At the meeting, we inquired about the entrepreneur's education. He replied that he had worked and supported himself through engineering school. How much salary was he drawing from the business? . . . It was a modest amount of money. How did he rationalize his low salary? . . . He wanted to make his money on the long-range growth of the company. We liked his attitude, despite the fact that his company had a net worth of only $400 thousand, and they were seeking $300 thousand in capital. We gave them the money for 5 percent of the equity.

The investment could have been one of our notable mistakes, but everything turned out all right. We were able to have a distribution of the company's stock, which was worth $1 million—and it was tax-free. First Midwest also made an additional $500 thousand profit on this maneuver.

Doing one's homework is the key to success in the venture capital business . . . although, frequently, it is better to be lucky than to be smart.

PROCEDURES

We have a number of affirmative covenants in the content of our debentures, but they are common as far as the venture investors are concerned. Generally, the instrumentation is as good or as bad as the people with whom one is doing business. A debenture may make formidable reading, but it is essentially nothing more than a promissory note with deferred payment dates.

Warrants are pieces of paper indicating the price and terms under which we can acquire equity. The stock we purchase is the same stock that is bought and sold in the marketplace, except that in our case it is generally restricted as to our rights to sell on the market without a long list of required procedures.

PRESENT PORTFOLIO

A brief run-through of our present portfolio will offer some insight into the activities of our firm. The various types of businesses include: manufacturers of—graphic arts and electronic equipment; janitorial and maintenance supplies; plastic products; boats . . . a chain of retail auto supply stores . . . a premium service company . . . a bakery and pastry dough company.

So far as our investment record is concerned, we have had a mixture of successes and failures. Approximately five out of our twenty-seven investments were losers in one form or another. We do not like to quote numbers, but our average annual return on capital, including distributions, unrealized and realized profits and losses, had been substantial. (It has diminished recently because of a decline in the market value of our publicly-held portfolio companies.)

We think that the future for venture capital is good; but there is a "time to reap and a time to sow." The year 1968 was a time to reap in terms of realizing gains and raising money. The period 1969-1970 was a good time to sow, to get into deals on an attractive basis.

Our success in the SBIC industry is not unique; many others have done as well. We are a little older, and probably have had an opportunity to learn from our mistakes over the years. There are now a dozen publicly-held SBIC's with creditable track records. In addition to paying dividends to their stockholders, they have done an excellent job in supporting small business—the backbone of the American economy.

14

How Banks And SBIC'S Work Together

Dale S. Hanson

The best way to describe how banks work with SBIC's is to review briefly four actual situations. These examples will also illustrate the advantages to the bank as well as to the mutual customer in working with an SBIC.

WORKING WITH SBIC's: PRIME EXAMPLES

Crown Auto Stores

Crown Auto Stores is a retailer of automotive parts, supplies and accessories. The company operates primarily through its own independent stores, but also operates departments in space leased from discount department stores. The company established itself as a partnership in 1961, operating profitably from its inception.

Due to rapid expansion, by 1965 the company seemed to reach a plateau. It was limited in not having enough capital to expand as rapidly as it had expanded earlier. In addition to needing capital funds at that time, it would also need bank funds if it were to continue to grow at a healthy pace. On December 31,

Mr. Hanson is vice-president of the First National Bank of Saint Paul, Minnesota, and head of a commercial lending division.

1965, Crown had a net worth of $198 thousand. The firm had total liabilities of $537 thousand, or debt of at least three times its capital, so that it was difficult for a bank to do more than simply provide revolving credit secured by accounts receivable and inventory. This kind of financial help would not provide the needed expansion money.

In early 1966, First Midwest Capital purchased Crown's $81,430 in subordinated notes and extended an unsecured term loan for an additional $68,570.

With this money, Crown was able to expand, and it began to open new stores. Because this was capital money, it broadened the company's base, thus enabling the bank to provide an increased revolving credit line along with the expansion of the Crown Stores. By the end of 1966, the company's financial picture was vastly improved. Its total liabilities were less than two times its capital—and all this had occurred in less than one year.

The capital quickly turned into sales. In 1966, Crown's sales increased 30 percent—up to $2,300,000—while earnings doubled to nearly $75 thousand. As the company continued its expansion, the bank increased its credit facilities so that by late 1967 the firm's credit line was up to $350 thousand secured by accounts receivable and inventory.

In early 1966, due to its good track record, Crown was able to receive a $275 thousand unsecured loan from the Prudential Insurance Company. A solid track record is required before an insurance company will make this kind of commitment. With the insurance company's commitment and Crown's excellent progress, we were able to change our line of credit from a secured accounts receivable inventory line to a straight unsecured seasonal line of credit for $250 thousand.

The next major advance in the company's financial structure came in May 1968 when Crown went public and raised approximately $300 thousand. During the next two years, even though Crown continued to have a $250 thousand unsecured bank line, they used it for only sixty days to build up inventory for a seasonal item. Further, they maintained excellent balances with the bank.

In retrospect, it was the money that First Midwest had invested that helped Crown get over this major expansion plateau. First Midwest Capital supported the Crown financial statements so that the bank could take a more aggressive position.

The company's management was young, and the supplemental management created a favorably balanced management picture.

This was really a success story.

Colight, Inc.

First Midwest had already invested in Crown Auto before our bank was introduced to the company. Colight, Inc. was a case in reverse. The company, established in 1951, was family-owned. In 1964, we became the company's bank and set up a $100 thousand line of credit. It was secured by accounts receivable and inventory, and guaranteed by the principals. At that time, the company had a net worth of $65 thousand, with total liabilities of $151 thousand. Sales were less than $500 thousand . . . and the company was not making money.

The principals were young, but we felt that they were capable of building a good business. The firm was engaged in extensive research and development which proved successful, and the future prospects for Colight looked attractive.

The company stabilized, but the pattern remained the same. Sales did not increase rapidly and the firm did not make much money. In mid-1965 the company had the opportunity to purchase the Miller-Trojan Division of the Clary Corporation. Colight did not have the necessary capital, and the financing of this acquisition could not be handled through our bank. Moreover, Colight was not ready to go to the public with a stock issue.

The company was introduced to First Midwest, and the firm subsequently purchased a $210 thousand subordinated note. There were warrants attached, but this capital provided the acquisition money that Colight needed to purchase the Miller-Trojan Division. Coupled with some key success in R&D, this was a turning-point in the company's history.

With the injection of the First Midwest money, the bank continued it's revolving line of $125 thousand, still secured by accounts receivable and inventory, though we were able to release the individual guarantees. The balance sheet of the company was considerably strengthened and by the end of 1965, Colight had total liabilities of $341 thousand and a capital base of $344 thousand. However, they continued to lose a little money.

It was not until 1967 that both acquisitions and the R&D efforts began to pay off. In 1967, 1968, and 1969 Colight began to show strong earnings. Also, the company raised $300 thousand through a public offering in 1969, paying off all loans to the bank. We continued to offer the company an annual line of credit because theirs was such an excellent success story.

Midtown Park, Inc.

Midtown Park, Inc., was not a success story—or at least not by 1970. This example illustrates how an SBIC can increase capital investment when a portfolio company runs into unforeseen difficulties. To bankers, it is a situation that occurs periodically. It is helpful to the banker to have a partner ready with additional capital if needed.

In 1964, First Midwest, three other SBIC's and several individual investors provided the capital for Midtown Park, Inc., to own and operate a 588-car parking facility with 18,000 square feet of retail rental space in downtown Minneapolis. The location of the facility was excellent. It was near the center of the city and a major urban renewal project. In addition to 25 percent equity, First Midwest purchased Midtown's subordinated note for $220 thousand. Initially the project was to cost $1,800,000, including $400 thousand in land. Midtown had a capital base of $800 thousand, which included $550 thousand in subordinated notes. Another Minneapolis bank committed first mortgage money totaling $1,200,000 with an insurance company take-out.

As the facility neared completion, several major difficulties—such as construction overruns and a long delay caused by a steel strike—forced the total cost to approach $2.3 million, $500 thousand over the original projection.

In March 1967, we were introduced to Midtown and they requested a $400 thousand term loan to fill the gap between the initial projection and current cost—a very "sporty" loan. Projections showed that our loan could be properly serviced along with the first mortgage loan.

The facility was completed in the fall of 1967, but two serious problems arose: the president of the firm had a heart attack; and traffic on the two main streets leading to the ramp was partially blocked for street repairs for six months.

In late 1968, just as things started to look up, the company lost its major retail space tenant, a large restaurant leasing 16,500 square feet of space. By early 1969, it was quite obvious that Midtown needed additional capital.

The firm had not defaulted on either the first mortgage or the bank's term loan; but without immediate capital it soon would default. First Midwest came to us and said that all Midtown stockholders had approved a plan to add another $100 thousand within a month. Based on a verbal commitment from the president of First Midwest, we added another $100 thousand to cover property taxes and other pressing financial needs.

By June 1969, the additional $100 thousand was committed and the short-term notes for property taxes and other debts paid. By 1970, Midtown was in a better position, but still not out of the woods. We are confident that if the firm gets to a point where it needs additional capital, First Midwest and its partners are in a position to protect the earlier investment and add whatever capital may be needed.

Interplastic Corporation

Interplastic Corporation was publicly-held when the bank came upon the scene.

Interplastic produces polyester resins and gel coats, and manufactures a variety of polyethylene containers. The firm was formed in 1962 by the merging of three small companies, each of which was losing money.

The company progressed steadily until 1965, when it was able to gain an SBA loan to purchase needed equipment. By 1967, when we became interested, sales were $1,900,000 with net earnings of $100 thousand. Total liabilities were $541 thousand and the company had a net worth of $492 thousand. We offered them a $250 thousand loan secured by Interplastic's accounts receivable and inventory.

We continued to follow the company, and in 1968 offered them a $600 thousand credit line secured by accounts receivable and inventory. Because of the company's rapid growth and the need for additional equipment, we were attempting to finance capital expenditures with a short-term vehicle. This was an improper approach, but the company was pressed for capital.

Interplastic was faced with several choices. It could seek long-term insurance company money, an additional sale of stock to the public, or a venture capital or SBIC investment.

The problem was solved when First Midwest purchased a $500 thousand subordinated note with warrants from Interplastic. This provided the funds for the needed capital expansion and the required purchases. It strengthened the company's balance sheet so that the bank was able to provide a $250 thousand unsecured term loan and a $300 thousand unsecured seasonal line.

KEY ADVANTAGES IN WORKING WITH SBIC's

To summarize the advantages to a bank and its customers in working with an SBIC, two other important points should be noted:

1. *Money.* It is generally equity-type money, as opposed to a banker's or an insurance company's capital.
2. *"Supplemental managment."* This is the manner in which SBIC's pitch in and help with professional management counsel. In addition, when needed, SBIC's can also help recruit the best possible personnel to eliminate weak spots or bolster management.

15

SBIC Laws And Regulations

Charles M. Noone

Under the regulations that govern investment companies, the Federal Investment Company Act of 1940, a firm is an "investment company" and subject to registration if:

- at least 60 percent of its assets are devoted to investment;
- it is currently in the process of a public offering of stock;
- it is publicly-owned;
- it has more than 100 stockholders.

Generally, most venture capital firms are not subject to the 1940 Act. American Research and Development, the prototype of venture capital firms, is publicly-held and subject to the 1940 legislation. The venture capital firms with which we have worked (other than SBIC's), however, are largely partnerships.

From an overall industry view, the forms of venture capital organization appear to be as varied and infinite as their numbers. In fact, within many venture capital firms each deal may create

Mr. Noone is a partner in the law firm of McCarty & Noone, in Washington, D.C.; he is also general counsel for the National Association of Small Business Investment Companies (NASBIC), and General Chairman, Committee on Banking Institutions & Regulated Investment Companies, Taxation Section, of the American Bar Association.

different participation groups. There is no standard pattern for a venture capital organization. Those companies subject to the Investment Company Act of 1940, however, must operate under stringent federal requirements.

Over 900 venture capital companies across the country have been licensed as SBIC's since the inception of the program in 1958. Due to mergers, liquidations and various other business factors, there are currently under 400 SBIC's. Of these, 250 to 275 are viable SBIC's, including 26 that are publicly-traded and registered under the 1940 Act. In addition, there are about 30 to 40 SBIC's registered under the 1940 Act primarily for the purpose of qualifying to be taxed as regulated investment companies under Section 851 of the Internal Revenue Code. This section qualifies mutual funds to pass their earnings to their shareholders without the imposition of the corporate income tax.

A few other SBIC's have accidentally fallen under the 1940 Act. A group of Chinese businessmen organized a small SBIC in Washington with a minimal capitalization of $150 thousand. As is their custom, these people brought in their relatives and friends for stock purchases ranging from $1 thousand to $2 thousand. Before they realized the extent of the complication, the company had more than 100 shareholders and they were obliged to register under the Act. The company has since left the program.

For venture capital companies—and particularly for SBIC's—the 1940 Act presents numerous problems. There were several traps lying unnoticed for the unwary until our discovery of them. There are still some unexplored legal areas that affect the operations of both SBIC and venture capital companies.

CLEARING THE LEGAL PATH

One of the earliest problems that developed related to Section 30-F. The section stipulates that closed-end investment companies are subject to Section 16 of the Securities Exchange Act of 1934, the so-called "insider trading" provision of the 1934 Act.

One of the first of the publicly-owned companies was Growth Capital, Inc., of Cleveland, Ohio. The firm had a public offering in 1960 and raised approximately $10 million. A partner in the investment banking firm that underwrote the offering of Growth Capital, Inc. had been elected to the firm's board of directors. Meanwhile, his firm continued to make a market in the shares of Growth Capital.

A stockholder of Growth Capital brought suit against the company pursuant to Section 30-F and, after much litigation, the board member and his partner in the investment banking firm were compelled to pay Growth Capital a sum of several thousand dollars, which was theoretically realized through the banking firm's buying and selling Growth Capital stock within a six-month period. This situation was partially alleviated by the 1966 Securities Acts Amendments; the problem remains, however, for publicly-owned and registered SBIC's.

Another complication which develops for companies registered under the 1940 Act is Section 47 (b). Many people believe this Section to be a time bomb—with a short fuse. Section 47 (b) provides, in essence, that any contract entered into by a registered company in violation of any provision of the Act, or any rule or order issued by the Commission, is void. This is strong language and has been a fearsome element in the Act for venture capital, particularly for SBIC's.

As a result of these problems, the SBIC industry sought several times to get specific relief from Congress, including exemptions from the 1940 Act. The industry asserted that the SBA, which licenses and regulates these companies, should regulate them for all purposes. Congress was sympathetic to the idea, but each time the subject arose, a spokesman for the Commission maintained that legislation was not necessary, that the Commission had adequate authority under Section 6-C of the Investment Company Act to grant any requested exemptions either to individual companies or to the industry as a whole.

Some exemptions have been granted. For example, in the area of affiliated transactions covered under Section 17 of the 1940 Act, the Commission promulgated a rule—17a-6—which to an extent alleviates many problems that SBIC's encountered in dealing with their portfolio companies.

Problems remained with the basic difficulties of dual regulation, causing companies to consider both SBA regulations and SEC regulations. As a result, an application was filed in March 1968 with the Commission requesting that it defer to SBA regulation on those provisions of the 1940 Act applicable to SBIC's. In December 1969, the Hearing Examiner handed down an initial decision granting two of the principal requests: exemption from Section 17, and permission to issue stock options.

This decision was, at this writing, under review. The government's Division of Corporate Regulation had filed its opposition to the initial decision, and the industry's trade association—the National Association of Small Business Investment Companies (NASBIC)—had filed its answer.

The Investment Company Act of 1940 is something to reckon with when considering a public offering to raise capital.

SBIC's VS. OTHER VENTURE CAPITAL FIRMS

Organizational and Operating Differences

SBIC's are licensed and regulated by SBA. After more than a decade of revisions, the regulations are now in operable condition. To receive an SBIC license, a detailed plan of proposed operation and organization must first be submitted to SBA. This must include evidence that the applicant has complied with applicable securities laws. This evidence normally takes the form of a no-action letter from the SEC to the applicant based on representations from the firm as to how the company will be organized and how the initial capital will be raised. A person can buy a license of an SBIC situated in one state and transfer it to another. SBA also reserves the right to approve transfer of the ownership of 10 percent or more of the stock of all SBIC's.

After receiving a license, the SBIC is subject to SBA regulations. Foremost, an SBIC can invest only in small businesses, firms which have assets not exceeding $5 million, net worth not exceeding $2½ million, and average net income after tax for two years not exceeding $250 thousand.

There are also alternative size regulations. If a prospective company does not fit the standard small business definition, but meets SBA size qualifications for an SBA loan, the investment could be acceptable. SBA size standards are related either to the number of employees of the company (particularly in the manufacturing industries) or to annual gross income of the company in the service industries.

Another limitation is that financing must cover for a minimal period of five years. On loans, amortization cannot exceed an average rate of 20 percent per annum over the first five years except for one approved exception. Also, an SBIC cannot put more than 20 percent of its private, paid-in capital in surplus in any one transaction.

There are stringent regulations guarding against an SBIC's acquiring control of a portfolio company. Unless unusual circumstances arise, an SBIC cannot legally take more than 50 percent of the stock of a portfolio company. If it does, then the SBIC must enter into an agreement to divest of the excess stock within a period of seven years, and that agreement must be legally enforceable by the portfolio company.

These and other rules are the result of the Congressional attitudes and concern that that SBIC program is principally designed to augment and strengthen independent small business, the heart of the free enterprise system.

THE NON-SBIC VENTURE CAPITAL ORGANIZATIONS

The Other Side of the Coin

Non-SBIC venture capital companies carefully consider the stringent regulation by SBA before determining whether or not to become an SBIC. Some venture capitalists who were in business before the program was launched elected to remain outside the SBIC industry to avoid the limitations and regulations placed on such firms.

LIVING WITH REGULATIONS FOR FUND SOURCES

What brings people into the SBIC program?

Principally, it is the availability—and the continual promise—of government funds. At the inception of the program in 1958, Congress provided that a company could be licensed with a minimum of $150 thousand paid-in private capital. Such a company could acquire from SBA up to $150 thousand in the form of a subordinated debenture having a term of twenty years, with principal payment due only in the last ten years. In addition, the SBIC could borrow up to 50 percent of its statutory capital from SBA, its capital consisting of the private paid-in capital and the SBA's subordinated debenture funds.

In 1963, Congress put a limitation on these funds: not more than $4 million could be lent to any one company. The subordinated maximum amount also was increased to $700 thousand. Thus, until 1967, a company with $800 million of private capital could qualify for a maximum of $4.7 million of SBA money.

THE AMENDMENTS OF 1967

In 1967, some radical changes were made in the statute, particularly in the manner of funding. In place of the two types of financing instruments previously used by SBA, a single subordinated debenture with a term of up to fifteen years was substituted.

Under the 1967 amendments, an SBIC can qualify for two dollars of government funds for every dollar of private capital up to a maximum of $7.5 million. This means that with net worth of $3.75 million, an SBIC could theoretically borrow $7.5 million in government funds. Furthermore, a new concept was adopted: a third dollar of loan funds from SBA was to be provided for companies with private capital in excess of $1 million and with at least 65 percent of their investable funds in venture capital investments. For each dollar of net worth in excess of one million dollars, the "venture capital" SBIC qualifies for government loans of three dollars up to an aggregate maximum of $10 million. Whereas an $8 million company previously could borrow up to $4.7 million, under the present law, an SBIC could borrow $10 million. The maximum leverage would be possible, for example, for SBIC's with net worth of $3.667 million as follows: $2 for $1 on $1,000,000 = $2,000,000; plus $3 for $1 on $2.667 million equals $8 million—or a total borrowing power of $10 million.

AVAILABILITY OF GOVERNMENT FUNDS

A Dangling Federal Apple

Major problems arose when the money supply was turned off in Washington. Effective July 1, 1968, budget cuts resulted in cutting off all new loans to SBIC's. But the management of SBA and the SBIC industry have never stopped trying, and their efforts continue to pay off. Prior to this writing, a major funding came in January 1970, when SBA received authorization to disburse $70 million to SBIC's through the last half of the fiscal year, June 1970. In 1971, a bond issue brought an additional $55 million into the SBIC program.

Non-SBIC venture capital firms seldom use borrowed funds. Normally, the bulk of their capital is contributed. Some of these firms, however, are concerned about leverage, inasmuch as on the downside, heavy debt structure can ruin a company. Furthermore, there are no sources of long-term loans available to most venture capital firms.

AN APPEALING SBIC TAX CONSIDERATION

Tax considerations also distinguish SBIC's from other venture capital companies. The Technical Amendments Act of 1958, amending the Internal Revenue Code of 1954, added new provisions to the Code. Three of them have particular significance for this discussion:

1. Section 243 (b) gives an SBIC a 100 percent deduction for dividends received from portfolio companies.
2. Section 1242 grants a stockholder in an SBIC an unlimited ordinary loss deduction where he incurs a loss on the sale or exchange of his stock in an SBIC.
3. Section 1243 allows the SBIC an unlimited ordinary loss deduction where it incurs a loss on a convertible debenture of a portfolio company or on stock acquired through exercise of the conversion privilege.

   (This should not be confused with Section 1244 relating to so-called "small business stock." Under Section 1244, certain small corporations with not more than $500 thousand paid-in capital, can create a special class of stock—"small business stock"—not exceeding $500 thousand in value. If the initial holders incur a loss on the sale or exchange of that stock, they will be entitled to an ordinary loss deduction. However, it is limited to $25 thousand per annum on an individual return and $50 thousand on a joint return, and the loss deduction is available only to the original holder of the stock, not the transferees.)

Even before the program got off the ground, it was recognized that, on the whole, small business investment companies were going to be small, closely-held companies, and potentially subject to the personal holding company surtax.

Senator Sparkman in the Senate and Congressman Patman in the House introduced legislation to except SBIC's from the definition of a personal holding company. The legislation became law in September 1959. The result was that SBIC's were added to the list of companies or taxpayers exempted from personal holding company penalties.

The second sentence of the new law stated that this exemption would not apply where a shareholder in the SBIC owns, directly or indirectly, an equity or proprietary interest of 5 percent or more in a small business concern receiving financing from the SBIC. This is regarded merely as a tough, self-dealing rule, and it was not until some years later that a spokesman from the Internal Revenue Service clarified the situation. He stated that the attribution rules under the Code apply to the SBIC as well as to its shareholders with this result: if a closely-held SBIC owned equally by two individuals acquires a 10 percent stock interest in a small business concern, although there is no other connection between the stockholder of the SBIC and that small business concern, by application of the attribution rules the SBIC's 10 percent stock ownership is attributed to its shareholders. The result is that each is regarded as owning 5 percent of the portfolio company—and thus the personal holding company exemption is lost.

After working many years to have the rule clarified, it now appears as though the attribution rule will not be applied; thus SBIC's will be able to qualify effectively for the exemption.

IRS REGULATIONS

Some Unique Advantages

By regulation, the Internal Revenue Service has given SBIC's additional unique advantages. It was clear at the outset of the program that if SBIC's were to be venturesome and take risks, they were going to incur losses and should be allowed to establish realistic loss reserves.

The industry failed to get a statutory reserve enacted by legislation; but in 1964 the Internal Revenue Service promulgated Revenue Ruling 64-48, which provided that SBIC's would be allowed to establish bad debt reserves equal to 10 percent of their outstanding loans for a period of ten years. At the expiration of the ten years, the SBIC's would have to rely on their own loss experience to increase the reserves. If the SBIC was not sufficiently seasoned, it would be permitted to rely on an industry average.

The initial 10 percent ruling expired December 31, 1968. Unfortunately, the industry average was never developed and the result is something of a hiatus. SBA has compiled statistical data on realized losses of SBIC's going back to the first license. Statistics indicate that the industry has realized losses of approximately 8 percent on its investments throughout the history of the program. Eliminating the amount of loans and investments that are less than three years old, the realized loss experience goes up to a figure in excess of 12 percent of industry investments.

The Tax Reform Act of 1969 changed all this by trying to bring uniformity to the tax treatment of financial institutions. New provisions with reference to bad debt reserves of financial institutions were added to the Code. For SBIC's, a moving six-year average is the rule. A basic rule dictates what is a reasonable reserve under Code Section 166. SBIC's that are less than ten years old, however, will be permitted to rely on an industry average, to be determined by the Secretary of the Treasury.

A HOPEFUL MESSAGE FROM PRESIDENT NIXON

While the entire venture capital industry is in a stage of growth and development, legislative ramifications are even more in flux.

In early 1970, President Nixon sent a message concerning Small Business to Congress. It contained certain intriguing proposals which could have a long-range effect on venture capitalists.

For example, the President spoke about Minority Enterprise Small Business Investment Companies (MESBIC's), a slightly different type of SBIC. Key officials of the Small Business Administration, working with United States Secretary of Commerce Maurice Stans, have been encouraging major corporations to organize MESBIC's as wholly-owned subsidiaries. These companies can be organized for a paid-in minimum capital of only $150 thousand. There are special provisions with reference to the availability of government funds for MESBIC's, and several major corporations recently organized such concerns.

There are certain advantages to a corporation in forming a MESBIC. There is no doubt that there are minority-owned business enterprises that need high-risk, long-term loans and equity capital. A corporation that forms a MESBIC and finances this type of business can extend its own area of activities.

The President's Small Business message dwelt at length on the need for increasing the availability of credit and capital for small business, and primarily for the MESBIC's. He recommended that the Sub-chapter S section of the Code be amended to permit a MESBIC to be a shareholder in a Sub-chapter S corporation—something that SBIC's have been seeking for a number of years. Under present Sub-chapter S rules, a corporation's stock must be owned by ten or fewer stockholders who must all be individuals or estates. A corporation cannot be a shareholder in a Sub-chapter S corporation under the present law. The President recommended that the number of allowable shareholders of Sub-chapter S corporations be increased from ten to twenty.

For many years, the SBIC industry has been seeking modifications of the Investment Company Act of 1940 and the Internal

Revenue Code to permit all SBIC's to elect to be taxed as regulated investment companies in order to avoid double taxation. This effort has not succeeded.

The alternative is to permit SBIC's and other types of financing institutions to qualify as Sub-chapter S corporations. (Under present rules, a Sub-chapter S corporation may not receive more than 20 percent of its income from interest, dividends or personal holding company type income.) To this end, the Tax Committees are reviewing a proposal of the former administration to eliminate the income test with reference to corporations qualifying to elect to be taxed under Sub-chapter S. The President appeared to be recommending that this be modified to liberalize and extend the opportunities for MESBIC's. Presumably, other types of venture capital companies might also enjoy these added tax benefits.

INDUSTRY GROWTH

When the SBIC program was launched in 1958, the nation's venture capital companies could almost be counted on the fingers of one hand. If the SBIC program has accomplished nothing else, it has led to the formation of an entirely new industry—organized venture capital companies.

16
Investing In The Computer Field

B. J. Brooks

What follows might be called the successful case history of a venture capital offspring nurtured by the expert care and training of a vigorous young parent. And stemming from this example and related experience over a period of years, we will explore some of the principal dynamics of venturing now and for the near future.

BACKGROUND OF A PARENT

Boothe Computer Investment Corporation is a wholly-owned subsidiary of Boothe Computer Corporation. The parent company is two and one-half years old, although chairman of the board D.P. Boothe has had some twenty years' experience in the business of leasing capital equipment. Many other management members also have had extensive experience in the leasing business.

Boothe Computer was organized and began operations as a third-party computer leasing company, concentrating on non-payout leases of IBM System 360 computers, along with associated peripheral gear. The company currently owns and has leased computer equipment worth approximately $150 million,

Mr. Brooks is president of Boothe Computer Investment Corporations, in San Francisco, Calif.

valued at cost. It consists of some 250 separate installations, leased to some 170 lessees.

In addition, Boothe has $20 million invested in Canada, $20 million in Europe, and owns 10 percent of a South African computer leasing company. We are also investigating the leasing market in South and Central America and Australia.

Boothe has approximately 1.7 million shares issued and outstanding, a little over 2 million shares on a fully-diluted basis. Approximately 10 percent of the stock is publicly traded, and 90 percent is held on an investment basis by major United States corporations and other investors.

Soon after the leasing company was founded, the corporation actively embarked upon a program of growing into a fully-integrated computer company. There are now five subsidiaries: a full-service software company; a manufacturer of high-precision optical equipment; a consulting company specializing in transportation; a company engaged in marketing computer and peripheral equipment; and—Boothe Computer Investment Corporation, an investment company providing equity funds to new and young companies in computer-related industries.

BASIC LOGIC FOR FORMING A VENTURE CAPITAL DIVISION

About two years ago, the parent company decided to establish a venture capital subsidiary. Several reasons combined to produce this decision:

1. Boothe Computer Corporation's objective was to become a complete computer company with activities in areas of the industry other than leasing.

2. The nature of the leasing business is such that the cash flow resulting from lease payments must be used constructively to maintain investor interest and enthusiasm.
3. A management team was developed that would not be fully utilized by remaining solely in the leasing and re-leasing business.
4. The management team had specific expertise and experience in the computer industry which would make the company an intelligent and knowledgeable investor, both in the initial decision-making process and in working with investees or portfolio companies after an investment had been made.
5. The cash requirements of a venture capital program dovetail with the cash flow generated by leases—that is, periodic requirements for relatively small amounts of capital.
6. Its location in San Francisco, near the peninsula and Southern California's spawning-grounds for new companies, was ideal.
7. As a business, venture capital had been an exciting industry over the past decade and the successes were well-known.

Boothe Computer Investment Corporation

Consequently, Boothe Computer Investment Corporation was formed as a wholly-owned subsidiary in May 1968.

BCIC's primary objective is to realize capital gains on venture capital equity investments over a three- to five-year period. As a secondary objective, this activity provides convenient exposure to new developments within the industry. Thirdly, the venture capital operation provides Boothe with the opportunity to become aware of the specific characteristics and peculiarities of various areas of the overall computer industry.

Since BCIC's first investment in August 1968, we had committed $3.5 million to investments in eleven companies as of the beginning of 1970. Commitments range in size from $96 thousand to $600 thousand. A conservative estimate of the value of the investment portfolio as of early 1970 was over $5 million. The investees cover a wide spectrum of business activities, but the common thread is that they are all somehow involved with the computer industry.

Assisting Investees

BCIC feels that there are a number of areas in which we can be helpful to our portfolio companies. In general, we provide assistance in the following areas, similar to the services provided by all professional venture capitalists: We—

- listen to management and react as a sounding-board for their plans and ideas;
- act as a buffer, or even arbiter, between conflicting management personnel;
- perform a monitoring function by requiring regular formal and informal reporting;
- offer general business and financial advice, based upon experience with a number of small companies;
- provide contacts and suggestions regarding, for instance, accountants and auditors, banks, consultants, attorneys, potential suppliers and/or customers.

Special BCIC Services

Based upon our experience as a leasing company, as well as the specific experience of management, we feel that there are also other areas where BCIC can be uniquely helpful:

Marketing

Marketing policies and plans

Market research and product development

Selection of personnel

Developing compensation plans

Knowledge of large users

Knowledge of configuration of typical IBM installation

Finance

Development of vendor lease plans

Accounting questions connected with leasing programs

Banking contacts and ideas for dealing with banks

Additional financing—private and public

Contacts

Number of specific contacts within the computer and banking industries

Large potential users who are either investors in or lessees of Boothe

Other investees in similar areas of activity

BCIC has limited capabilities in these areas:

Engineering

Manufacturing

Purchasing and inventory control

Cost accounting

It is interesting and, BCIC believes, significant to note that the strong and limited capability areas dovetail with those of the typical investee, in that new and young companies are usually stronger in engineering and manufacturing than in marketing and finance.

CRITERIA

In terse outline form, here are the general criteria BCIC has set for making investments:

Management

Experience in similar or related areas

History as a team

Profit responsibilities in previous positions

Success-oriented

Growth potential as managers

Market

Favorable, with growth possibilities

Obtainable through reasonable efforts in marketing

Room for a small company

Product

Appropriate for management capability and capability of manufacture

Patent protection, when necessary

Financial

Plan is feasible, with a determinable amount of funds

Additional capital will be reasonably available, when and if required

Overall, BCIC looks for a situation in which the proper combination of our criteria is available at a price that affords an opportunity to realize capital gains commensurate with the risk involved.

CURRENT TRENDS IN VENTURE CAPITAL

The Long and Short of It

In a tight money market, when venture capital commands a greater percentage of ownership, this situation will continue to fluctuate with the economy as the stock market does—and for similar basic reasons.

As for the long-term trend in the venture capital business, there is no question that we will see during the next decade not only a continuation, but an acceleration of the trend for an entrepreneur and groups of entrepreneurs to form their own companies. Many of these groups will come from major corporations. A disproportionate number of the groups will be in the high-technology areas. Here is some of the reasoning behind our thinking:

- Dedication and loyalty to main corporations, which many of us saw in our father's generation, are anachronisms. We are living in an age when unquestioned loyalty is not tolerated conceptually.
- There is a growing and apparent desire among young people to "do their own thing."

- The general affluence of America permits risk-taking, without the threat of sacrificing, for a long period of time, the family's food, housing, and general welfare.
- High-technology industries are based upon creative technology, which can be painfully and effectively stifled in large companies.
- The ratio between the brains and capital necessary for success is heavily weighted in favor of brains in high-technology industries, particularly when compared to traditional industries of the past.
- The recent general attitudes of the courts has been in favor of the small entrepreneur; lawsuits from ex-employers usually are not considered serious threats.
- A number of different—and differing—pools of capital are available and visible.

POOLS OF AVAILABLE VENTURE CAPITAL

Available to small companies are several types of venture capital which have been divided, somewhat arbitrarily here, into ten basic categories:

1. Individuals and consortia of individuals
2. Private venture capital partnerships, such as the Rockefellers, the Whitneys, Bessemer Securities, Payson & Trask
3. Investment bankers—consortia of partners, often combined with wealthy clients
4. The public market, usually obtained through an underwriting
5. Large publicly-held venture capital companies and SBIC's
6. Bank-owned SBIC's

7. Performance (or "go-go") funds
8. Insurance companies and pension funds
9. Industrial and commercial firms supplying capital primarily as an investment, such as Allstate, Boothe Computer, Singer, Dupont and others
10. Industrial and commercial firms supplying capital primarily as a form of vertical or horizontal integration, such as Electronic Memories, Memorex, CalComp, Marshall Industries and Data Products

It is apparent that there is plenty of capital available for investment in promising, new, young companies. It is also apparent that each venture capitalist, even those in the same general category, is unique. Therefore, it would further benefit companies seeking venture capital to attempt to get as much as possible in needed services in addition to capital.

To make the most intelligent decision, it is necessary to do a considerable amount of research and self-evaluation, both external and internal. A company must be sufficiently self-critical to recognize its basic strengths and weaknesses and, subsequently, what it should be seeking from a venture capitalist—now and as the company grows in the future. Because each source of funds has its own "personality," it is necessary to determine experience and expertise, and to investigate the firm's reputation for fairness, integrity, ability and willingness to be helpful.

In attempting to see how venture capital firms in these categories differ, let us take a brief, overall look at each.

Individuals and Consortia of Individuals

Capital from these sources usually consists of funds from relatives, in-laws, friends and "angels." When available, it is the easiest to gain. This type of investor, typically, is not critical when things are going well, but he is highly critical of management when faith is lost and fear appears. Moreover, these investors often lack expertise in the entrepreneur's business and are unable to offer specific constructive advice. Also, they are usually unable or reluctant to put up substantial amounts of additional funds when needed.

This source of funds is most appropriate for the garage-shop operation, where large amounts of capital are not required. One must realize that second- or third-round financing, even for the successful company, probably will not be available from this capital source.

Private Venture Capital Partnerships

Generally, these groups are run by professionals with a wealth of experience in structuring a financing plan which can satisfy everyone's requirements. They often have extensive experience in a number of industries, although each has his own favorite industry, as a rule. They can provide important, high-level contacts in a number of diverse areas. Most importantly, these partnerships usually have a large capacity for patience when things do not go according to original projections.

However, because of the experience and the number of situations they review, they can write a tougher deal, from an ownership percentage standpoint, than less-experienced investors. They also demand a substantial amount of reporting, formal and informal, and may prove to be intractable regarding subsequent financings. They often demand a voice in policy decisions—such as board seats—and can be hypercritical of a company's plans and financial and production projections.

Financing from these partnerships is appropriate and obtainable for those companies with an understandable product and business plan. It is also appropriate for those who will accept a rein on, or at least a sophisticated questioning of their activities and plans. Those who object to someone's looking over their shoulders should avoid this category.

Investment Bankers

These sources of funds are easily identifiable, particularly during bull markets. For example, during 1969 everyone knew a broker whose firm's partners invested in venture capital. These groups are usually not as critical of plans and operations as the venture capital partnerships because of their lack of industry experience. They look more to possible returns than to basic industry considerations. The money is somewhat easier to obtain because "high-income" money is willing to take high risks for high returns.

Obviously, if a company is successful, an association with partners in investment banking firms provides a running start on subsequent financing. Also, these groups usually provide a better deal for the management team in terms of ownership.

As a group, these investors vary more than in any other category. Although some are sophisticated, for the most part they are not in a position to offer any depth of helpful advice. They can also be persistent nags if operations are not up to projections.

This source of financing is best for those who are unprepared to do the detailed work necessary to sell a professional venture capital partnership. It is advantageous to those who want, or are willing to give up, good professional advice in return for a higher management stake in the young company. There are now some excellent investment bankers providing venture capital. Unfortunately, most investment bankers do not fall into this category. Furthermore, during down markets, such as developed in 1970, this source of financing becomes exceedingly scarce.

The Public Market

At certain times, this pool of capital offers the best situation for management in terms of ownership because the public is, by and large, willing to pay more money with less control than any other capital source. If a company is successful—success measured by rising stock price—subsequent financings are relatively easy. A stock selling publicly at a high price/earnings ratio provides an excellent medium for purposes of acquisitions. Publicly-traded stock also gives employees the opportunity to ascertain accurately their paper profits on stock options or low-priced stock. There is also an excellent public relations value to having a publicly-traded stock.

On the negative side, the public is fickle and generally requires steadily increasing earnings to maintain a high stock price. This means that a company might be tempted to indulge in questionable accounting to keep earnings rising. Disclosure requirements are considered onerous by many managements. Also, the effective use of stock options to attract key personnel is severely hampered by a high-priced stock. In contrast, subsequent financing can be difficult if a stock has had poor or lackluster performance.

The cost of underwriting—at least $50 thousand plus commissions—can be a back-breaking expense for a small company. Overall, however, public offerings can be the best source of capital for those companies who are convinced that they will have *no* bad quarters ahead. They are also best for companies who need stock for acquisition programs or who need to see regular evaluation of their worth. However, public underwriting can be quite uncertain. Many of the underwritings from 1968 to early 1970 could occur only during a "hot new issue" period. By March 1970 many such financings became impossible and numerous companies incurred major legal and accounting expenses without raising a single penny. Others that had planned expansion programs, or debt reduction, from such financings, were put in difficult positions.

Publicly-held Venture Capital Companies

These large companies are almost identical to the venture capital partnerships, as far as the investee company is concerned. However, they may be required to disclose more about their portfolio companies' activities to the various government agencies and to the public. They also tend to have a preference for convertible debentures or debt with warrants, rather than common stock.

Bank-owned SBIC's

These SBIC's are not substantively different from the other SBIC's. They are in a position to be helpful in obtaining loan money from the parent bank, although, as a matter of practice, they typically do not put undue pressure on the parent bank.

Performance, "Go-Go" Funds or Letter Stock Funds

It is difficult to list any advantages that this group offers a company other than capital. Because of the number of investments they make, they are unable to know enough of any one investee to be more than cursorily helpful. They are, by definition, mainly interested in the short-term performance of the securities they purchase.

Insurance Companies and Pension Funds

These sources, like the performance funds, usually do not have anything to offer but capital. They also invest in too many companies to follow any one closely, and most of them have no experienced venture capitalists on their staffs. Because of their fiduciary responsibilities, they are apt to be interested in debt securities, such as convertible debentures or notes with warrants.

Industrial and Commercial Firms Supplying Capital Primarily as an Investment

It is difficult to generalize in this category. Besides specific expertise, each investor has his own reason for being in the venture capital business. For example, Boothe Computer has marketing and computer industry expertise, the Friden division of Singer has 2,000 salesmen and 1,500 servicemen in the field, and Dupont is seeking scientific breakthroughs.

It is imperative to analyze these companies individually, with the objective of determining where their strengths would be most helpful to the young company seeking funds.

Industrial and Commercial Firms Supplying Capital Primarily as a Form of Vertical or Horizontal Integration

These companies have the obvious advantage of being particularly knowledgeable about the industries in which they finance new companies. They offer many of the advantages of a parent-subsidiary opportunity to realize capital gains. They also offer a ready buyer of the outstanding stock, when and if it is determined to merge the subsidiary into the parent.

The major disadvantage, however, is the genuine lack of operating autonomy.

WHICH PATH TO CHOOSE?

For most new or young firms seeking capital, there is no simple formula for obtaining funds. Each situation requires a different approach to the specific capital pool, and the deal that one firm negotiates can be as different as day-and-night from the funding of his competition.

What is most important to remember, however, is that a little research into venture capital funding, and the particular firm chosen to make the investment, can put a company in a better position at the bargaining table—and help to obtain vital capital when it is needed.

17

Venturing In High Technology

Morton Collins

The field of venturing is noted for wide variety, both among the entities who invest and in the enterprises that receive support. In the following discussion, we will focus on a hybrid organization that demonstrates the variety among venture capital organizations by serving a unique function.

DSV: AN INTRODUCTION

Data Science Ventures, Inc., formed in July 1968, is structured as a corporation with one class of common stock, of which management owns a substantial share. Our investment technique is different from that of most venture capital organizations in that we consider only ventures within the high-technology field of data processing.

DSV also represents a new vehicle for traditional sources of venture capital. We are a private company, and our stockholders all represent established sources of private capital. In essence, we constitute the front line in data processing for a large group of traditional venture sources. In this manner we do not compete in the arena with other venture capitalists, inasmuch as many of them are our backers.

Dr. Collins is president of Data Science Ventures, Inc., in Princeton, N.J.

> DSV is staffed on a functional basis. We are split along two lines: The first line is composed of high-technology personnel who have substantial expertise in some area of data processing. We do not cover the whole field, in that the firm has expanded so rapidly; but we cover the key areas and hope to capture the others through the spill-over in each other's knowledge.
>
> The other line consists of management people who have technical backgrounds and business degrees. Their prime mission is to work with companies after the investment is made, and to see that the companies are managed in a fashion that will optimize the return to the investor.

We have no magic formula for making companies successful. We have observed certain factors that always seem to be present in successful companies, and other factors which always seem to be present in companies that fail. We try to exclude the latter and include the former in our companies. Our function, pure and simple, is to seek capital appreciation. We invest on a long-term basis and tend to think in five-year quanta as a minimum. Basically, we are in the money business. Our business is to create companies that are successful, and to make money for them.

OBSERVATION TRANSLATED TO ACTION

DSV was formed as the result of several observations.

First, the data processing industry has grown rapidly and will continue to grow in the foreseeable future. It has more potential growth than any other single area in the economy.

Second, there is a general lack of technological expertise among financial institutions, particularly those which are the traditional sources of private capital. This weakness is even greater in the data processing area. This is coupled with the fact that their available expertise has come from the wrong sources, such as a university professor who is an expert in this area. The professor may know all there is to know about the architecture of a new computer, but he may be consummately unqualified to judge the size of the total market for such a product. (Perhaps this is an overly-cynical view; however, having been both a university professor and a consultant to the financial industry, I am indicting myself along with the rest.)

There is a substantial difference in degree of objectivity when one is advising someone else to take a risk—or considering taking the risk oneself. It is relatively easy as a fee-paid consultant to size up a situation briefly and say, "Yes, this appears to have the proper technical ingredients; I think that you should bet $500 thousand or $1 million on the company." If it is one's own money, there is a tendency to be more careful and objective.

DEVELOPMENT OF AN OPERATIONAL PHILOSOPHY

Operational philosophy at our firm has come about largely through interaction with the venture capital community. Some ideas resulted from watching the financial community in operation and trying to correct the operations or techniques we considered to be wrong.

We have four key operational concepts:

1. Maintaining a current blueprint of the data processing industry and its related technology;
2. Evaluating new investment opportunities;
3. Developing specific techniques of interaction with portfolio or affiliate companies;
4. Reviewing and adjusting active investments.

With regard to the development and maintenance of a blueprint of data processing and related technology, we have spent a substantial part of our total effort in dividing the data processing industry into segments, and analyzing such factors as size of the markets, their likely growth, types of products, technologies, and changes that will probably develop within these segments. By definition, we cannot predict breakthroughs. It is possible, however, to project the likely changes in a technology, at least over a five-year period. Compiling this information, which obviously changes daily, is a herculean task. Therefore, we do a poor job of it at best, but we do not depend on our own efforts entirely. We purchase information from other sources, particularly information of a statistical nature.

Judging the Investment

We look at all the projections that various people make, and put these into our matrix to arrive at a continuously changing blueprint. This material provides an excellent sounding-board for prospective investments. When someone calls us with an investment opportunity, such as a new terminal device, we look at our blueprint in that area and ask ourselves if this represents something for which the market is substantial enough to result in an interesting company. If not, we will not be interested.

Creating the Investment

Our philosophy also enables us to create investment opportunities rather than simply react to investment opportunities that are presented. This is a growing trend in the venture capital business.

It enables us to see holes in the marketplace—needs that are not being fulfilled.

Overall, three things are needed to create a good company: viable ideas, good men and capital. If we have the capital and the ideas from the blueprint, then all we need to do is seek out the men. The difficulty of doing this cannot be minimized; but by utilizing this blueprint, we can at least judge our investments and occasionally create an investment opportunity.

NEGOTIATING THE DEAL: PRELIMINARIES

With respect to the techniques of evaluating new investment opportunities, we do not differ materially from any other firm that operates in the venture capital industry. We require a written proposal or a business plan. We would prefer that the people who prepare the business plan not tell us about the financial requirements or their cash flow projections, as we would rather work with them to structure the financing. We would rather not have them say, "We are a startup venture; we need $3 million to get through the first year; we are not willing to give up more than 20 percent of our company." Such over-definition occurs often and creates many problems. We prefer that the proposal not specify such matters.

Next, we consider the written proposal to determine how the company's plan fits with our working philosophy. If it fits, we then conduct initial interviews with the management to find out how they think. We attempt to take them through circular paths of logic, to find out if they are only trying to tell us what we want to hear or if they really have something to say. This is followed by more in-depth interviews with the management or proposed management people. We also complete fairly lengthy market and technical analyses, with emphasis on the market side.

Usually, it is detrimental for the technology to be in the forefront without a practical—and marketable—solution in sight. We like to see a technology that is being employed in ways which can generate solutions to people's problems. After all, this is what the customer wants—products and services, not elegant computer hardware.

Following this, we structure an investment or deal with the management people. We attempt to select people for the group who can be helpful to the company or with whom we have established a working relationship.

We have working relationships with several firms on the West Coast. Because we are located on the East Coast and cannot visit the area more than once a month, it is very convenient for us to have someone "down the street" who can watch out for deals there. In addition, there are people in our investor group who are related to commercial banks. They can help obtain the proper introductions to help our portfolio companies with appropriate lines of credit. We try to help the companies in any way we can by structuring the investment group appropriately.

RISKS IN HIGH-TECHNOLOGY SPECIALIZATION

Because we deal only with high technology, the people who start the companies in which we make investments are people versed in technology rather than business experience. Thus, startups in high technology are fraught with risks. A look at the statistics will demonstrate that from a risk position, it is the least attractive area of venture capital investment.

Who Takes the Risk?

We have tried to look at this objectively to determine who takes the risk in a technological startup situation. In general, we find that the man who is to be the president of the new company currently works for a sizable corporation. Among other factors, he has a good income by professional standards. Although he is temporarily giving up a guaranteed income to start a new company, he receives the opportunity to make considerable money in capital gains. Actually, he gives up very little; in fact, his salary is generally directly translated, and he is left with nearly the same net income as if he had remained in his secure position. In addition, he often tries to install the kinds of benefit program formerly offered by the large company. So the overall situation does not change for many entrepreneurs.

What really changes for him is the fact that he now works sixteen or twenty hours a day, instead of eight or ten. If his company goes down the drain one or two years later, what has he lost? He goes back to another company similar to the one of his original employer. He is richer for his entrepreneurial experience and probably will get an increase in salary. He has risked nothing more than a little pride.

We take the view that essentially all the risk is borne by capital investors in a technological startup situation. The venture capitalist must be wary of the attraction of such a situation just because it is fresh and interesting.

A typical startup fantasy is that a company will develop a wonderful new device and sell it to everyone. The market will be enormous and the world will rush to buy it.

In reality, this "better mousetrap" story does not exist. The greatest single problem the technologically-oriented manager has is a lack of appreciation for marketing expertise and financial knowledge, although from our experience financial knowledge can be instilled more easily than marketing expertise. It is difficult to convince some company presidents that their marketing vice-president or sales manager should receive the highest salary in the firm.

We are interested in startup companies when certain mitigating circumstances prevail; the strongest is a previous track record. This means that management has had prior successful experience in running a small company or division of a large concern. Furthermore, there must be a functional balance in the management: marketing expertise, engineering expertise, a strong central leader, financial expertise, and other success elements.

If the company is properly financed and has a strong leader, there is no reason to suspect that it will not do well. The major risk is that the product may not be salable for one reason or another. However, if the marketing is handled properly, there is no reason to feel that this will occur.

Going back to our original premise that capital takes all the risks in a startup, then how is a deal structured? We take a very hard line on this subject. We will be perfectly happy to finance a startup if we can be shown that a prospective situation has the proper management balance, that there is a reasonable and feasible business plan, and if we are given the right to absolute control of the new company.

SETTING UP A PERFORMANCE FORMULA

We are not interested in owning small pieces of very large pies. We want to control the temperature of the oven. In nearly every startup situation in which we have invested, we have structured a performance formula with the company.

Inasmuch as we are taking substantially all of the risks, we deserve the right to control the company. If a year from now the company makes no progress toward its goal, we want to be able to pull the rug out from under if necessary, so that we can recover whatever possible. However, if the company performs as projected, the entrepreneurs earn back the share of the company which is properly theirs.

In essence, we turn a startup into a continuing situation, or a situation looked at two or three years later, through the formula. There are many ways in which this can be accomplished; among them, by creating performance goals, or structuring multi-stage financing with a minimum of two, or perhaps three, stages of financing involving combinations of equity, convertible debt, straight debt, warrants with milestones for achievement. In this manner, the company gets the capital it needs to begin to develop its prototype; this could be one of the milestones.

We also have set time goals, financial and performance goals, some of which have been technological in nature. After meeting these goals, the company can have more financing as needed. Performance periods may range from a minimum of three years to a maximum of forty months. This is a tight period in which the company must perform at a maximum. We generally measure performance by pre-tax net income. We also enable management to earn back from our ownership of two-thirds of the company to a fifty-fifty situation, or even more if they exceed their goals. Our situations are very flexible.

We will not make an investment unless we judge that it is possible to work closely with a company. We try to create a partnership and meet at least weekly with each of our portfolio companies. We have no desire to control the company for the sake of control, nor do we think we can run other people's companies. Our primary mission is to help solve and avoid problems.

We have not demanded, but have always accepted board representation.

Also, sometimes a growing company might reach the stage where a new manager is required to handle the next stage of the company's development. In these cases, we have always tied his compensation to profit.

Corporate Spending Vs. Performance

A venture capitalist must ask: are the appropriate funds being spent for development in a company, if it is trying to achieve performance? We do not know how to handle this problem except to say we must live with it. We like to think that our goals and management's goals precisely coincide: to build the largest company possible in the shortest period of time. We are willing to sacrifice whatever is needed in order to do this.

Having a performance formula, however, does not mean that we will hold to it in an iron-clad fashion if it does not make sense. One of the obvious problems that arises is a public offering occuring within the time span of the performance period. We try to structure such factors into the initial performance formula to decide how the equity will be split at that time.

When we started out, one of our principal concerns was that we would not worry about conflict of interest; but we soon found that this was not a good idea. We will not make obvious conflicting investments.

We have thought about merging one or more of our companies in the event that one falls into troubled times. We believe our area to be sufficiently interesting to traditional manufacturing companies that the merger or acquisition route is open to us for a troubled company, particularly if it requires more capital and time than we can invest.

REVIEW AND ADJUSTMENT OF ACTIVE INVESTMENTS

Our job is to learn how we can improve our client companies, and how we should prepare for new financings or other aspects of the planning function through periodic review.

During the period from our beginning until the spring of 1970, we considered a total of 862 investment opportunities, and received 414 formal written proposals. In that period, we completed a total of nine investments involving $3 million of our capital. The total dollars invested in those nine companies was $16.9 million. Our average investment was $410 thousand—our largest investment $1.42 million, and our smallest $100 thousand.

DSV Portfolio Examples

The companies in which we have invested are primarily engaged in the manufacture of computer and electronic equipment; they are all privately-held. The financing—and equity ownership—varies in each case. For instance, in the case of—

- a California manufacturer of removable media, disc storage equipment for small digital computers: financing–combination of convertible debentures and common stock; equity–we own 6.7 percent, the investors 67 percent;
- a New England manufacturer of mini-computers: financing–common stock; equity–we own 26.9 percent (and vote 54 percent), the investors own 69 percent;

- a New England manufacturer of high-speed memory devices utilized with small mini-computers, etc.: financing—common stock; equity—we own 21.8 percent, the investors 55 percent;
- a California-based manufacturer of IBM compatible tape equipment: equity—we own .4 percent, the investors 40 percent;
- a California manufacturer of tele-communications equipment for supermarket chains: financing—combination of straight debt, common stock and warrants; equity—we own 7.3 and 9.8 percent, depending on a performance formula;
- a midwestern manufacturer of tele-communications modems: financing—combination of common stock and warrants; equity—we own 5.6 percent, the investors 56 percent;
- a California manufacturer of computers: financing—combination of preferred and common stock and convertible debt; equity—we own between 22.7 and 31.8 percent, the investors between 50 and 70 percent, depending on a performance formula.

The common thread in these and other companies in which we have invested (except for a marketing company in Germany) is that they are all manufacturers of hardware.

UNPREDICTABLE PROBLEMS

Some people say that venture capital is a business fraught with danger. We believe it is a succession of crises. Any given company has a succession of crises in its history, and a venture capitalist who is intimately related to a number of companies must know how to survive.

We have had problems come up in our companies—problems which never exist or can be predicted in the business plan. For instance, we had one situation in which the principal technical man in the company became enamored of a religion. The local religious leader of his sect passed away, and he felt that he had to take over the flock, which greatly reduced his time input to the company. That kind of circumstance is hardly predictable.

In another situation, one of our companies had approximately $96 thousand in escrow with a law firm for a property purchase. The law firm misused the escrow funds and we suddenly had a negative cash flow of $96 thousand.

We have had several situations in this very difficult money market where investment bankers have been committed to do private placements for companies, and have failed. We then had to put on our track-shoes and play the role of investment banker.

We had another frightening situation in which a vice-president of a portfolio company became involved with the president's personal secretary, creating major problems with the vice-president's wife.

In the future we will see more venture capital funds available and more companies participating in venture capital activities. We are finding that entrepreneurs are increasingly astute, and are more aware of sources of financing and techniques of financing.

As time goes on, we expect to see more industry-specialized venture capital companies. The concept seems to make sense in view of an expanding marketplace and a greater variety of high-technology industries.

18

Packaging The New Invention

Roger Shashoua

Patents International Affiliates, Ltd., was formed in 1965 to finance new inventions and to introduce inventors to manufacturers.

We felt that a vehicle was needed for working with bright, young inventors and to instill faith in them. To achieve this goal, we created the first International Inventor's Show in 1965. It turned out to be an amateurish conglomeration of flying submarines, golf balls that sent out smoke signals, and other items of that ilk—hardly destined to be big sellers.

We could not take an equity position in any invention. If we did, inventors would not buy space for the show. If we charged industry, they would not attend because of the quality of the inventions exhibited. This continued for three years, during which time we slowly built a solid foundation and earned the respect of inventors around the world. It is important to understand that the majority of inventors are not professional people. They are usually basement operators, not polished businessmen in paneled offices.

In August 1968, we were able to find someone who believed in what we were doing, and our company become publicly-held. We had sufficient capital to eliminate dependence on industry, and

Mr. Shashoua is chairman of the board of Patent International Affiliates, Ltd.

financing was now available to inventors to repay their years of confidence in our efforts.

As of now, 156,000 inventors in fourteen nations participate in our activities, which include major exhibits in Brussels, London, Chicago, Los Angeles and New York. We now package the inventor's product for 25 percent of the equity. Industry is also served with a total package, rather than a Buck Rogers fantasy.

CRITERIA

Amidst 30,000 New Products Annually

Approximately thirty thousand new products come across our desk every year. We manage twelve major expositions, and are affiliated with fourteen others operated by other groups. For these fourteen shows, we have the new products, publishing and advance information rights to their inventors.

For the tremendous overflow of products, we use straight-forward criteria: we invite industry to attend the trade shows and evaluate products. They no longer can attend shows for a two-dollar charge, but they pay a full membership fee to the International New Products Center, our information division.

Judging from the companies that have attended and investigated the products, however, approximately 60 percent of the businessmen seem to lack the necessary imagination to commit their firms to the venture. They are interested in the patent stage, but hesitate to underwrite the necessary development stages.

DEALING WITH THE INVENTOR

We deal with volume business, and feel that the screening and testing of new inventions is better left to the corporate backers. Most of the interested businesses are blue-chip companies, and have excellent research departments. With first option on inventions with attractive potential, as well as 25 percent interest if a major company becomes interested in an invention, we go to the inventor and point out the increased protection in dealing with our firm. It has been a determining factor in our growth.

Many inventors want money as soon as possible. They have worked hard and want a cash advance; but most companies cannot offer this. Some companies require that the inventor sign a statement to the effect that if the company can prove they thought of the idea first, the inventor has lost the contract. The poor inventor has little recourse against the corporate giant if it comes to a costly legal battle.

The basic reason for our company's success is that we are a buffer between the inventor and industry. Companies prefer doing business through us because they do not want to become entangled with complications, such as lawsuits with inventors. Inventors, on the other hand, like to do business with us because we can advance cash if we find a company that is interested in the particular product.

In return for our efforts on behalf of the company, we take equity participation in the firm. Before putting our company's name on anything, we look for three things: management, concept and distribution. Where there is excellent distribution and aggressive, competent management, anything can be sold. This is our business philosophy.

TESTING CONCEPTS: A UNIQUE APPROACH

Our approach to testing concepts is unique:

1. We send a publication about new products available for licensing to a broad spectrum of major corporations, including the leading blue-chip firms.
2. If we receive a 5 percent return, our staff reviews the project.
3. With a 10 percent return, my partner looks at the new product.
4. If our returns tally 25 percent or over, I interrupt vacation and return home immediately to personally investigate the invention.

With such projects we then arrange for a private placement. We do not approach corporate finance firms in the United States because they have rules and policies which we respect but cannot work with easily.

We have found huge sums of capital in Europe for new inventions. This "new product participation," as we refer to it, can be better understood by a typical example:

Our company owns 25 percent of a revolutionary product called "Carbolok," a chemical additive which provides forty-eight hours' carbonation. Because we believe this new process is great, we decided to develop the project ourselves, rather than give it to one of the leading soft drink firms.

Currently we are involved in approximately 120 projects out of several thousand we reviewed. For years this has been the approach in the oil business . . . An oilman cannot ask for $200 million to develop 200 acres. He must raise his money an acre at a time. We also take the total capital needed and divide it among participating finance houses. For example, a particular project may need $2.5 million. We say we can raise 2,500 participations. In the United States, we cannot sell privately to more than eight investors; nine would require our going through a full securities registration. However, in Europe there is no limit to the number of investors, so it is possible to gather 2,500 participants at $1 thousand each.

If someone is interested in meeting venture capital principals in Europe, he should contact his banker for help. The banker's overseas branch office will bring him together with companies that are looking for new products. There are hundred of outlets and each one leads to another. He should not hesitate to shop the marketplace in Europe, for he will not be respected unless he does.

DEALING WITH THE CREATIVE PERSONALITY

We came into the venture capital industry because many inventors refused to give up 80 percent of their rights to a broker in order to receive the necessary $20 thousand to develop a patent. We know that inventors are different from average people because they have already done something which sets them apart from others: they took a bold step—and created something.

Most people do not have the managerial ability to be able to form a company and move it ahead. Our company looks for management ability and other prime criteria. If a particular group meets our requirements, we will package a new company and place it in the form of product participation.

Overall, our most successful project is—Patents International Affiliates, Ltd. In 1970, we held a major inventors show in London. This was the first show in which we instituted the policy of receiving 25 percent equity in everything exhibited. Approximately 400 products were exhibited, including the innovative coin-operated tennis court.

The next step was to publicize the new idea. It just happened that a new firm, Tennis Unlimited, was entering the tennis field and planned to franchise courts. We approached the firm and pointed out the advantages of the coin-operated system, including the lack of competition. When negotiations were over, we sold the rights for $300 thousand—$150 thousand in cash and $150 thousand in stock, plus 5 percent royalties. For an idea of the profit potential in this business, it should be noted that we paid only $30 thousand for the full rights to the system.

We then advised the company to set up a special subsidiary to sell coin-operated tennis courts in the United States; thus, Pay Tennis International was formed. Currently the firm is seeking additional financing through outlets in London, Paris and Switzerland. We will sell small participations now and will approach the corporate finance departments later.

19

Financing Franchise Firms

Marvin Meit

Venture capital means taking a plunge—winding up neck-deep in risk, fully immersed in the trials and tribulations of a small company.

Some of today's venture capitalists are fulfilling the function formerly performed by bankers: making loans to companies and receiving equity rights when money is tight. Madison Consultants, Inc., would rather be involved with a company from its founding, and work to help it achieve a successful operating level as quickly as possible. We look for three basic factors in the companies we assist. The first is "people." Without good people, a venture that is turning out the best possible product or service will never become more than mediocre.

The second factor—is the company in a growth industry? Is it a new industry? Is the company marketing a new concept?

A successful executive runs his company by asking probing questions. If he is in an industry where he does not know the proper questions to ask, he cannot possibly get the correct answers. We are not interested in new companies in fields that we do not fully understand. Because we take an active role in our companies, they must be in areas in which we have competence. We do not want a scientist or a technician telling us that things

Mr. Meit is president of Madison Consultants, Inc., in New York City.

are going well. We want to know it; we must be able to determine whether he is telling us the truth.

The third factor we require is stock market acceptability. This is very important to venture capitalists because no one wants to remain a minority shareholder of a private corporation. The big payoff eventually must be a public offering.

If we investigate a company, and the people and industry appeal to us, we run a check through our underwriting friends. We want to know if this kind of company could qualify for a public offering, and what goals must be achieved in order for this to occur. Several deals that we thought were exceptional opportunities were turned down by the underwriters.

STARTUP COMPANIES—WHY THEY FAIL

There are two major reasons that startup companies fail: insufficient working capital and/or poor financial control. One of the key roles of a venture capitalist is to help the company avoid these two problem areas.

We attempt to fund our companies with enough initial cash to carry them through to the point where they become successful companies. This may not be feasible in certain technically-oriented companies which must set up plants with machinery and equipment. Except in rare instances, the funds for such capital requirements could not possibly be generated from private placements.

The risks in the market arena are so great that we will not become involved if the company must depend on a successful public offering for its final funding. To us, "going public" represents the return of capital to original investors, or raising additional working capital to achieve the next projected plateau, but not the money needed for the company to become a success.

RAISING CAPITAL: TWO "CRIMES"

There are two "crimes" perpetrated when people raise capital: first is, raising too little money; the penalty for this is that the firm probably will go out of business. The second is, raising too much money; this results in poor use of capital.

Raising too much money will force a company to give up more equity than is necessary. Furthermore, the capital will be lying idle. We have been offered situations where entrepreneurs request one million dollars, but the cash flow indicates the need for only $250 thousand. When the entrepreneur is confronted with this truth, his response is that he only wanted to sleep at night.

PROVIDING FINANCIAL EXPERTISE

Our firm likes to assume the position of "financial vice-president" of each of the situations in which we become involved. The irony is that young companies need financial controls mostly when they are beginning their businesses. Many entrepreneurs do not plan to hire a CPA or a qualified controller until they hit the $3—to $5-million mark. Unfortunately, they need this kind of financial expertise at the outset. We fulfil this vital function, setting up the accounting and financial controls, arranging for the public auditors, and helping determine proper budgets. When necessary, we also arrange for the underwriting. Inasmuch as we are principals of the firm, we do not take finders' fees from the underwriters. We also help to arrange for additional leasing contracts or bank lines. Overall, we function as an employee of the company, doing the best job we can.

TYPICAL FUNCTIONS

When an individual comes to us with an idea, product or concept for a new industry, we study the entrepreneur and complete extensive investigations.

We then research the industry. For example, our latest venture capital investment is in the retail optical industry. We examined all the companies that have gone public in that industry. We try to determine where the company is going, what it will be worth, and how much capital is needed.

When a deal is accepted, our firm does not invest its own money. Utilizing a list of investors, we package the deal and raise the money. If we were to receive 40 percent of the equity and the investors 30 percent, our participation usually would be 10 percent. In some situations, we may receive as much as 25 percent of the equity. This may sound high, but we do not get involved in situations where we cannot make an active contribution to the company. We justify our equity through our activities, and our portfolio companies or investor partners do not frown upon our equity position.

Our investors place their money into our situations in a unique manner. Typically, the investor is not a fund or someone who is willing to have his money tied up for five to seven years. Our investors want to get into a deal, see if it goes, then get out again within a short period of time. We provide this avenue of recapturing captial by a combination of equity and subordinate debenture which we sell to our investors as a unit. Our debenture agreement is constructed so that it will pay out over the projected cash flow of the company, which might be in a three-year or five-year period. In order to maximize our earnings, we have no interest payment the first year. The loans always carry a provision that the investors will be repaid for the proceeds of an underwriting if the proceeds exceed a fixed amount.

Basically, our motivation is to protect the company. By doing so, we automatically improve the position of the investor, although investors do not always see it in this way.

We also attempt to determine the true cash requirements of the business. If $1 million is needed, there must be an underwriting for $1.25 million, because fees, printing, legal and accounting costs could be as high as $250 thousand. Also, the proceeds from an underwriting in excess of $1.25 million will be used to repay the debenture holder. We are not forced to do an underwriting due to pressure from our investors. In a good market, if a $1.25 million offering can succeed, $200 thousand or $300 thousand more can be underwritten to repay the debenture holders. The investors are then left with investment letter stock, although they receive the bulk of their money. But our firm is locked in with the entrepreneur; and we will tell him that we will work side-by-side with the new venture since we have a sizeable amount of stock.

The reaction from our fledgling companies is usually very favorable, and we enjoy an excellent psychological relationship. Also we are directors or officers in each of our portfolio companies.

CASES IN POINT

In February 1969, we received a proposition from a day care center business. We spent several days with the entrepreneur, liked the way he talked and thought, and were impressed by his track record in successful management. However, we did not like the situation in which he was getting involved. He wanted to purchase a franchise from an existing firm and go into business. We did not like the franchisor, a weak company with a poor track record.

We have been able to find ideas and concepts which were valid and rewarding. For example, one of our first situations was a franchise company in the food business, Roy Rogers Roast Beef, a Division of the Marriott Corporation. We learned quickly that no one today is interested in financing a single-purpose building, such as a drive-in restaurant structure with unusual architecture. The day care center we investigated utilized a free-standing building; it was carpeted and air-conditioned, designed for the latest innovations in child education. However, when it came to yesterday's building designers, they felt the franchise needed unique shapes to create identity.

The day care center we supported was designed as a square box in an Early American style. The building could be used for a doctor's office, an insurance company's or a real estate broker's office, if we ran into trouble with the day care center.

The proof of success is that we invested in the day care center using our building design, and we have now established franchises in many states with multiple investor owners who wanted to own these buildings at reasonable returns, considering the tight money market.

We decided to raise a quarter of a million dollars for the new company, Day Care Centers of America. This seemed to be a reasonable amount of money in terms of the six to eight months required to work out corporate strategy before any income could be generated. The president of the company had about $22 thousand, which he put into the company; our investors contributed $250 thousand.

Because of the high-risk nature of this situation, we capitalized the company at an authorized one million shares. We issued 180,000 shares; 90,000 shares to our investors, which cost them $25 thousand. At the same time, they lent the company $225 thousand on a subordinate debenture. Our investors paid twenty-eight cents a share for the stock. The founders paid par value, which is four cents a share, and the president of the company also took $18 thousand in the debenture issue.

The debenture has a three-year term, 7 percent interest with no interest the first year. In less than one year, we opened three schools and began our franchise program. At this point we had approximately $50 thousand left in the bank and had begun to generate cash flow from the schools and franchisees.

We had three discussions with underwriters, with commitments from two of them to underwrite at $8.50 a share. This means that each of our investors would get part of their $225 thousand back from the proceeds of the underwriting, and will be left with 8,700 shares worth $75 thousand, but which cost only $2,500.

That is an extreme example of the best possible situation.

Anyone For Roast Beef?

We also put together a successful financing package for Ram Hart Systems, Inc., a franchise of Roy Rogers Roast Beef. We sold units at $30 thousand, which consisted of a $20 thousand debenture and 10,000 shares at $1.00 a share. This was our first situation, and it was a pure startup company with a negative cash flow. But we lined up an underwriting in 1968 when the market was quite different, especially for franchising stocks. The roast beef company had a successful underwriting exactly six months to the day after the money was put up as risk capital. Those people who bought a $30 thousand unit received their $20 thousand debenture, and were left with 10,000 shares of stock for which they had paid $1.00 . . . and initial offering price for the stock was $10.00 per share.

These examples demonstrate how we structure our investments to obtain the maximum leverage and get the capital back for our investors.

20

The Multi-Million Dollar Startup Business

David M. Goodman

Among the fascinations of the venture capital business are the fast pace, and the unusual ways in which practitioners become involved in the field. The circumstances to be discussed next are a good example. In addition, some of the problems and rewards we have experienced are noted in hopes they will prove interesting to neophyte and practiced venturer alike.

SOME BACKGROUND

Goodman

As a note of encouragement to late starters, I was thirty-five years old before I read a financial page; and I had to then because I had become the *de facto* executive vice-president of a company listed on the New York Stock Exchange. The president liked to sit by his swimming-pool in Beverly Hills (between trips to Las Vegas) and telephone me at 10:30 sharp every morning to find out what was going on. I always replied, "Everything is great."

Mr. Goodman is chairman of the board and chief executive officer in the firm of Goodman & Mautner, in Los Angeles, California, specializing in servicing portfolio companies.

And he would predictably answer, "Well, then I think I'll go to Vegas."

This man was a "financial genius." One day he told me, "We need $2 million to expand our leasing activities. You're running the company; so go to New York and get the money." It was then that I first learned about registrations and the Securities Acts of 1933 and 1934, and the Investment Act of 1940. Never having taken a course in corporation finance, I learned to rely on good investemnt bankers and attorneys. After a month in New York City, I became a full-fledged "financial genius," too.

Many years later, someone came into the office with a venture capital deal and handed me a business card that stated he was an "investment banker." The card carried the man's home address. In reply to what his qualifications were as an investment banker, he said, "I have lots of money and I am going to put it in a lot of ventures." This is one of the big problems with investing . . . many amateurs believe that the mere possession of money is the only qualification needed to join the professional investment community.

Mautner

My partner, Mr. Mautner, at one point in his career, had used his own money to help fund Capital for Small Business (CSB)—the first SBIC registered in Los Angeles. One of his earliest investments was a small computer company, Scientific Data Systems (now SDS). It took three passes at his group to get them to put up $100 thousand, a sum which has grown many times over since. Because of that investment, the record of Capital for Small Business was outstanding. Eventually the company was liquidated; return to the original investors was 35-to-1, in only six years.

The firm of Goodman and Mautner is a venture capital partnership which began business in August 1969. Mr. Mautner and I are equal partners; we must agree on all decisions.

THE SEARCH FOR CAPITAL

Funding of Scientific Data Systems

As a management consultant, I helped a newly-formed venture capital company, Davis & Rock, make one of their first investments—an investment that later accounted for about 80 percent of their portfolio, the same Scientific Data Systems.

The deal involved my assisting a friend who had shopped for capital all over Wall Street, in the erroneous belief that he needed $1½ million. He had found only one man who would agree to form a group to invest $500 thousand, and he could not raise the remainder of the capital. I suggested that he revamp his financial plan, stop shopping the deal and let me help in the search for capital.

Among those whom I contacted was a close friend who was forming his own venture capital company (Davis & Rock); however, he felt that it would be impossible to compete successfully with IBM. I expressed my opinion that the young entrepreneurs were good managers, excellent engineers, and had found a great potential gap in the market.

After one day of meetings, Davis & Rock agreed with my feeling about the entrepreneurs—that one was a great engineer; the other a brilliant intellectual with excellent marketing potential. Soon thereafter, the group made the investment.

This was a case of merely helping a friend solve a funding problem by changing his planning scheme. He cut the size of the original financing from $1½ million to $1 million by widening his profit margins, achieving an earlier break-even and qualifying for commercial bank loans.

How much equity must management lose? In this deal, management received 40 percent of the SDS deal and the investors took 60 percent. This was an excellent investment: my friend, who originally owned approximately 20 percent of SDS, recently estimated his Xerox holdings in excess of 416,000 shares (current value $45 million).

It makes little difference what the numerical split is—60/40, 51/49, 49/51 or 55/45. What is important, however, is the rate of growth and the long-range growth potential. Will the new company grow at 25 percent per annum in sales and net earnings—or better?

Continental Devices Corporation

Before the SDS deal, some people who had worked with me at Hughes Aircraft wanted to form a new company of their own. They planned to make silicon diodes. In those days, Hughes Aircraft was the largest supplier of glass-encapsulated germanium diodes, and was very proud of its highly-profitable semi-conductor division. But the division managers had a great deal of difficulty in trying to get top management to listen to new product and process ideas; so, in 1958, they decided to set up their own business—Continental Devices Corporation.

Together with the young entrepreneurs, we wrote a long-range management plan and took it to the East where we raised $1.25 million. The split was 40 percent for management, 60 percent for the investor. There was also an understanding that if we wanted to develop a transistor line, after being successful with the silicone diode line, the investors would lend another $800 thousand to

$900 thousand—which they later did. For the additional funds, we had to give up less than 5 percent of the company, because by that time we had far exceeded our break-even projections and the company was very profitable. The firm later went public and merged into Teledyne on very favorable terms.

VENTURING WITH AN ON-GOING COMPANY

From $1.6- to $14-Million with a "Flaky" Electronics Company

Bissett-Berman Corporations (BBC) had been in the electronics business for five years. The company was shipping $4 million and breaking even. The firm had attempted unsuccessful mergers with two corporations, but both arrangements failed to work, tossing the company back to independent status. The latest sponsor was a large company which owned 52 percent of Bissett-Berman. The sponsor was tired of BBC management's excuses for not having become a leading conglomerate in five years. They wanted to sell out of the company, and told management that if they could not find a buyer within ninety days, the sponsor would find a marriage-partner. The proposed spouse was Bell & Howell.

BBC management felt that they did not want to become involved with Bell and Howell and experience the same kinds of problems that had plagued them with the two former merger attempts. However, this latest proposal would have been profitable for them in terms of immediate income and capital gains. They wanted to obtain outside financing to buy out the control stock and move forward with an aggressive marketing program. The company's management contacted us through an attorney. When we met, we told management that if they went to work immediately, both goals could be accomplished within sixty days.

Twenty-three days later, a sound, long-range management plan was produced. The marketing projections also checked out well. Inasmuch as the firm's electronics products were to be sold to prime contractors who were depending upon Air Force programs, we made contacts at the Pentagon to verify long-range plans and Department of Defense program budgets.

Based on a variety of favorable factors, we raised $1.6 million for Bissett-Berman. We bought out the control shares for $800 thousand, which represented the original investment. The balance of $800 thousand was to be used to develop a new product which the original sponsor believed to be another "flaky" electronics component.

In 1969, the "flaky" electronics component, the "E-Cell"—a unique electronic energy cell—helped BBC ship approximately $20 million and show a profit of $1 million after taxes. The company, after two-and-one-half years of effort, was merged because the owners wanted liquidity—not because they had to sell. Overall, in less than three years, $1.6 million for 52 percent equity became $14 million, which is an excellent return on paper for venture capital investors.

OUR PREFERENCES

A controller of our acquaintance had an interesting financial rule-of-thumb: "Whatever you buy for a dollar, you should sell for two. That way you always get your 1 percent."

Our firm always tries to get its "1 percent." We looked at over 170 deals during an eight-month period between mid-1969 and early 1970, and invested in only four of them. These four companies met a predetermined set of criteria. They were in industries that were growing much faster than the gross national product —preferably at a rate of 52 to 30 percent per annum.

They all had excellent management. If management had worked for a large company, they were division managers and had their own P&L responsibility. If they had small business experience, they learned that the object of the exercise is to accumulate large black figures at the southeast corner of the P&L statement.

Another factor is that they were in technologies that have had high price-earnings ratios. The markets and the products were interesting, and there seemed to be a reasonable chance that they would succeed.

Some References

We like startup situations. We prefer applied technology, but do not avoid mundane industries, such as pharmaceuticals or the food industry. We are ready to look at any deal that will provide a ten-to-one return in five years. The average life of our partnership with portfolio companies is seven years. And we want to make our limited partners even richer and more sophisticated than they are.

We also invest in classic venture capital deals—going firms that need capital and prefer a private placement to a public issue. Sometimes firms come to us for private placement after a public offer has failed; and sometimes it is possible to help them.

As a partnership, we are able to purchase stock positions or debentures in existing private or public companies. We are not an SBIC, and are not limited to the amounts of capital we invest. Our average placement goal is $300 thousand to $400 thousand. Two or three of our limited partners, however, are among the wealthier investment bankers in the United States. They are "merchant bankers," and deal mainly with corporate finance and institutional placements. Thus we have capital sources to raise funds for our client companies if they need additional financing. Our limited partners, for example, will consider participation with us in a deal that requires upwards of $500 thousand to as high as $2 million.

THE "TEN-FOR-ONE RIDE"

When $500 thousand is needed, some venture capitalists want to gain $5 million out of that investment in public market value in five to seven years, depending upon their criteria.

If the investor gets 50 percent of the company for his $500 thousand and it grows in market value by ten-for-one, management's 50 percent would also be worth $5 million. The total company would be worth $10 million in a public market in five years.

Value depends on the price-earnings ratio. If a company plans to ship $4 million worth of electronic components at the end of the fifth year, and sets a goal to earn $400 thousand net profit after taxes, the company will be valued at roughly 20 times earnings, or only $8 million. This company does not meet our qualifications.

In this case, the total valuation should be $10 million. Applying classic price-earnings ratios of leading growth companies during the bull markets of the 1950's and '60's, most of the stocks sold at fifteen to twenty times' earnings when they first went public. A venture capitalist is interested in a long-term capital gain. This is why many look for a "ten-to-one ride." This is true whether the venturer is an investment banker or a private venture capital fund.

The price-earnings ratios and sales multiples are arrived at by historical valuations and the particular industry involved. Beckman Instruments, for example, sold for twenty-five to thirty times' yearly earnings for several years.

In a tight money market, a venture capitalist is reluctant to invest in a typical instrumentation company. If he does invest, he will place a fifteen-times multiple on the company. The market also helps determine the multiple. The historical nature of the product line, the kind of business it is going to be, management quality, current investment fads and fashions—all play a part in the overall decision.

If a venture capitalist were asked to put money into an electronics instrument company, he would instinctively compare it to leaders in the field and study the industry's price-earnings multiples. If the company involved is in the steel business, a venture capitalist is not likely to be interested in making a private placement.

Approximate price-earnings ratios for various industries can be gained through any large brokerage firm. Most securities analysts also have a feel for price-earnings ratios and industry trends.

The essential goal of a venture capitalist is to make millionaires out of teams of engineers and managers who are tired of earning profits for major corporations. Unfortunately, the federal government now views this approach with alarm. The Tax Reform Act of 1969 discourages capital gains risk-takers and appears to encourage corporate wage slavery.

A LOOK AT THE OTHER SIDE OF THE COIN

We know of at least five fellows in the United States, investment advisory partners in large investment banking firms, who have produced over the six- to seven-year period through 1969 between

25 and 40 percent per year increase in market value on $100 thousand or more invested with them on a discretionary basis.

Sophisticated men who have money know that an alternative to high-risk private placement of venture capital is to place it with an investment counselor to manage, or allow an institutional research department to invest it for their accounts. Why should sophisticated investors become involved in a locked-up situation and hold unregistered stock for three to five years when they can make money in an investment banking firm, or hire a professional investment counselor?

One answer is that these investors may do much better than 25 percent per annum—perhaps as high as "ten-to-one." For example, we invested in a small firm, Technical Associates, in which our four-member group raised $50 thousand to purchase the company. Within eighteen months, we had an offer for the company of $900 thousand in a listed stock. We could not believe it, but we checked out the offer and it was valid. This was when the company's stock was trading at $18. In early 1970, the stock rose to $200, split two-and-one-half-for-one, and then split two-for-one. We did far better than "ten-to-one" in this situation. If someone wants to put capital to work, there are many ways to accomplish this goal.

OUR POLICIES

How do we differ from other venture capital firms?

In our agreement, the two general partners cannot benefit personally from any fees charged to a client company in which we invest funds. Generally, the legal costs of putting a deal together will be charged to the company, but we try not to burden the company with excess fees. We are, after all, interested in long-term capital gains derived from high profits and price-earnings.

We also have a loose network agreement with other venture capital firms. One or two in New York call us when they have a deal in California and we check it over for them. If we approve it, we do the deal formally and they may participate. If we are not sure of the quality of the investment, we write up the facts and send a copy to our associates. We then decide whether to continue the study.

We have invested in deals with individuals, SBIC's and investment bankers. We do not necessarily ask to become directors on the boards of our portfolio companies. We will act as directors, if asked—if we feel we can make valuable contributions. If asked, we will also actively aid in management problems.

A UNIQUE VIEWPOINT

Having grown up in production, management control and operations, I have a different viewpoint than most investment bankers: hard experience versus extensive post-graduate financial background. My partner, with an extensive academic technical background, has another way of thinking. Together, we can be useful to the client firm in almost any industry, even in a high-technology company. We know what management, marketing and production mean—mundane operations too many investment bankers take for granted. Our firm provides operating advice as well as financial aid to our portfolio clients.

We are committed to the belief that there is always capital for an outstanding deal. We have the cash, convertible debentures, and Treasury Bills on hand to prove it.

21

Forming A Venture Capital Firm

William R. Hambrecht

The firm of Hambrecht and Quist was formed in 1968. My partner had been the head of Small Business Enterprises, the SBIC subsidiary of the Bank of America. I had been on the staff of a New York Stock Exchange brokerage firm. We were close friends, and had syndicated a few venture capital deals together. Having studied the venture capital field, we concluded that there were major changes taking place.

We saw opportunity in the form of two trends that were altering the buying pattern of venture deals:

- There was a marked increase in the number of new venture capital firms. The day of only half a dozen venture capital specialists in New York appeared to be past.

- The major institutions were changing their attitude about venture capital. Eight or ten years ago, for example, we would not go to Boston because there was no one to talk to there about venture capital deals. Today, many major institutions in Boston have committed a definite portion of their available capital to venture capital investments, and we make it a point to go there regularly.

During the last decade, venture capital has become a natural

Mr. Hambrecht is a senior partner in the firm of Hambrecht & Quist, in San Francisco, California

extension of the performance criteria under which many institutional money-managers operate.

With these factors in mind, we felt that there was money to be made if we could develop a method to be exposed to as many venture deals as possible. If only one deal a month is reviewed, that particular situation may appear quite appealing; if a hundred deals a month are seen, a sense of relative values and stringent criteria are soon developed. To achieve this broad exposure, we had to design a unique corporate structure. After scrutinizing some of the most successful venture capital firms on the West Coast, we decided upon an organizational design similar to that of a West Coast venture capital partnership (Davis & Rock) that has been liquidated at great profit.

JOINING FORCES

Our firm possessed a degree of this success formula owing to my partner's venture capital experience. We contacted a half-dozen leading venture capital investors in San Francisco and brought them into our group as limited partners. These men included the two brothers who had put up the original money for Ampex, Prentice Hale of the Broadway Hale chain, and John Bryan, who had participated in the original Memorex financing.

Thus, we associated ourselves with people who were venture capital professionals and were successful. More importantly, these people could bring deals to us.

FINANCIAL SERVICE

We also felt that it was necessary to provide a complete financial service for the small- to medium-sized company. We wanted to look a company in the eye and honestly say, "Yes, you ought to go public;" or, "No, you should not go public," or, "Yes, there is cheaper money at a commercial bank or through an institution than from venture capital sources."

To do this, we needed an investment banking firm that could offer an entire range of services—from venture capital investment to commercial bank financing, institutional capital, and, if needed, public financing.

We took a long, serious look at the investment banking business and decided that the trends made it propitious for us to start our business immediately. The business was very profitable in 1968 and major firms were preoccupied with the larger deals, so they passed by smaller financings. At that time it also appeared that very few major Wall Street firms were serious about the venture capital business. On Wall Street, there is a pathological fear of being wrong and there is, therefore, little interest in high-risk startup investments. Moreover, the local finance firms with whom we had good connections were retail-oriented because they had been formed by retail brokerage salesmen. They did not have the staff to properly process venture capital investments.

After several years of hard work, we now have a firm with a broad range of venture capital experience. The principles are primarily venture capital professionals and the firm is financed by venture capital investors.

CREDENTIALS

The heart of every good venture capital firm lies in the quality of the staff. We now have six full-time people within the firm who work on evaluating and processing venture capital proposals.

They include a technology analyst, an attorney, a business consultant and a former corporate treasurer, who is also a certified public accountant.

Our firm's philosophy is that each man generally oversees six portfolio companies, but also offers his talents, where needed, on other deals. Each individual in the firm calls on his fellow staff workers for their particular discipline, a team approach that has been very successful.

From an investment banking point of view, we have established an underwriting capability. We make markets in stocks and have a brokerage operation with a New York Stock Exchange membership which (hopefully) pays for itself.

We were able to do this while still avoiding the retail stock brokerage business. Retail operations create constraints that make it difficult to deal with venture capital. For example, every time I would bring in an interesting deal to my old firm they would say, "Well, if we do this, somebody in our Iowa office is going to sell it to a widow. If it doesn't work out we will hear from her lawyer." We solved this by not having either an Iowa office or salesmen.

From late 1968 to early 1970, we made eighteen private placements for a total of approximately $28 million. We brought seven companies public for a total of $13.4 million. At this point, we had forty-two investments in our firm representing a portion of the eighteen original deals that we purchased. Some of the seven firms were involved in the public offerings, and the remainder were participations in syndications with other venture capitalists.

THE FIRST DEAL

Getting Wet

The first deal in which we participated was a firm named Teller Industries. It was formed by four officers of Litton Industries, one of whom had been the general manager of the component division. It was an interesting deal with a technology that was frankly uninteresting—the circuit-board business.

We invested $400 thousand and received about 35 percent of the company. The company founders put up $100 thousand in cash, which represented practically everything they owned.

Everything that could go wrong soon went wrong. Litton Industries went to the Corporate Commissioner's office and found that the august firm of Hambrecht and Quist had provided the financing. They immediately sued us for providing the capital.

Luckily, the suit was not a problem. Since that time, we have handled two subsequent financings for Teller, and have acquired a number of other small companies in the circuit field.

THE ORIGINAL "DIRTY DOZEN"

We are very proud of our second venture, known as Information Storage Systems (ISS). For those who keep up with the data-processing world, this group was founded by twelve men from IBM's Direct Access Storage Division in San Jose; and when they left the computer giant a few years ago, IBM nicknamed them the "Dirty Dozen." They started their company to develop a disc-drive capability to compete with the IBM 2311 and 2314.

By 1970, we had raised a total of $11 million for ISS. The company was a $45-million backlog, and we think it has a bright future. It got in under the wire with a very exciting product. They now have a contractual relationship in which ITT's Telex distributes their drives to the domestic IBM market. In addition, they have the Hewlett-Packard OEM business.

DIFFERENT APPROACH

Subsequent Ventures

For Optical Coating Laboratories, we placed $1 million worth of stock with several insurance companies. This company, located in Santa Rosa, is in the thin film optical coating business. The public soured on the company because of a management change when the market dropped from $65 a share to about $30. Feeling that the company had merit, we brought it to the insurance companies and were able to place $1 million worth of stock at about a 20 percent discount from the public market price.

The next deal we did reveals a different approach. We were invited by Donaldson, Lufkin and Jenrette to participate with them in a corporation named Environtech. Environtech was formed to purchase divisions of major companies operating in the pollution control field. The company started with sales of $40 million and is now quite profitable.

Another company in which we invested (Tymshare) was originally backed by the Bank of America, which put about a half-million dollars into the company in 1966 to get it started. By 1970, they were the only profitable privately-held time sharing company.

We also participated in a West Coast private placement for Viatron Corporation. We have yet to find ourselves in any group of venture capitalists in which there was not strong opinion one way or the other on this particular deal. The company raised huge amounts of money to capture a market in which they hoped to be able to deliver hardware at a cost basis dependent upon advanced technology.

We went into the deal because we had an investment in a company called American Micro Systems, one of the leaders in MOS chip technology.

We raised $3 million to start Electroprint in a joint venture with White Weld. The technology was developed at Stanford Research to develop an electrostatic method of printing through an electronic grid. It is a process that is technically superior to anything around, including the Xerography process. This was an unusual kind of deal. Our typical approach is to follow a management group, but in this case, we did the deal because of the fascinating technology involved. This is the first deal in which Stanford Research has ever taken an equity position. Sun Chemical, Time, Inc., Arcada Corporation and several leading investors were also involved. We were called in for advice and ended up with a piece of the deal.

Other investments include Edutronics, a million-dollar offering of privately-placed stock for a group that grew out of IBM and Standard Oil of Indiana in the customer education field. The Harper Group, an air-freight forwarding company, was another of our venture capital deals.

Anita Lynn, Inc., can only be described as a crazy kind of situation. One of our associates, a very bright and usually conservative man, looked at the deal and said, "We have to invest in this company." We raised $350 thousand for the firm. This was a difficult task in that the company sells cosmetics through milkmen. Surely every investment man in the business was terrified of having to go before his financial committee and explain how he lost money in that deal. If the goods can be sold, this is a highly profitable business. The company appears to be doing well, but it is still a little frightening.

Dycom is a magnetic tape transport device for small computers. We raised a total of $750 thousand for this firm. Technology for Communications was also a startup venture we did jointly with White Weld.

Lastly, Engineering Data Peripheral required $350 thousand to make a head per-track disc system.

THE IMPORTANCE OF PEOPLE VERSUS PRODUCTS

This review of our recent investments points up the fact that we look for management groups and attempt to stay away from buying products. At the same time, if an idea is good enough we will always look at it.

From the underwriting point of view, it is interesting to see how the pieces all fit together. We participated in a total of about forty-two syndicates, but we also brought seven companies public. In doing so, we opened the opportunity for venture capital investment in five of the seven companies. These included: Spectra Physics, the largest independent laser company; Behavioral Research Laboratories, a publishing firm; Combined Communications, a TV and outdoor advertising company; Computer Terminal Corporation and Bio-Cal Instrument Company.

We are also the investment manager for an off-shore venture capital mutual fund. We have European shareholders in the fund representing some of the leading banks and merchant bankers in England, Scotland and Switzerland. We felt that Europe would soon be a very important source of venture capital, so we founded this small fund with about $4 million. In the process, we are also educating investors about the companies we are backing, for the day when they will need more capital.

We started our firm in 1968 with $1.1 million. By 1970, we had capital of $4 million; we carry our own portfolio at cost. In most deals, we typically invest $50 thousand to $100 thousand.

We have found that out of every twelve deals we do, one is a write-off. On eight, the venture capitalist can expect to muddle his way through—perhaps doubling or tripling his money; but he should have three good deals, and one or two must be very big winners. They may return twenty, thirty—as much as forty—times his capital. This makes the long days of work and the sleepless nights of worry worthwhile.

22
Competitive Industry Trends

Charles L. Lea, Jr.

Despite cyclical trends in the stock market, the venture capital business continues to grow. The period 1968 through early 1970 revealed rapid acceleration, a trend that was reversed by mid-1970. By mid-1971, signs pointed to another shift in an upward direction.

Over time, sources of capital are expanding, and new sources are becoming available. During the 1968 rise, these were for the most part institutional; banks and insurance companies entered the field primarily due to the demand of their customers who had seen results achieved by others in this activity.

Capital also became increasingly available from corporate sources. Many major corporations in the country during this period organized independent venture capital efforts which, we believe, have a good chance for success in the field.

Growth, Specialization . . .

The striking quality about many of these funds is their size. The $84 million Heizer Fund is an excellent example. Our own New

Mr. Lea is executive vice-president of New Court Securities Corporation (New Court Private Equity Fund), in New York City.

Court Private Equities Fund, with a capitalization of $50 million, runs a close second. It has become apparent that the small venture capital fund, with capitalization under $10 million, unless coupled with some other activity, cannot sustain the operating expenses or maintain the liquidity necessary to protect the position it ultimately would achieve. The best answer to this problem is syndication. We have always believed in partnership arrangements. For the small fund, this is a very sound concept.

These new funds also have been able to articulate a special business point of view. They are interested in making investments in specialized fields, such as high technology, buy-outs, turnarounds, or even control situations. Some of these have even identified specialists within specialties.

PROFESSIONAL STAFFS

Another characteristic of most of these funds is the professionalism of their staffs. The fund managers have experienced operating and technical people close at hand, if not on the firm's payroll. In the last few years, we have sat through a number of investment meetings which evolved into technical discussions on a Ph.D. level. There is clearly a trend toward the sophistication of the venture manager, and it is going to be harder to sell deals to these managers without thorough preparation. On the other hand, they will pay premium prices for quality—and they will move quicker when they find it.

We are now able to assess and measure the risks and probabilities in a situation more rapidly and with greater technical efficiency than ever before. Because we are able to identify better quality, we can pay higher prices for the securities offered. On the other hand, if the deal has many holes in it, it is going to be more difficult to sell.

Wealth versus Experience

The venture capital business, however, may never be a purely professional one. In a very individualistic endeavor, there will always be the wealthy individual with available capital, or even financial organizations that take on the personalities of the individuals who run them. Quite often these will be affected by the emotions of the times: when the market is booming, they are big buyers; if gloom is descending, you hear from them only through their lawyers.

INCREASED PLACEMENT SIZE

One of the competitive trends in the business is the increasing size of the transactions. During our years in the field, our thinking has changed a great deal as to how to look at a venture capital deal. When in my twenties and thirties, I was inclined to believe in leverage. In my forties I am inclined to overcapitalize things, and as a result, sleep a little better at night. Leverage is no longer available. When your friendly commercial bank lending officer is presented with a projected cash flow statement for six months or a year hence, the bank, because of tight money conditions, can no longer be expected to play along. Today's deals must be larger because the money requirement falls on the venture capitalist. The insurance companies now want too much of a deal (sometimes as much as half), so we do not utilize them. By and large, we are putting up much larger pieces of the total pie than we have in the past. The smaller deal is anathema to the investor. The problems in the small transaction are identical to the large ones. The investor's responsibilities are equal in both; yet financial rewards, in relation to time expended, are relatively low in the small deal.

TOMORROW'S SMALL DEALS

Increased Risk and Time Involvement

As the major companies—insurance firms, banks, large capital pools—move into the venture capital industry, and as money generally becomes more available via lower interest rates, the entrepreneur will be in a better position to dictate his terms for financing. The small individual venture capitalist in competition with the larger firms will probably be forced to accept more risk and spend more time financing startups.

Anyone selling a deal is going to go where the money is, and he will try to do his deal with as few people as possible. As major investment pools grow, they will obviously be the most efficient place to go.

Though smaller pools of capital may come along as junior partners in some of these larger transactions, the more efficient function of these smaller funds may be to look at small deals. Small deals also involve the highest degree of risk, including the startup type of situation.

THE ECONOMICS OF PACKAGING

From the point of view of the investment banker, finder or promoter, the economics of packaging dictates larger size. It takes anywhere from three to six months to complete a transaction. Expenses entail finders' fees, investigation, writing of the proposal, consultants, travel, telephone and legal fees, and possibly, several groups of attorneys. To this, add overhead—and we can very easily come up with between $25 thousand to $50 thousand invested in a transaction. Understandably, the venture capitalist can get quite nervous at closings.

Today's small deal is under a million dollars—and it must be absolutely unique to be of interest. The largest private high-risk deal that we have participated in was about $9½ million. About ten years ago, we raised the original capital for the now well-known Damon Corporation. The financing involved about a half-million dollars. If we were doing the same job today, we would probably be out to raise $1.5 million.

SOPHISTICATION . . .

Another of the competitive trends in the business is the sophistication of the deals. We feel that if there is any art to our business, it is the art of keeping things simple. Deals that tend to become overly complicated usually turn out to be inequitable or unsound. Business is difficult enough without adding complications.

On the other hand, when times are difficult, the stock market shaky, and the banks and insurance companies sitting on the sidelines, we have to be resourceful and imaginative in the manner in which we buy and sell. Negotiators at those times may well consider such devices as performance convertibles, installment purchases and sales, sale and leaseback partnerships (of plant as well as equipment), and soft dollar research and development contracts (high tax-bracket dollars) with wealthy investors.

TOMORROW'S WORLD OF VENTURE CAPITAL

The Great American Market

Some of our colleagues suggest that the infusion of large amounts of capital into the industry will drive the prices of good deals up to a point where returns will be depressed to unattractive levels. We do not share this point of view, although we believe that periodic imbalances may occur.

Further, we believe that we have not yet begun to tap our available creative human resources. Our hunch is that the unruly generation coming onto the scene right now may contain some of the greatest entrepreneurs in the last hundred years. It will be interesting to watch their progress as they move into the work force.

Another observation: as an industry, we have focused too much on Boston and Palo Alto as sources of the best ideas, while great things are happening all over the country. Our current interest is the Middle-South, the Piedmont area, where we have found interesting and attractive situations. Some amazing things are developing on a regional basis.

In our view, America is the best market in the world for venture capital investment. Europe and other foreign areas are not particularly attractive prospects at this time. Venture capital has become successful in America because of the size of our domestic market and the ability to get a new idea into the market quickly. We do not see this happening in foreign markets, segmented or compartmentalized as they are now.

Overall, in our opinion, these are good times to be in the venture capital business. In many ways they are the most demanding of times. But we believe that those who are willing to invest their time and effort as well as capital, with patience, will be well-rewarded.

23

Venture Capital Techniques... And Tomorrow

Peter D. Danforth

Gunwyn Ventures celebrated its first birthday in 1970. In most industries one year of existence hardly represents a significant milepost. However, new pools of private, public, corporate and institutional capital are now being formed at such a rapid rate that somehow one year does not seem particularly young.

We entered our second year with bated breath. The only investment more venturesome than backing a startup commercial or industrial enterprise is backing a startup venture capital firm. Mistakes are quickly visible and losses are apt to be taken early. On the other hand, successes emerge slowly, and meaningful gains are often five years or more in the making.

We have developed some strong opinions in the short history of our firm, some of which may be useful to those who are exploring the wisdom of a private financing, or those who are in the business of identifying, counseling and servicing young businesses and businessmen seeking venture financing.

We would like to touch briefly on three major areas:

1. A review of our organization and investment activities to date.

Mr. Danforth is general partner in the venture capital firm of Gunwyn Ventures, in New York City.

2. Our investment philosophy and several aphorisms concerning the industry.
3. Some hunches as to what the 1970's may bring for firms such as ours and for small businesses in general.

ORGANIZING OUR FIRM

Gunwyn was organized as a limited partnership, with capital provided by four brothers and a sister—children of the late George Gund of Cleveland, Ohio. The family's interests are widely diversified, and they want a portion of their resources to be oriented toward supporting deserving young businesses in exciting areas of the economy. Like most people who have supported private venturing firms, the Gunds are willing and able to withstand the high risks associated with such an activity and are enthusiastic about the possible rewards, intangible as well as financial. Our sole mandate is to seek out, evaluate, invest in and support venture projects.

In our first twelve months in the venture capital business, we were exposed to almost five hundred investment proposals. These were referred to us, in approximately equal proportion, by investment bankers, commercial banks, business brokers, public accounting firms, other venture capital firms and friends. Had we believed every story we were told and agreed to every equity valuation, we estimate we would have invested over $250 million in companies whose total valuation after the infusion of our capital would have exceeded $3 billion.

Of the total number of projects brought to our attention, we elected to seriously investigate thirty. From that small group, we made nine investments totaling slightly under $2 million, an average of about $225 thousand per investment. Our immediate or potential equity interest in these companies ranges from 8 percent to 25 percent. When added to the interests of our co-investing partners, total equity participation ranges from 22 to 72 percent.

Our experience suggests that, in any given year, a venture capital firm will invest in about 1 percent of all proposals screened. The fact that we financed 2 percent is ascribable to the non-recurring factors associated with opening a new business. In an effort to establish investment momentum, we have elected to participate occasionally with other venture capital firms in instances where we know our partners extremely well, and where we can rely heavily upon the excellence of their investment evaluation and leadership.

OUR PORTFOLIO

Our portfolio presently includes the following investments:

- A twenty-year-old educational publishing company in Connecticut which creates and distributes a variety of subscription materials to school administrators, principals and school boards, as well as enrichment programs to teaching professionals in the public school sector.
- A four-year-old Massachusetts corporation which has developed highly-proprietary industrial air pollution control equipment. Although fully commercial models are not yet available, production prototypes are entering environmental testing.
- A three-year-old computer-based systems and time-sharing company in New England.
- A sporting goods manufacturing company, with plants in New York State, Puerto Rico and Japan. We believe this firm will grow rapidly in both sales and earnings because of its ability to

excell in carefully-defined markets, where profit margins are strengthened through product quality and brand recognition.

- A New Jersey enterprise started in 1969 by three capable young scientists who left a large technically-based company. This business custom-manufactures ceramic metal devices used to "package" large scale, integrated circuits and metal-oxide semi-conductor devices.
- A new stationery products company in California founded by an outstanding young manager, well-versed in finance and marketing, who has perceived a more efficient way of manufacturing, merchandising and distributing office supplies and stationery products.
- An Ohio manufacturer of industrial process control instrumentation, which has developed new ways of measuring basic physical properties of sheet products produced in the paper, plastics and filmcoating industries.
- A young New England company which manufactures test equipment used in the production of microminiature electronic circuits.
- A West Coast producer and distributor of specialty food products.

What do these companies have in common?

First, they are either in rapidly growing technical areas of the economy or they are more mundane businesses operated, in our opinion, by highly-talented management teams with exciting and believable programs for corporate growth.

Second, not one of these companies could have financed its capital requirements through a more conventional source (a public offering of equity securities or conventional bank credit from commercial sources).

Third, in all cases our investment decision was based on incomplete data. As in stud poker, we could discern from the up-cards certain corporate strengths, such as prior management success, stability or growth of the industry, patent protection . . . As with stud poker, however, winning is usually determined by the down-cards. In this analogy the down-cards are the answers to questions such as:

> Can a successful management from one company operate effectively in a new business?
>
> Will the market respond favorably to a new product?
>
> Will the highly-technical area become obsolete overnight?

Again, as in poker, the venture capitalist has to pay to see the down-cards.

Another common bond of these companies is that each requires a great deal of advice and counsel at the policy level. Contrary to popular opinion, discussions with operating management at this level do not normally center around such questions as:

> What is our long-range acquisition program?
>
> Should our surplus cash flow be diverted into ninety-day treasury bills or tax-free municipals?
>
> What should be our stance regarding anti-trust legislation?

Rather, the questions we wrestle with are apt to be:

> How can we cut the engineering budget by 80 percent?
>
> Where is our next line of bank credit coming from?
>
> How do we meet next Friday's payroll?

A final common thread is that while there is a natural inclination to feel somewhat bullish about some, and exceedingly apprehensive about others, our history with these companies has simply been too short to warrant a write-up or write-down of our investment basis. If forced to make a guess, we would predict that a few of our original nine investments will be extremely disappointing; with others we will no more than recoup our original investment—plus, perhaps, the imputed cost of capital; and the remainder (perhaps one or two of the original nine) will realize an extremely satisfactory return for our firm. It is the remaining one or two that makes the entire exercise interesting. The one thing we cannot predict, unfortunately, is which of each of our current investments falls into each of the three categories mentioned.

OUR FORMULA FOR RETURNS

What constitutes an extremely satisfactory return?

Venture capital firms are constantly asked this question, and it is doubtful that any two share exactly the same opinion. Our objective in any given investment is to see a minimum return of three times to five times in as many years, as well as an upside potential for considerably greater return if everything falls into place.

The problem is that too frequently everything falls out of place and, as a consequence, the overall returns to venturing firms are seldom as breathtaking as many believe. If rate of return in a venture capital firm can be accurately measured, we believe that a consistent 15 percent realized rate of return compounded over many years would cause most venturers to jump with joy.

Considering the youth of our organization, we have elected for the time being not to finance startups, as these are extremely time-consuming investments, are difficult to investigate thoroughly—and, even more difficult, to value fairly for investment purposes.

Also, at times we have invested jointly with other venturers whom we know and trust. Of the nine investments listed, Gunwyn is the lead (major investor) or co-lead investor in six of them, as measured in both dollars and involvement. In the remaining three, we frankly look to our investment partners for a major share of the workload.

MAXIMS FOR INVESTING

We would like to cover a few of the maxims which have evolved concerning proper techniques of venture capital investing. Some of these we totally subscribe to as part of our own investment philosophy . . .

Buy Well and Buy Enough

We are often appalled by the outlandish valuations placed on young companies either by their owners or, as frequently, by their investment bankers. There was a time when the venturer looked to the balance sheet as a means of determining investment value. Then it was the income statement. Later it became a forecast of the company's profits for the next year. We are asked to accept valuations based upon multiples of such useless factors as next year's projected order backlog, or the number of parts in the company's end product.

No young company wants to give up more ownership in an equity financing than is absolutely necessary. This is logical and understandable to the venture investor. However, for his part, the owner/manager must realize these other factors:

> A responsible private investor should and will contribute more than dollars—namely, his firm's involvement and commitment to the enterprise.
>
> The new investment most likely will not be liquid for a number of years, perhaps five or more.
>
> The investment will probably not represent control of the business.

Venturers, as a rule, do not want control. They do, however, seek a minority interest which is meaningful enough to justify extensive involvement. If a young company expects a venturer to pay an inordinately high "going-in" price, one that is justified more by fashions in the "new issues" market than by current corporate facts or short-term expectations, then the company will be doing itself a disservice over the long run.

A related aspect of "buy well and buy enough" is the stressing of equity, not credit. Our firm prefers to purchase straight common stock for a significant minority interest. We seek to establish strong relationships with owner/management groups based on mutual confidence and earned respect. We do not believe that our counsel concerning posture is that of a creditor with only a contingent equity interest based on future success.

Doing Your Own Homework

We believe that it is very important to do our own homework. This principle frequently is not understood by companies seeking financing.

A venturing firm cannot and should not be expected to make an investment decision after reading a fifty-page investment memorandum, or spending a few hours with the management group. Admittedly, a private financing should be completed faster than a full public underwriting; but a young company with a sketchy track record should not expect miracles. We are often asked how soon we can give an answer. Our typical reply is, "If you want a 'no,' that can be arranged tomorrow. If you want a 'yes,' that might take four to six weeks."

Venturing firms must develop as much data as possible to fortify their investment decision. A consideration frequently overlooked or discounted by a young company is that a thorough pre-investment study enables the investment partner to make a more useful future contribution. Even if a negative investment decision is reached, the information gathered can be of great use to the company itself.

Don't Fall in Love with Your Ventures

There is a double meaning to the adage, "Don't fall in love with your ventures." More often it suggests that a venturer's vision is narrowed by involvement. Over a period of time, close working relationships are formed in this business. When the operations of a portfolio company take a turn for the worse, it is too easy to assign responsibility to factors over which management has little control. The capacity of a venturing partner to become involved, yet retain a high degree of objectivity, is a factor which must be kept in mind constantly by the venturer himself and by the owner/manager group as well.

The other aspect of this maxim relates to conditions associated with success. Once an investment has been successful and satisfactory liquidity has been established, many firms find it difficult to let go. We have not yet had to wrestle with this high-grade problem, but when our capital has served its purpose, we hope we will be willing to take our gains and reinvest the proceeds into other deserving young enterprises.

Have Fun

The last, but possibly most important tenet of our business is to "have fun." There are easier, more comfortable ways to make money than by venture capital investing which is emotionally exhausting and, if executed classically, a constant flirtation with disaster. So, accounting for all of the pitfalls, there is no consideration higher on our list than identifying and sponsoring happy businesses and happy people.

FOUR MAJOR TRENDS IN THE INDUSTRY

It is important to mention a few of the trends which we see in the venture capital industry.

First, for a considerable period prior to mid-1970, the field was becoming intensely competitive and a variety of new sources of high-risk capital were organized. Although this intensity subsided in the market of the latter half of that year and on into 1971, whenever a favorable business climate exists, such competition is likely to recur. Such a trend should be beneficial to all small businesses, providing these new sources of high-risk capital exhibit statesmanship in the conduct of their business.

By statesmanship, we mean:

- insisting on realistic valuations;
- carefully studying and checking business plans to insure future corporate viability;

- thorough appraisal of management competence;
- continuing involvement in affairs of a business after an investment is made.

Lax ground rules invariably result in the wasteful employment of capital resources.

A second trend—not likely to be permanently affected by cyclical considerations—in the future, just as there will be more firms with more dollars to invest, there will also be more young businesses to finance. The overall quality of this increased corporate population may not be significantly higher than in the past, but there are bound to be many more. Over time, it becomes increasingly difficult for large corporations to retain outstanding managers. More and more of these men are considering going it alone.

Third, the combination of these first two developments suggests that future projects will require more dollars to finance. Our experience suggests that the average capital requirement of a young business has increased over the last decade from the $100 thousand range to perhaps $1 million or more. Should this trend continue, venture capital firms will tend to syndicate high-risk investments more frequently. In so doing, both risk and workload are shared.

And fourth, venture capital firms of the future will initiate many more investment ideas internally than they have in the past.

AN OUTLOOK FOR SMALL BUSINESS

All of these trends ultimately bode well for small business. Access to organized sources of high-risk capital will be better-defined, and channels of communication to the professional staffs of these firms will be more direct. We hope to see more opportunities where the final investment terms have yet to be set, and fewer investments so tightly structured that an affirmative investment decision is virtually impossible.

So long as the entrepreneur remains imaginative, dedicated and realistic as to the value of his business, somewhere there should be an imaginative, dedicated and realistic venture capitalist to help him finance his dream.

The principal conclusion we would like to leave with you is that today's venture capital industry is very "approachable." Investors want to have a continuing input of new ideas, innovative situations. They are looking for sound business principles and profitable operations.

NOTES

CHAPTER 8

1, Page 101 Disclosure Policy Study Report—"Disclosure to Investors—a Reappraisal of Administrative Policies Under the '33 and '34 Acts." (Under the direction of then Commissioner Francis M. Wheat of the Securities and Exchange Commission, and frequently referred to as "The Wheat Report.") (Superintendent of Documents, Government Printing Office, Washington, D.C., 1969.)

CHAPTER 9

1, Page 106 Securities Act of 1933 (Superintendent of Documents, Government Printing Office, Washington, D.C.)

2, Page 106 Securities Exchange Act of 1934 (Superintendent of Documents, Government Printing Office, Washington, D.C.)

3, Page 106 The Wheat Report—"Disclosure to Investors—a Reappraisal of Administrative Policies Under the '33 and '34 Acts." *See* Notes, Chapter 8, Number 1.

4, Page 106 Public Utility Holding Company Act of 1934 (Superintendent of Documents, Government Printing Office, Washington, D.C.)

5, Page 106 Trust Indenture Act of 1939 (Superintendent of Documents, Government Printing Office, Washington, D.C.)

6, Page 106 Investment Company Act of 1940 (Superintendent of Documents, Government Printing Office, Washington, D.C.)

7, Page 106 Small Business Investment Act of 1958 (Superintendent of Documents, Government Printing Office, Washington, D.C.)

8, Page 111 Securities Act, Release 4997—"Proposals To Adopt Rules Relating To Underwriters, Non-Public Offerings, And Brokerage Transactions Under Section 2(11), 4(2), 4(1), and 4(4) Of The '33 Act." (Superintendent of Documents, Government Printing Office, Washington, D.C., 1969)

9, Page 126 Securities Act of 1933, Release 4982 and Securities Exchange Act of 1934, Release 8638—"Application of the Securities Act of 1933 and the Securities Exchange Act of 1934 to Spin-Offs of Securities and Trading in the Securities of Inactive or Shell Corporations." (Superintendent of Documents, Government Printing Office, Washington, D.C., 1969)

CHAPTER 10

1, Page 129 (Supt. of Documents, Govt. Printing Office, Wash., D.C.)

2, Page 141 Disclosure Policy Study Report under the direction of SEC Commissioner Francis M. Wheat. *See* Note: Chapter 8, Number 1.

BIBLIOGRAPHY

To date, relatively little has been published about the venture capital industry and how it works. This is due not only to the fact that the industry is still quite new, but also—to write effectively about how companies in the field really operate is a difficult task. So much of this business is the result of individual experience and intuitive judgment that "how to" books of specific guidelines simply do not seem applicable.

The following is a select list of sources of materials currently available on the subject:

Boston College School of Management. *Proceedings from the 1970 Boston College College Management Institute.* "Venture Capital and Management: The Art of Joining Innovative Technology, Management and Capital," 1971

——— *Proceedings from the 1969 Boston College Management Institute.* "New Business: The Art of Joining Innovative Technology, Management and Capital," 1971

Hutchison, G. Scott. *The Strategy of Corporate Financing.* New York: Presidents Publishing House, Inc., 1971

Makela, Benjamin R. *How to Use and Invest in Letter Stock.* New York: Presidents Publishing House, Inc., 1970

National Association of Small Business Investment Companies. Allen Neece, Jr., associate director, Washington, D.C.

Noone, Charles M. and Rubel, Stanley M. *SBICS: Pioneers in Organized Venture Capital.* Chicago: Capital Publishing Corporation, 1970

Practicing Law Institute. *Venture Capital, Legal and Business Problems.* New York: Practising Law Institute, 1970

Rubel, Stanley M. *Guide to Venture Capital Sources.* Chicago: Capital Publishing Corporation, 1971

Small Business and Venture Capital Associates. *Encouraging Venture Capital for Small Business.* New York: Associated Educational Services Corporation, 1967

United States Department of Commerce. *Technological Innovation: Its Environment and Management.* Washington, D.C.: Government Printing Office, 1967

U.S. Small Business Administration, Investment Division. "Reports on SBIC Industry, small company financing, etc.," Washington, D.C.

PERIODICAL PUBLICATIONS

Business Management. "RX for Venture Capitalists," (April, 1970), Vol. 38, No. 1, p. 16.

BUSINESS WEEK. "Brave Brokers Take the Plunge," (March 21, 1970), pp. 116-118.

——— "How the High-Fliers Take Off," (November 22, 1969), pp. 112-116.

——— "Letter Stock Is Worth the Worry," (January 18, 1969), pp. 108-114.

——— "The 'Smart Money' Draws a Crowd," (February 28, 1970), pp. 92-95.

——— "They Gamble on New Technology," (November 1, 1969), p. 128.

Dun's Review. "The Golden Equation of Venture Capital," (September, 1969), pp. 43-45.

——— "Golden Touch of American Research and Development," (November, 1968), pp. 40-45.

——— "Singer: A New Way to Make Money," A. Hershman, (January, 1970), pp. 23-37.

Electronic News. "Venture Capital Game Popular in West," Neil Kelley, (December 2, 1968), p. 42.

Financial Analysts Journal. "Pattern of Success in Venture Capital Financing," W. Rotch, (September, 1968).

Financial World. "Focus on Funds," Edward Ryan (July 23, 1969).

——— "SBICs: Best Hope for Small Business," (May 20, 1970), pp. 10 and 30.

——— "SBICs: Venturing into New Fields," (November 19, 1969), pp. 8 and 25.

Forbes. "Has the Bear Market Killed Venture Capital?", (June 15, 1970), p. 28.

——— "Improving on the General," Dr. Morton Collins, (April 15, 1970), pp. 78-81.

——— "Very Special Affair," American Research and Development, (October 15, 1969), p. 42.

Generation. "A View of the Venture Capital Industry," Stanley M. Rubel, (April, 1971), pp. 47-51.

Investment Dealer's Digest. "SBICs, Venture Capital Companies Continue to Gain Investor Confidence," Stanley M. Rubel, (June 19, 1969), pp. 66-67.

Institutional Investor. "Venture Capital: The Biggest Mousetrap of the 1970's?" Chris Welles, (January, 1970), pp. 37-52.

Journal of Commerce. "Venture Capital 'Golden Age' Seen," William Pengra, (January 13, 1970), p. 3.

Los Angeles Times. "Venture Capitalists Banking on Future: Angels of Wall Street to Step Up Activities," Ron S. Heinzel, (January 15, 1970).

Modern Data. "Has the Well Run Dry?" Robert F. Johnston, (April, 1970), pp. 164-165.

New York Times. "Small Business is Becoming Big Business in the U.S.," Elizabeth M. Fowler, (May 26, 1968).

——— "Venture Capital Aids 5 Winners," Robert Metz, (July 8, 1969).

Securities. "Something Ventured," (January, 1970), pp. 14-18.

The Wall Street Journal. "SEC Examiner Urges Publicly Held SBICs Be Freed of 2 Curbs," (December 3), 1969.

INDEX